The Lone Pine
PICNIC
GUIDE
To Ontario

Nancy Gibson
John Whittaker

Maps & Illustrations
by Diana Gibson

LONE
PINE

The Publisher:
Lone Pine Publishing
#206, 10426-81 Avenue
Edmonton, Alberta, Canada
T6E 1X5

Canadian Cataloguing in Publication Data
Gibson, Nancy.
  The Lone Pine picnic guide to Ontario

  (Lone Pine picnic guides)
  Includes bibliographical references and index.
  ISBN 0-919433-69-3

  1. Ontario — Description and travel — 1981- — Guide books.
2. Picnicking. 3. Outdoor cookery.
I. Whittaker, John, 1940-   II. Title.   III. Series.
FC3057.G52 1991   917.1304'4   C91-091438-9
F1057.G52 1991

Front cover photo: A. Michael Kundu
Cover design: Yuet Chan
Layout and design: Lloyd Dick, Phillip Kennedy
Editorial: Jane Spalding, Phillip Kennedy
Printing: Gagne Printing Ltd., Louiseville, Québec, Canada

Publisher's Acknowledgement
    The publisher gratefully acknowledges the assistance of the Federal
Department of Communications, Alberta Culture and Multiculturalism, the
Canada Council, and the Alberta Foundation for the Literary Arts in the
production of this book.

Ce livre est imprimé sur
du papier contenant plus
de 50% de papier recyclé
dont 5% de fibres recyclées.

For Helen and Hugh

Marion and Denis

Hope and Ross

In remembrance of picnics past

Table of Contents

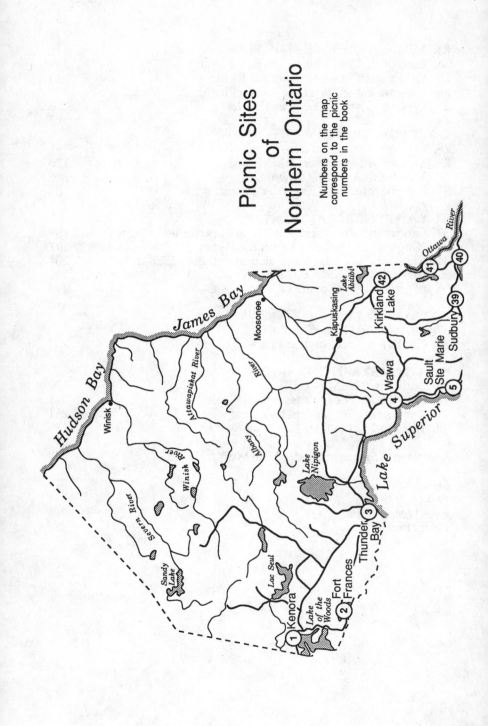

Picnic Sites
of
Northern Ontario

Numbers on the map
correspond to the picnic
numbers in the book

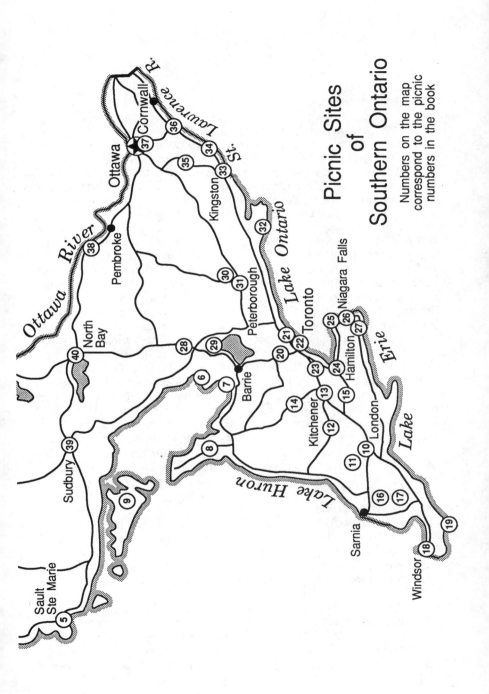

Picnic Sites
of
Southern Ontario

Numbers on the map
correspond to the picnic
numbers in the book

Acknowledgements

This book reflects the willingness of many people to share with us their favourite picnic places. Our Ontario friends helped us in many ways. We are grateful to Penny and Dale Bent, who housed and fed us in London while we explored southern Ontario and the Niagara Peninsula. Penny and Elizabeth Bent also assisted with the research for the Lucan picnic. Mrs. Leona Bent helped with the Guy Lombardo picnic in London. Our thanks go also to Valerie Shypit, whose home is always our base in Toronto. Peter, Karen and Jeremy Sadlier-Brown kindly loaned us their cabin on the Ottawa River which served as a base for our northern Ontario explorations. Sheelagh Whittaker and Bill Morgan not only fed us, but served as our consultants on things yuppyish in Toronto. Maureen and John Monk provided a bed and a picnic lunch. Pat and Dave Story put us up in their cottage in Sault Ste. Marie, and provided valuable background information on Francis Clergue. A special thank you, also, to Judy Botterill and Ron Farino, who with Bert and Karen Berger, supplied much material from their explorations of the eastern shore of Lake Superior, and who proved that they understood the "magic" in a picnic by introducing us to Mr. Vallée in Wawa. We are grateful for the assistance of Matt Ward at the Public Works office in Wawa, and of Mr. Vallée, himself, for showing us his special park. Jane and Ian Henderson, with their luncheon guests and Ian's library, helped us to plan our research of the Trent-Severn Canal. Joe and Joan Stevens of Winnipeg steered us in the right direction for the Fort Frances picnic, and Ruth and Rudy Freisen, also of Winnipeg, provided us with an authentic Mennonite feast while telling us about Mennonite history in Ontario. Martin Lynch of Kaslo, B.C. let us tap his great knowledge of Ontario history, and helped with the Harry Oakes story.

As with each of our earlier picnic books—British Columbia and Alberta—this book has been enriched and polished by the editing of Uncle Nowell Sadlier-Brown, and of Helen and Hugh Lavender. The careful copy editing done by Jane Spalding and Phillip Kennedy at Lone Pine Publishing added the final flourish. Mary Walters Riskin, along with every member of the staff at Lone Pine, offered continual encouragement and support through all three picnic projects—thank you all!

We are deeply indebted to many people who work in the fields of tourism and environmentalism in Ontario for their help in identifying and researching the picnic sites, and for subsequently proofreading our drafts of the picnic in their locale. Some of them are Sheridan Alder, Darryl Allan, Ralph Beaumont, Noel Buckley, Theresa Bunbury,

Acknowledgements

Curtis Brubacher, Don Cecile, Alex Clark, Karen Coburn, Maryellen Corcelli, Luanne Crilly, Paul Deault, Keith Dewar, Elizabeth-Ann Fauteux, John P. Good, John Hamilton, Gay Hemsley, Judy Henderson, Brian Huis, Linda Kearns, Rob MacDonald, Robert McLelland, Judy McGonigal, Ken McIlwrick, Barry McKnight, Dave McLennan, Steven Mecredy, Doris Medlock, E.J. Melanson, L. Meleg, Mark Michenko, Brian Moulder, Maureen O'Rourke, Arthur Pegg, Betty Popelier, Kate Proctor, Heather Resvick, Donna Roach, Sandra Saddy, Terry Sprague, Dave Stepanik, Marlene Steele and her daughter, Debbie Stevens, Elizabeth Stewart, Lorenzo Wheatung, Nancy White, Bob Whittam and Keith Winterhalder.

We are equally grateful to those whose names we have missed inadvertently. We found the staff of the Ministry of Natural Resources of Ontario, the Provincial Parks and Parks Canada especially helpful throughout the province.

We are grateful to McGraw-Hill Ryerson for permission to use the three historical drawings by C.W. Jefferys; to the St. Lawrence Seaway Authority for permission to use the profile of the seaway; to the Grey Sauble Conservation Authority for the photograph of the McNeill mansion; to the Sault Ste. Marie Museum and Archives for the photograph of Frances Clergue; to Gateway Publishing in Winnipeg for permission to use several recipes; to the Provincial Archives of Ontario and the National Archives for permission to use several photographs.

We would like to thank our daughter, Diana Gibson, for the pleasure of her company throughout the research trip, and for her production of the excellent picnic maps and drawings in this book. Our daughters, Carolyn and Katy Whittaker, also helped with some of the research during their summer "holidays." Picnics have always been a family enterprise with us, and so has this book. Each and every one of our nine children has, over the years, introduced major innovations and refinements to our picnicking. Thank you Michael, Carolyn, Diana, Steven, Ginger, Justin, Jason, Annthea and Katy.

There have been so many friends who have taken us on picnics, lent us their books, and shared their ideas, which we have shamelessly adopted—thank you all.

This is the place to admit that despite the help of so many knowledgeable people, there may still be errors and misinterpretations in the book, for which we assume sole responsibility. In some cases facilities change over time, and these changes will conflict with information in this book. We sincerely regret any consequent inconvenience.

Finally, we would like to thank Grant Kennedy, president of Lone Pine Publishing, for taking serious picnicking seriously!

Key to Symbols

 Picnic Tables

 Water Source

 Toilets

 Fires Allowed
(stoves/pits and wood available)

 Shelter

 No Pets Allowed

 Telephone

 Boat Launch

 Swimming

INTRODUCTION

Picnic Preamble

In our family a picnic is a very special thing. It is a delicate blending of the right people, the right setting, a suitable menu, interesting activities and conversation, and nice weather. When all these elements coincide, the result is inevitably a delightful memory for the participants. Our picnics are recorded in "memory pictures" by one of our daughters, and in photographs by some of the rest of us. Many a family reunion at Christmas is peppered with each of us remembering a different, but splendid, picnic and revitalizing the memories for each other with the full colours of both kinds of pictures.

This book is designed to help you make your picnics memorable occasions, replete with historical anecdotes, legends, adventurous menus and recipes, things to see and do nearby, and a touch of magic here and there. There is no particular logic to the selection of places—we simply followed our whims and instincts. Occasionally we sought the settings for history we already knew; places with strong auras of the past are Sainte Marie Among the Hurons at Midland, for example, or Petrolia, where the first oil well was drilled in 1858. Sometimes we were overcome by the natural beauty of a site, like Elora, or Middle Falls near Thunder Bay. Several of our picnics, like Crawford Lake at Milton, reflect the history of native Canadians, since we are aware that they have been visiting or living in many of the best picnic sites for at least 10,000 years. And sometimes our sense of fun triumphed, and the result is exemplified in the Stratford and Orillia picnics.

Pages of Picnics

Everyone loves a picnic, so we selected spots which are easily reached by car, usually involving no more than a hundred metres of walking so that each picnic would be accessible to most senior citizens and to small children. Thus, with reluctance, we turned down the wonderful site that required eight kilometres of steep hiking, and islands accessible only by private boat. Most of the picnics are small-scale, meant for friends, couples, and families. We have, however, included a chapter on planning picnics for large groups, with a few recipes for 100, and the rules to some games which we remember playing in our youths. The picnic at Toronto Island includes recipes for 40 people, in case your large groups aren't so large.

Most of our picnic places were discovered as we explored Canada in the summer on our old school bus. We found that theme picnics were a great way to educate ourselves and our kids, and the kids quickly became experts in identifying magic picnic places—sometimes even in the heart of a city.

Each of the picnics included in this book has a theme, which may be suggested by the place, the history, or the name; sometimes the connection is a bit far-fetched, as you will see.

Picnics in Perspective

Why would any sane person leave all the comforts of a modern home to venture off to a wild, untamed place to eat a meal prepared over a campfire, sitting on an old blanket or a rough bench amid ants and mosquitoes, when the most meticulous preparation may get rained on anyway?

Anthropologists tell us that the human species is driven to interact with the elements, to conquer nature, to reaffirm dominance in the natural order of things. This urge to control the wilderness leads to isolated episodes wherein the human species attempts to "civilize" the wild by using propane stoves, deck chairs, plastic canopies, battery-operated fire starters, and in extreme cases, recreation vehicles, to establish a crude replica of the suburban homestead upon a piece of unsettled land.

The first picnics weren't imitations of anything—people ate out and cooked over campfires on nice days because it got stuffy in the caves. As technology went along, cooking methods became refined, and with the concept of the chimney, moved permanently indoors in most societies, ending forever the annoyance of trying to start a fire in the rain.

But not quite forever. It has been speculated that the notion of picnicking crossed the channel to England from France in the nineteenth century along with the "cult of nature" influence spawned by Jean Jacques Rousseau and fueled by the romantic poets. By now, people were living comfortably inside relatively permanent dwellings with such conveniences as indoor plumbing and windows. The simple life of the past was idealized, and living in harmony with nature took on a certain romantic appeal. Romantic idealism is rarely pragmatic, but the adoption of picnicking by the British is either an example of monumental blindness or determined self-deception, given the usual climate of the British Isles. In the never-ending contest between people and nature, it is during the act of picnicking that people are most vulnerable to the elements; to be "rained out" means that nature remains dominant despite technology.

There are several sociological explanations for the peculiar behaviour displayed by picnickers. These outings can be interpreted as an attempt to escape from the urban industrial environment, an escape from artificiality. Picnic participants may be seeking temporary informality to balance the enforced rigidity of modern daily life. Alternatively, picnics can be seen in a positive light as the reaffirmation of a social unit. For example, making a morose fourteen-year-old son attend a family picnic reaffirms parental power within the family. (But is it worth it?)

The Spanish carry this group affirmation to an extreme, collecting 10,000 people for a week once a year on a mountain top, or alternatively in a swamp, and picnicking and dancing day and night for the duration, without even a Port-a-Potty in sight! During this religious picnic, called a *romeria*, rain does not diminish the festivities, but is simply ignored; dancing continues, parades march on, masses are held, and fires miraculously continue to burn. Our equivalent of the *romeria* is the community picnic or agricultural fair but, unlike the Spaniards, we usually go home at night.

Pique-Niques Past

According to the Oxford Dictionary, the word picnic did not occur in English in literature until 1748. The word is probably derived from the French *pique-nique*. In England, nineteenth-century picnics were a pastime of the rich, involving an outing to a pastoral setting and a meal composed of contributions of food from each participant. Hence the rarely used word, picnickery, which implies "a collection of things from various sources, like the provisions at a picnic." The Picnic society in London was a group of people whose gatherings were characterized by dramatic presentations and other social entertainments to which each member of the society contributed. Finally, a picnickian is a person who takes part in a picnic. With this broader sense of the word picnic, our readers, fellow picnickians all, will understand our concept of the compleat, or in more contemporary terms, the magic picnic, the components of which are not limited to victuals, but must include an appropriate setting, congenial company, and a mystique. This last component is intangible, but essential. It provides the theme—and the magic part of the picnic. A magic picnic is one in which all components are in place and are savoured and enjoyed by each picnickian.

The art of picnickery is flexible, limited only by the standards and requirements of the particular picnickians. Some issues may be taken for granted, and remain unspoken, such as clothing. What to wear on a picnic is a personal question. It has been addressed by some of our greatest minds at some length, and here we refer you to the famous painting by Edouard Manet entitled "Déjeuner sur l'herbe" (less elegant in English—Lunch on the grass) in which one of the female picnickians elected to wear nothing at all. We leave these delicate issues to the reader, although we discuss clothes in a general, objective way in our chapter on equipment.

Particularly Precious Picnics

Our family tradition of picnicking was elevated to an art form one day beneath the ruins of an old Spanish fort as we sat (fully dressed) in the shade of a silvery olive orchard, transported by the beauty of the afternoon, the compelling history of the place, and the wonderful tastes of the Andalusian foods and wines which composed our seven-course feast, complete with china and crystal! After our return to Canada we continued to seek out "magic" picnics at home, picnics which had the right combination of elements—and we have discovered many.

Some of our picnics are less serious than others. The first of these began when we tried to find Black Forest Cake to eat in the German Black Forest. After many stores and bakeries let us down, we finally found a frozen cake in a supermarket and then drove back into the Black Forest from the village to thaw the cake and have our picnic. This sort of theme picnic challenges everyone's imagination, and permits the corny members of the group to display the full range of their talents.

We would be dishonest if we didn't acknowledge a debt to James Michener, who expounded on the art of picnicking before we did in his book on Spain, *Iberia*. He had discovered the Spanish penchant for picnicking, and later so did we, as we meandered through Spain with our five children in an ancient but loyal Volkswagen van called Vincent (see photo on back cover). This van carried all seven of us, our packs and the thirteen boxes of books that always seem to accompany us throughout Europe, at a steady but slowish speed. Vincent took us to many picnics throughout Spain as we read bits of Michener aloud. The van was probably the best-equipped picnic-mobile in Europe—carrying a portable table, a portable propane paella cooker, cutlery, china and linens, and a couple of pretty vases for flowers for table settings.

We have developed and refined our picnic equipment since then, and our suggestions are offered in the next chapter of this book. Many picnic sites are equipped with tables and grills and shelters, but some of the sites that we especially like have no amenities whatsoever, other than the magic of the place. You may choose to have an elaborate formal picnic, complete with your own portable table, or you may choose to have a sandwich on a blanket. In some of our picnics we offer both options. We have provided an index of the recipes from all the picnics at the back of the book so that you can mix and match them.

Proximate Proportions

Our picnic recipes are expressed sometimes in metric units, sometimes imperial, and sometimes both. Indeed, it is in the kitchen that Canada's conversion to metric is at its most confusing. Exact conversion produces ridiculous quantities: for example, 1 cup is equal to 236.6 millilitres. The usual way that a Canadian cook copes is by having measuring devices calibrated in both cups and millilitres. Then it is easy to switch systems to match the recipes. The important thing is to stick to the same system throughout the recipe, as it is generally proportion that is more important than actual quantity. For those who have only one kind of measuring cup, the following approximate conversion table is offered.

Approximate Metric Conversions

1/4 tsp.	1 ml
1/2 tsp.	2 ml
1 tsp.	5 ml
1 Tbsp.	15 ml
1/4 cup	50 ml
1/2 cup	125 ml
1 cup	250 ml
41/2 cups	1 L

Picnics in Public Parks

The Ontario Liquor Control Act prohibits consumption of alcohol in public parks without a permit. The inclusion of spirits in some of our menus is not to be interpreted as an invitation to disobey the laws of the Province of Ontario.

Pursuing Picnic Perfection

We expect our readers to fall into three groups: those who already picnic seriously and want to compare their spots with ours; those who want to become serious picnickers, and just need a little push; and armchair picnickers who will enjoy the stories, prepare the recipes, and eat in front of a cozy fire in their warm, dry living rooms.

We must acknowledge the suggestions from friends, many of whom will recognize elements of their own picnics in these pages. Our friends did help us as we went along, although they flatly refused to take us seriously as we described the magnitude of the task of picnic-book writing facing our family. In fact, the most empathetic comment came from our publisher. "Ah, a tough job, but someone has to do it!" he said. But was that compassion or envy in his tone?

Everyone has a favourite picnic. As we wandered the province doing our research we found that people who had been strangers to us a moment before had warmed to the word "picnic" and were suddenly confiding intimate family picnic secrets to us in exhaustive detail! There was the family in the pick-up truck who, when asked if there were any good picnic spots in the area, turned their truck around, yelled, "Follow us!" and led us along a logging road partway up a mountain to their favourite place. They told us vignettes of local history that wouldn't be found in reference books, but which added the touch of "magic" to the picnic. This wasn't an isolated example. When we asked one man in a small town museum about local history, he quickly telephoned to his wife to ask her to make up a picnic basket, drove us to his farm to pick her up, and took us all on one of the best picnics we've ever had.

We know that we have not seen, discovered nor even heard of all the great picnic places in Ontario. In fact, we would find it very distressing if we had, for much of the fun comes with the joy of discovering a new site, and this is our challenge to our readers. A picnic is an adventure that you share; we invite—nay, we encourage—readers to share their special picnic places for possible future editions of this book. Write to us, care of the publisher. All letters will be answered and suggestions acknowledged, if used.

And now, let's go on a picnic!

Picnic Paraphernalia

In this chapter we provide a checklist which progresses from the very basic kit for the occasional picnicker to the sophisticated gear of the serious dilettante. There is also discussion of the relative merits of different items which reflects our personal biases, but acknowledges other points of view, so that you can make your own informed selections. The following sections are arranged in a progression from a simple picnic kit to a more elaborate set-up.

The Absolute Basics

Also known as the "boy scout" or the "be prepared" kit, this consists of one Swiss army knife carried at all times in the jacket pocket. This isn't as simple as it seems. Care must be taken when selecting a Swiss army knife because they come with such a delightful array of pop-up gadgets that one is tempted to get the one that does everything including pick teeth, darn socks and yodel. This is unfortunate because knives with all those attachments, if they can still be called knives, weigh so much that they can no longer reside in a pocket but require a belt pouch or pick-up truck to carry them around. Fortunately, the Swiss have priced these knives beyond the reach of most wage-earning picnickers and so, while the temptation may be there, the wherewithal is often not. Our knife, which serves us well, has attachments that:

flip bottle caps,
pull corks,
open cans,
slice cheese, and
get the onion pickles from the bottom of the jar.

These are the essential functions, since smacking bottles against rocks to open them is ecologically unsound and potentially dangerous, and an inaccessible can of pâté de foie gras can spoil your whole day. These knives are still available for less than $20.

The Basic Picnic Kit

Do you travel often in your car, and do you like the occasional "impromptu" picnic? In that case, in your trunk along with the jumper cables, tire chains, and the half-filled bottle of windshield fluid, should be a basic picnic kit. This kit can be kept in a small box, taking up very little space, but permitting spontaneous picnicking without frills. It will do very well for the occasional picnicker, and you can add more equipment if you find you need to.

First there are the basics, the:

can opener,
bottle opener,
cork screw,
knife suitable for cheese.

While the all-purpose Swiss army machine will do, it also may introduce bits of cork into the wine, spray soda pop all over from punctured tops, and leave nasty jagged edges around the lips of tins. Thus we progress to special-purpose devices. The cost is truly a function of what you want to spend, with corkscrews and can openers varying in price from $1.98 to $20 each. Electric can openers are non-functional, of course, at most picnic sites, so purchase one of the more primitive manual models (or reclaim the old one from the back of the kitchen drawer).

Other convenient—and sometimes essential—bits of equipment that can be tucked into your picnic box are:

Bread knife: Although it may be fashionable to tear chunks of French bread from the loaf, there will be times when you want smooth slices, and this requires a knife with a serrated edge and a least an eight-inch (20 cm) blade. We prefer a serrated edge to a sharp French or German chef's knife because it tends to stay sharp longer, and is not quite so lethal when you are fishing around in the picnic kit for something else. This knife is also useful for slicing onions and tomatoes.

Insect repellent: Deep Woods Off is among the best.

Suntan lotion: It doesn't always rain on picnics. Get a high protection lotion, especially if near lakes, glaciers or the ocean.

Band-aids: Place a few in a plastic bag.

Matches: In the old days when smoking was socially acceptable, matches or other forms of fire-starting apparatus, like lighters, were always available. Now they are not, and one must make a special note to remember them. Bring lots, in a waterproof plastic bag or box. If you really want dependability, most camping stores sell waterproof matches.

Toilet paper: In boy scout camping days, this used to be referred to as 1001 because it has 1001 different uses. Keep in an old coffee can, with a tightly fitting plastic lid to keep it dry.

Garbage bags: Always pack out what you bring to any site.

Flashlight: It doesn't matter what time the picnic starts, at some point in the season you may find yourself stumbling around in the dark, possibly looking for something like car keys or a child's tooth retainer. Check the flashlight occasionally to make sure the batteries are not dead.

Binoculars: Whether you prefer the big field glasses, or one of the small but powerful sets, these are invaluable for spotting birds, looking at mountains, and spying on other picnickers.

Although it probably won't fit in your kit box, you will want a:

Blanket: Any old blanket will do, but there are good woolen blankets available in matching zipper cases which are sold as car blankets. These have the advantage of doubling as a pillow in the car for tired picnickers.

The final, but essential ingredients of a basic picnic kit are:

Flower, bird and tree identification books: Invaluable aids when wading through swamps, or wandering mountain meadows. There is something nice about knowing that the fuzzy pink plant you have found is really "Rosy Pussytoes."

Standard Equipment Package

Once you get beyond the impromptu picnic and onto a planned, or at least semi-planned, occasion there are certain items that become standard equipment. These items tend, in our case, to live in a cardboard box in the garage, where they can be quickly found. It is the presence of these items that moves picnicking from rustic ad-hockery to a pleasant art form. Since much of the picnicking takes place in parks, which usually have some of the rudiments of civilization such as toilets and fire pits or grills, the equipment package is directed at making the maximum use of those environments. These items, used in addition to the basic kit outlined above are:

Simple first aid kit: Antiseptic ointment; Lanacaine, to treat a cut, burn or bite; tweezers to remove the sliver or nettle; Dettol to kill the germs; an elastic bandage for the sprained or broken ankle; some Tylenol or Aspirin for pain or headache; and some antihistamines in case of that unlikely instance where someone stirs up a hornets' nest.

Fire makers: It is possible that someone else always gets to picnic spots just before we do and takes all the good wood; or maybe park staff have never tried to burn the firewood they supply. For whatever reason, our dominant impression of the firewood provided in parks is that it is green, impossible to split, and unwilling to burn. To alleviate the distress we take fire starter: nice little white squares of petroleum product that will eventually ignite the most stubborn of firewoods.

Splitting maul: We were originally of the opinion that little hatchets were a potential disaster, best left in the hardware store window, and that a three-pound, long-handled axe would look after most eventualities. Several frustrating years of trying to split the wood at parks has changed our minds, and we now carry a six-pound splitting maul (found in most hardware stores, about $25) which adequately serves the purpose. Although all of us can wield it when necessary, it is best to bring along a son still experiencing his "macho" period. Daughters' boyfriends are a satisfactory substitute.

The kitchen cupboard: A number of things which are always available in the cupboard or the fridge are rarely thought of until you are on a picnic and realize that you don't have them. Our little supply box contains: salt, pepper, soya sauce, Worcestershire sauce, mustard, sugar, ground coffee, a small bottle of cooking oil, and a small bottle of dishwashing detergent.

Pots and pans: The absolute minimum implements include: a cast iron frying pan, which will turn an uneven fire into an even heat; a pot for boiling things; a coffee pot; and a large plastic basin which does double duty as a food preparation basin and a washing-up bucket. Other items, woks and double boilers and the like, depend on the menu you propose to use, but are not part of the standard equipment. Our coffee pot is an old enamel camp coffee pot into which we throw water and grounds; it sits directly upon the fire. We did experiment for a while with a Melita pot, and one of those fancy Italian jobs that has a spring-mounted plunger to push the grounds to the bottom. These were unsuccessful because you want coffee the most when both you and the weather are cold and miserable. The fancy European jobs have no facility for rewarming the coffee, whereas the old pot can just be set, or left, among the coals. In addition, coffee from the fancy systems just doesn't have that nice chewy texture we associate with campfire coffee.

The kitchen sink: Basic items that make life over the coals more bearable are: an old glove for picking hot pots off the stove; a flipper for turning things in the pan; some tongs for grabbing things; a slotted spoon for fishing, and a serving spoon. Remember also to bring a dish rag, scouring pad, and some dish towels.

Coffee cups: Coffee cups merit a listing of their own since they are still an item that is in dispute in this family. There is a faction that likes the tin or enamel cups like the old miners had. Such a cup has the added appeal that when the coffee is cold, the cup can be placed directly on the grill to reheat. The other faction claims that tin cups burn your hands and lips initially, that the coffee cools down too fast, and finally that there is always a chip in the enamel right where your lips meet the rim. This second faction favors a simple Melmac cup (they are used in hospitals) which the first faction feels are ugly. A third faction has been attempting to introduce earthenware mugs, which are, of course, breakable.

The above list should reduce or eliminate most of the preparation hassles associated with picnics. Planning can then focus directly on the menu and on the central—and usually remembered—items such as the disposable plastic plates, cups and cutlery, the plastic table cloth, and the coffee Thermos.

The Garage Sale Picnic Kit

If you begin to picnic more frequently you may prefer not to use plastic disposable equipment. You may progress to the Garage Sale Picnic Kit, which includes:

Old, hard-sided suitcase: This will be your storage and carrying case, so give some thought to the size you want. It isn't an irrevocable decision, however, since these suitcases cost between about $1 and $5. Your sales resistance should prevent you from spending more than that.

Dishes: Select some that please you from the wide variety available at garage sales and flea markets. You may merely upgrade to a classier set of plastic dishes, or you may choose dinner plates of different, but complementary, antique patterns.

Glasses: Select some good glass or crystal goblets. After extensive research, supplemented by numerous field trials, we have discovered that wine tastes terrible when sipped from plastic glasses.

Table cloth: Linen or cotton, not plastic—and only occasionally found at garage sales. You may have to buy a length of pretty fabric and hem it.

Table cloth clips: Available in camping supply stores, these hold your table cloth down in a breeze (or even a gale-force wind).

Spices: In a small box in your suitcase/picnic kit place small quantities of your favourite spices. Use the little bottles they come in, or save old pill containers or small jars.

Bread board: Picnics often involve slicing and serving cheeses, cucumbers, pâté, tomatoes, and chunks of smoked salmon. Picnic tables, although they may possess interesting graffiti, sap drippings, and remnants of previous picnics, are not the most hygienic surfaces on which to work. We suggest that you bring your own bread or cheese cutting board. A slab of wood will likely do, but plastic cutting boards are lighter and easier to clean.

The Abercrombie and Fitch Picnic

We feel that we would be doing our readers an injustice if we did not mention that symbol of yuppie splendour, the Abercrombie and Fitch Picnic Basket. This will cost close to $300 for two, and almost $500 for the set for four. It comes with four dinner plates in an exclusive English bone china pattern, a Thermos, stainless steel cutlery, plastic mugs, glass wine glasses, plastic-covered storage containers, a table cloth, and salt and pepper, all neatly arranged in a wicker and leather basket.

Although basically a good idea, with a few first-rate features (we especially like the china pattern), the selection has a few flaws which must be overcome if it is to be a truly functional picnic basket. We suggest that you throw out the plastic mugs and replace them with china or pottery mugs; replace the stainless cutlery with sterling silver flatware; and replace the glass wine glasses with crystal.

One final accompaniment, absolutely essential if you expect to achieve recognition commensurate with the Yuppie status, is:

The matching table cloth, picnic blanket and helium-filled balloon. The balloon is anchored to your picnic table and enables friends and relatives to locate you on a crowded picnic turf. It also helps if the balloon is coordinated with your table cloth, sports clothes, and the upholstery of your BMW.

Quest for Fire

The metal grills and firewood provided at parks present a continuing challenge to the patience and resourcefulness of the picnic devotee. These pits can be used to cook the occasional hot dog and marshmallow, but for serious cooking they offer frustration, angst, and burned salmon. Thus, as your picnic menus move beyond hot dogs, we suggest you upgrade your fire sources to include some of the following items.

The Coleman naphtha gas stove: It's the sportsman's companion, the traditional camp cooker, the burner that always dies when you are not paying attention to it, and the one which causes you to bang your knuckles when pumping it up. The Coleman is cheap to operate, reliable, and reasonably safe. The problem is that you must love and understand your Coleman, know how much to pump it up, always have the little funnel for filling it, and generally pamper it. If you do, it will give you years of dependable service.

The portable hibachi: Shishkabobs grilling over a bed of coals. . . a picture postcard picnic. Our problem is that we never seem to be able to get the charcoal going properly and so the meat takes too long, or is still raw at serving time, and the beautiful bed of coals finally appears just about the time we are packing up to go. Also, we have not yet mastered the problem of transporting charcoal so that it doesn't make a mess in the trunk of the car.

Propane appliances: Fuel from a bottle. We must confess that we tend to like the neat, simple, reliable heat that comes from a propane fire. We do not believe that half the fun of a picnic is fiddling with a fire source; we prefer to transport the close control of a modern kitchen stove to our picnic table. The first of these devices we acquired was the single burner propane gas ring which is a little tripod with the propane bottle forming one leg. This works well for one-dish meals like stirfrys in a wok, or frittatas, or soups. It's also great for making coffee. It can change from simmer to boil instantly, and as long as you have a spare propane bottle, the heat goes on. We have been so happy with this little burner, that for cooking multi-pot meals, instead of going to a two- or three-burner stove, we take two or three single-burner units. This is, however, probably the most expensive means of cooking, since the little propane bottles cost about $5 each.

Propane portable barbecue: Recently introduced, this table-top item weighs about 20 pounds (9 kg), sells for about $50, and runs on propane. The control it offers means that steaks and chops can be grilled—not sacrificed—and since the lid closes, baking is now possible at a picnic.

Dutch oven: There is one historic cooking artifact that is great fun, and a source of excellent meals. This is the traditional Dutch oven which is neither Dutch, nor an oven, but rather is a big cast iron pot with a lid like a pie plate. The Dutch oven can be buried in a fire pit, with coals stacked up on the lid, and left to cook bread, casseroles, or stew.

Gilding the Lily

There are some items which may, by some, be judged as frivolous or decadent, but could still find their way into your picnic kit. These include:

Folding lawn chairs: For many these are not an extra, but mandatory. The picnic table that is comfortable to sit at for long periods of time has yet to be developed, and a few lawn chairs provide excellent thrones for elders.

The portable picnic table: Plastic folding picnic tables which seat four and can be easily carried are available for approximately $100. Ours folds into a flat case which remains in the trunk of our car and is useful in underdeveloped picnic spots.

Ice bucket: Used for serving chilled wine or champagne. It is also possible to get earthenware wine bottle coolers (they look like a plain flower vase) which you supercool in your freezer or in ice. The wine bottle (white or sparkling wine) rests inside the chilled container on the table, and the wine remains cold throughout the meal.

Portable blender: Battery-operated blenders are fairly new on the market and may take a bit of hunting, but they are perfect for mixing margueritas, daquiris, or sauces and salad dressings at the picnic site.

First aid kit: By the time you become a regular picnicker you will need to have a reliable first aid kit. Accidents do happen: ankles get twisted, fingers get cut, wrists get sprained, and people get bitten by all manner of insects. Many such ailments can be treated without spoiling the picnic. We have with us on all picnics a waterproof plastic case containing the following items:

Band-Aids

3" tensor bandage - extra support for sprains and twisted limbs

Dettol - disinfects wounds

Lanacaine - removes sting from burns and bites
several packages 4 x 4 gauze bandages
several packages 2 x 2 gauze bandages
one roll 2" gauze bandage
one roll low-allergy adhesive tape
scissors
Q-tip swabs
finger splint - to immobilize a sprained or broken finger
butterfly bandages - to pull together the edges of a cut after it has
     been cleaned
Tylenol or Aspirin
a mild antihistamine
a pocket guide to first aid - for the moments when you panic and
     can't remember what to do.

Clothing

Some people wear funny hats, others have a favourite jacket that is worn only on picnics. Fun and comfort are both important. Picnics are not to be confused with serious hikes, for which clothing can be prescribed. Picnics vary widely—what may be right for a city park picnic may not be right for a wilderness picnic. Still, there are a few general considerations. A light plastic jacket or poncho that folds up into a tiny pack will be appreciated time and time again during unexpected showers. Rubber boots are a good idea if there is a hike near the picnic ground, especially if it passes through boggy land. Generally we find that on a picnic there is no shortage of carrying space, as there is on a hike or a longer trip. There is usually lots of space in the trunk of the car, so the extra pair of boots or flippers are not a major inconvenience even if they are not used.

Food Storage and Handling

Food storage is an important issue, even if you are only moving the food a short distance. The danger of food poisoning is serious, although easily avoided by taking some sensible precautions. The simplest rule of all is: keep hot foods hot and cold foods cold.

This will require a bit of special equipment, and a little foresight. For example, if you prepare a casserole at home for the picnic, cook it just before you leave, wrap it in newspapers or other insulation material, and transport it in a box or, ideally, in a picnic cooler with other hot foods. A cooler can be used to transport both hot and cold foods, but not together. A cooler, after all, is only an insulated box with handles. The point is to keep the meal as hot as possible during transfer. Similarly, if a potato salad is included in your menu, make it the day of the picnic and chill it thoroughly in the refrigerator. Just before leaving, place it in an ice-filled cooler, or otherwise insulate it to keep it well-chilled all the way to the picnic table. When packing the cooler it is a good idea to place ice blocks or refreezable sacks on top of the food as well as in the bottom of the cooler.

Protein foods require special attention; eggs, meat and milk must be kept cold during transfer. This also applies to foods derived from dairy products, such as yogurt, mayonnaise and cheese. Here Thermos or vacuum bottles, long the mainstay of the hot coffee drinker, can also be used to keep milk, yogurt or a cold soup cold.

Foods containing acid should not be stored or transported in metal containers or pans, even if they have been prepared in them. Although the result is not dangerous, it is displeasing, as the acid will react with the metal to discolour the food, and there will be a slight metallic taste. Vinegar is dilute acetic acid, wine contains acid, and most fruits and vegetables contain acid, especially oranges, lemons, tomatoes and rhubarb. Store and transport these foods and their sauces and juices in plastic or glass containers.

Meat is one of the most dangerous sources of bacteria, and deserves a separate discussion. Buy only fresh meats. Keep them cold during transport and processing. Make sure that all meat is well cooked—rare steaks should be served only if the meat was freshly purchased just before the picnic and then transported at 4°C (40°F) or less. Your control of temperatures is much less accurate on a picnic, so it is easier to estimate doneness on pieces of meat that are about the same size and thickness.

Chicken is especially hard to judge, but as a precaution, ensure that there is no pink meat near the bones, and that all juices are white, before you serve the meat.

Cooking eventually kills the bacteria in meat, but there is a certain range of warmth, 4°C to 60°C (40° to 140°F), during which bacteria flourish. Be very sure that all meat has been cooked until it reaches a higher temperature than this. If you can't measure with a thermometer, carefully examine the meat before serving.

A word about cutting boards. You may have a nice clean piece of wood or plastic in your picnic kit which you then use to prepare the meat for barbecuing. If you later prepare vegetables or anything else on the cutting board, you will contaminate this food with the bacteria from the uncooked meat. There are two solutions: first, have two cutting boards, one for preparing raw meat and the other for everything else; second, carry with you a solution of Javex and water for washing down the cutting board each time it is used for preparation of raw meat.

One way to avoid some of the dangers of bacterial contamination of picnic meats is to use a marinade. The acid in the marinade slows the growth of bacteria. The marinating container (plastic or glass) should still be kept cold in transit.

This completes the summary of the results from our years of experimenting with picnic equipment. Undoubtedly everyone has his or her own personal preferences, and new gadgets continually appear on the market. We are fairly selective because we still want to keep spare tires in the trunk, and occasionally even carry loads of groceries. We only acquire what will fit in our existing picnic suitcase. A picnic kit is an expression of personal taste—give full rein to yours, to make your picnics easy and fun to organize.

KENORA

1 **Kenora**
A Burnt Out Picnic

In May 1980 a forest fire swept through northern Ontario devastating 280,500 acres of woodland in just two days. This fire is known as Kenora 23. Our picnic takes place in part of the regenerating burn area, on the north shore of Willard Lake.

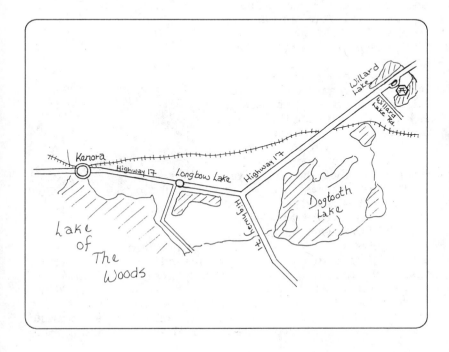

How to get there

Drive east from Kenora on Highway 17 for 42 km. The turn-off to the Willard Lake picnic area is on the south side of the highway, just after Willard Lake Road. You can park right beside your picnic table on the north shore of the little lake.

Kenora 23

There was quite a lot of lightning in the air during the early weeks of May 1980, and when lightning strikes dry trees, it can start a fire. Most such fires just burn themselves out quickly. But there was a strong, dry wind on the morning of May 19th, 1980, and it caught one of the many little fires and turned it into a raging forest fire. A wind-driven fire is wide; it moves very fast, leaving behind some undamaged trees and underbrush because it passes over them: this is called crowning. Kenora 23 began well south of the highway, and was carried north by the wind. The fire reached the south side of Willard Lake at night, burning less intensely, and you can see that some trees were left unburned there. In the morning when the fire reached the north side it was much more intense, and much hotter. The damage here was therefore more severe, as the skeletons of the pre-1980 forest behind your picnic table will attest.

Skeletons from Kenora 23

In just two days the fire burned over 30 km along the Trans-Canada Highway, almost as far as George Lake. At times during the fire the authorities closed the highway, but since it was a key route for evacuation it was kept open as much as possible. Two thousand people lived in the area that was damaged, in villages, cottages and camps. Most area residents were evacuated and many buildings were burned.

Speed of response is of paramount importance in fighting a forest fire. There are two strategies: one is to send in ground crews to try to slow the progress of the fire by digging ditches and creating clearings to contain the fire in as small an area as possible. Over 1,500 firefighters worked round the clock for 48 hours to control Kenora 23 in this way. The other approach is an initial attack with helicopters and water bombers. The helicopters are used to bring crews and supplies in and out. The planes carry water to the edges of the burn to help create a protected margin. The foremen and supervisors of the operation conduct their reconnaissance from planes, too. Both strategies were used to fight Kenora 23. At the peak of the fire, 123 aircraft were in use.

Although the planes are quick and efficient, there are serious dangers involved in flying near or above a fire—the heat causes unpredictable updrafts and air currents. One supervisor told us about having his little plane suddenly flip over just above Willard Lake.

Regardless of the strategies used by the forestry department, weather remains the dominant influence on the life of a forest fire. After 48 hours a gentle rain relieved the hot windy weather which had promoted Kenora 23, and the crew were able to get the fire under control.

Regeneration

There have always been forest fires. They are part of the cycle of the woodlands, and regeneration is part of that process, too. In time the forest heals itself. The pattern of regeneration depends very much upon the intensity of the fire. If the fire has been extremely hot, all the hardwood will be consumed; if it burns at a lower temperature, only the birch and poplar are likely to burn completely. Other factors which affect regeneration are: the thickness of the duff layer—the moss, needles and mold on the ground; the moisture patterns of the soils and the air; and the amount of residual timber (deadfall). Forestry departments nowadays often aid the process of regeneration. Assessment and planning are done with ground crews and with aerial infra-red photographs. In the northern part of the Kenora 23 burn area, jackpine was seeded from the air.

In the picnic area, since the damage was limited, jack pine is regenerating naturally. Jackpine benefits from a fire because the cones, or seeds, are only released in intense heat. That's why they are among the first new plants. There is also about ten percent of black spruce on the northern shore. The south shore is also regenerating naturally with about 20 percent black spruce, mixed with the jackpine and some poplar.

The Kenora district has an especially rich variety of plants and trees because it is a transition area. Situated on the edge of the Precambrian Shield, it lies between the boreal forest and the southern forest zones, and displays elements of both.

A forest fire is cleansing to an area. After it has passed, a richer mosaic of vegetation grows. The forest canopy is reduced or removed, and more light means a wider range of plant life. Moose, bear, deer and beaver thrive in a post-burn region. This positive aspect of forest fires has long been known by Indian peoples, who lit fires in the spring to create optimal hunting areas, to control grass, to create clearings for villages and pasture lands for animals, and for many other ecological reasons. They knew that an early spring burning warms the soil, removes dead material and releases soil nutrients, promoting a longer growing season. For some years the forestry department outlawed intentional burning because it was seen as a cause of uncontrolled forest fires. Now, however, forest officials have begun to recognize the potential advantages of controlled burns, and are using the technique themselves.

Things to do

1. Bring along your canoe and enjoy the peace and beauty of Willard Lake. You might even catch a fish for your picnic.

2. Enjoy an aerial view of the forest by taking a seaplane tour. The floatplane base is in Kenora harbour at 2nd Street Dock.

3. Take a boat cruise for several hours on the Lake of the Woods. The MS *Kenora* ticket office is at the Harbourfront dock in Kenora. There are over 14,500 islands in this lake. (A note to trivia buffs: this is the second largest of the roughly three-quarters of a million lakes in the province in Ontario.) The uneven coastline of the Lake of the Woods is 65,000 miles long, and the lake itself stretches 65 miles north to south and 55 miles east to west. The beauty of this lake is world renowned. You can see this for yourself on a luncheon, afternoon, or dinner cruise. Reservations are advised for the lunch and dinner cruises—call (807) 468-9124.

4. While in Kenora tour the Boise Cascade Paper Mill, and learn about the process of newsprint production. Tours are available twice daily from 8 to 4, except on statutory holidays. Children must be over twelve years of age, and groups not larger than ten. Reservations are required. Call 468-6411.

Things to eat

Bring along your camp stove for this one so you can appreciate the effects of the forest fire without causing one. Since this is fishing country, we suggest that you catch a trout or bass in Willard Lake for the main course.

Pan-Fried Fresh Fish

Fillet your freshly caught fish and fry the fillets in butter in a medium hot heavy cast-iron frying pan. Fresh fish tastes so good that there is no need to augment the flavour, but you might bring along a handful of sliced almonds, and throw them into the hot butter once you have removed the cooked fish. While they are browning, sprinkle on a dash of lemon juice and freshly ground pepper, and pour the works over the fish fillets.

Spinach and Mushroom Salad

1 pound spinach leaves
1 1/2 cups fresh mushrooms
2 Tbsp. capers

Wash and sort the spinach leaves, and tear into bite-sized pieces. Clean and slice the mushrooms, and toss with the spinach and capers, and the following dressing:

Whisk:
1/3 cup vegetable or olive oil
2 Tbsp. tarragon vinegar

And add:
1 tsp. sugar
1 tsp. Dijon mustard

Bannock

3 cups flour
salt
1 tsp. baking powder
2 Tbsp. lard
3 cups cold water

Combine dry ingredients in a bowl. Make a well, and pour in the water. Mix into a dough and knead it; flatten out and place in a heavy frying pan with a bit more lard. Cook over low heat. Turn once.

We usually place the dry ingredients, pre-mixed, in a container, and do the rest at the picnic site.

Fresh berries and cream we leave for you to supply.

Spruce Tea

Since you are in the woodland, this seems especially appropriate. Collect half a cup of chopped or broken up young spruce twigs and needles, and place them in boiling water. Turn the heat off, but keep covered to steep for about 10 minutes.

It doesn't matter if you can't distinguish between spruce or pine—they both make good tea.

2 Fort Frances
Lady Frances's Wedding Trip

Frances Simpson married her cousin, George, in England in February, 1830. Since George's business responsibilities were pressing, they left almost immediately on an extensive honeymoon/business trip of several thousand miles. By June 1st they had reached the fort at Lac la Pluie, later to be renamed Fort Frances in honour of this adventurous young woman.

How to get there

The picnic takes place in Pither's Point Park, a peninsula at the junction of Rainy Lake and the Rainy River. Named after Robert J.N. Pither who was in charge of the Hudson's Bay Post at Fort Frances for many years, it is at the east end of the town of Fort Frances, just off Scott Street (Highway 11). The turn-off is well marked. Our favourite picnic site is near the end of the point, past the dry-docked tugboat, under a big tree, looking back toward the city.

Lady Frances' Honeymoon

Frances was eighteen years old when she married her 43-year-old cousin, George. George's letters of the time reveal that he was indeed in love with his bride-to-be; this was not merely a marriage for the sake of propriety. Almost immediately after their wedding, they set sail for Upper Canada. Resting only briefly at Montreal after the transatlantic voyage, they soon left Lachine, bound for the west. Their journey was made by canoe. Portages were mostly on foot, and only occasionally by cart. Mrs. Simpson was carried on the back of a husky voyageur through some of the more difficult portages. Throughout this trip, Frances kept a detailed diary.

George Simpson was well known for the astonishing speed at which he covered the vast distances of his territory. Frances's presence on this trip does not appear to have caused any slackening of his pace. The day began at about 2 a.m. Soon everyone was on the river, travelling by moonlight for the first few hours. The group stopped for breakfast at 9 a.m., but were back in the canoes within forty-five minutes. A typical day might include many miles covered by canoe, with several portages. Frances managed all of this in a long skirt! The day's journey often ended only at dark, when the group ate quickly, and slept soundly on the ground, cushioned only by their cloaks and a few blankets.

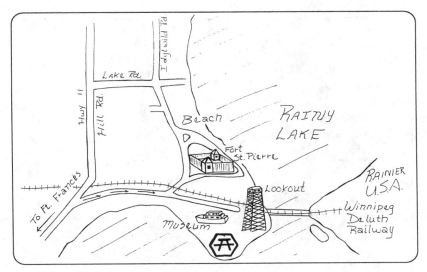

They reached Lac La Pluie at noon on June 1st, 1830, after an eventful morning. Their canoe had struck a rock, and was leaking badly. They pulled ashore, but discovered that the equipment for mending the canoes was in the other boat, far ahead of them. Frances pointed out in her diary that "Necessity . . . is the Mother of Invention: a piece of Oil-cloth answered as a substitute for bark; a piece of Twine for "Wattap," (or sewing roots) and the whole smeared over with Butter inside & out, (instead of Pine Pitch) which stopped the leak sufficiently . . . " They did arrive safely and, after a tour of the fort and its garden, dined on fresh sturgeon and dried beaver meat. A few months after the Simpsons' visit the fort at Lac La Pluie was renamed Fort Frances in honour of the governor's lady. The fort which Frances visited that day in 1830 was about 2.5 km downstream from our picnic site.

The other Mrs. Simpson

Before his marriage to Frances, George Simpson followed the custom of the time, and lived and travelled for many years with an Indian woman, or "country wife," as they were called. In choosing to marry his English cousin on a return trip to London headquarters, he was abandoning an already established family, with four children. This act had far-reaching effects on the families of the Canadian fur traders.

Until this time, relationships with native wives were considered official contracts by both parties. The marriages were arranged according to regular procedures, with a suitable bride price being paid

Pither's Point Park

to the bride's parents. Such marriages had many advantages for the fur trader. They secured the loyalty of the Indian tribe. Furthermore, these women served as interpreters for their husbands; often they were also guides because of their knowledge of the woods and waterways. Their familiarity with the regional flora and fauna made them invaluable suppliers of local foods, especially during winter. Country marriages were often life-long.

These women were treated with the greatest respect by both traders and Indians. They were enveloped into the culture of the fort, although their ties to their tribes were always maintained. Their children were raised according to British middle class traditions, with the boys expected to enter military service or the fur trade at maturity. Daughters often married other traders.

Margaret, daughter of a York Fort schooner captain and his native wife, was George Simpson's wife for at least ten years. She bore him four children: Maria, George, James and John. Nothing is known of Margaret's feelings regarding the arrival of Frances. It is known, however, that soon after, Margaret Taylor was married to Amable Hogue at the Red River Settlement. George remained in contact with his children.

Country marriages continued after 1830. However, many traders chose to follow the example of their leader and abandon their country wives in favour of British women. The strong puritanical influence of the missionaries also helped to push these native and mixed blood women into a subordinate position.

Things to do

1. Visit the museum housed in a replica of Fort St. Pierre. The original fort pre-dated the Simpsons' visit by a century. In his search for the great western sea about which he had heard from the Indians, La Vérendrye's explorations had led to the establishment of many important fur trading posts, including St. Pierre on Rainy Lake (Lac La Pluie then). The first fort was built in 1731 by La Jemeraye for his uncle, La Vérendrye. The museum features contemporary local art, native Indian crafts, and some historical displays.

2. Climb the lookout tower, also in the park. Vertigo sufferers will find that the view is worth being 100 feet up. The museum at the base of the tower also has historical displays, as well as displays about the lumber industry in the region.

3. Still in Pither's Point Park, you can tour the dry-docked tugboat, the *Hallett*, once the most powerful logging boat on Rainy Lake. It was used for hauling logging booms across Rainy Lake from 1941 to 1974, when it was replaced by the more economical logging trucks.

4. Visit the Fort Frances Museum and Cultural Centre, at 259

Fort St. Pierre

Scott Street. The museum, unlike the seasonal attractions at Pither's Point Park, is open daily year-round. Exhibits include historical and industrial artifacts. Upstairs there is a display of local arts and crafts in the summer season.

5. Whether or not there is an engineer in your family, you will marvel at the beauty and astonishing length of the Noden Causeway, eight kilometres east of Fort Frances on Highway 11. Completed in 1965, it is six kilometres long, and serves as part of the highway link between Toronto and Rainy River. It joins the banks of Rainy Lake by island hopping. One span is 12 metres above water level and permits the large lake vessels to pass beneath. The causeway was constructed entirely of materials quarried in the immediate area.

6. Experience part of the journey of Lady Frances by canoeing in Quetico Provincial Park, 180 km east of Fort Frances. It is clear from her diaries that Lady Frances passed through the rivers and lakes here to reach Lac La Pluie in 1830. The park remains much as it was then, and most of it is accessible only by canoe.

Things to eat

To stay true to our theme for this picnic we would have to serve fresh sturgeon and dried beaver meat, since this is what was served to the Simpsons on their arrival at Hungry Hall, the HBC fort. A loggers' feast is a suitable alternative. After all, Fort Frances is a pulp and paper town now, and you did visit the logging tug, the *Hallett*, didn't you? The following menu is what a logger might have for dinner in a bush camp around the turn of the century.

```
┌─────────────────────┐
│      MENU           │
└─────────────────────┘
```

Ham and Sausage
Baked Beans
Bread with Butter and Molasses
Dried Fruit Pie
Coffee

Try to find home-made sausages and thick slices of ham at a small butcher shop. They should be fried in lard in a big cast iron frying pan, over an open fire. Your bread should be made from whole wheat flour, sliced thick, slathered with butter, and then spread with molasses. You might even like this. (Purists will spread the bread with lard rather than butter.) Accompany the meal with lots of very strong coffee.

Loggers' Baked Beans
(Serves 4-6)

2 cups dried Great Northern beans

Wash and drain beans. Soak beans in cooking pot overnight. In the morning, cover and boil for 15 minutes. Drain, reserving the liquid.

Combine:
1 14 oz. tin stewed tomatoes
1 tsp. dry mustard

1 medium onion, chopped
1 Tbsp. brown sugar
2 Tbsp. molasses
oregano, marjoram, basil, and rosemary to taste

with the beans. Place the resulting mixture in a earthenware pot or crock.

Stir in:
1/2 pound salt pork or bacon in chunks

and bake in a slow oven for 4 to 6 hours. Use the reserved fluid to keep the beans from drying out. Alternatively, if you lack a crock or oven, the beans can be cooked on the top of the stove in a large pot, stirring occasionally and using the reserved fluid to keep them moist. Transport packed in newspapers to keep warm, or reheat at the picnic.

Dried Fruit Pie

The logging camps were often in remote places, and all supplies had to keep for a long time. Loggers were especially inventive with their dried foods.

Stew dried prunes, figs or apricots, or a mixture of dried fruits in water to cover. Add sugar or honey to taste. Bring to a boil and simmer uncovered until the fruit is tender. When only a half-cup or so of liquid is left, thicken with a tablespoon of cornstarch, and cook for a few minutes longer. Pour into cooked pie shell (see Aunt Nell's pie crust recipe, Wasaga Beach picnic). Bake at 325 °F for 20 minutes or until set. Cool and serve. You can update this recipe by serving it with ice cream or whipping cream.

LAKE SUPERIOR

3 Thunder Bay
A Portage Picnic

The voyageurs had to carry their canoes and supplies by land around rapids and waterfalls. Hence, this picnic takes place beside a waterfall, Middle Falls, on the Grand Portage.

How to get there

This picnic is in the picnic area/campground at Middle Falls Provincial Park. The site has few tourists, a beautiful waterfall, and is actually beside the Pigeon River, the route of the Grand Portage of the

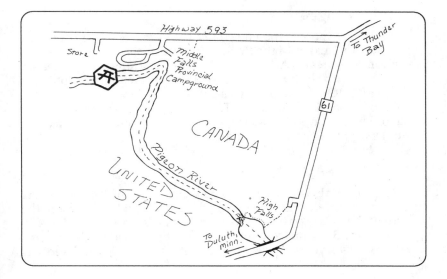

Middle Falls on the Grand Portage

voyagers. To get there drive south from Thunder Bay on Highway 61 for 59 kilometres. Turn west at the sign for the park, just before you reach the American border. Rather than turning in at the park entrance, continue along the road another few kilometres or so to the store, on your left. Turn in and park here, since it is closer to walk to the picnic from this end of the park, and the ice cream cones at the store are legendary—hence your picnic dessert.

The Voyageurs

Using fast canoes, the voyageurs could traverse the continent from the Great Lakes to the Rockies in four to six weeks. The route west from Montreal to Athabasca was over 3,000 miles long by water. It was divided into two main sections, with the halfway point at Thunder Bay. Once a year the western and the eastern canoes met at the Rendezvous in the summer. The western voyageurs brought fur pelts to be sent on to the markets of the east, while the easterners brought supplies and trade goods for the coming winter.

The Mountain Portage

The Mountain Portage is on the north side of the Kaministiquia River, around Kakabeka Falls. According to David Thompson, the length of the portage around the falls was 1,426 yards, which is 4/5 of a mile, or 1.3 kilometres. This route had been used by the Indians for thousands of years. A spear point dating from 5,000 years ago was found near the lower end of the portage. You can still walk along part of the portage trail. It crosses the picnic area on the north side of the falls—just follow the signs.

The Grand Portage

The Pigeon River is part of the boundary between Canada and the United States. From 1722 to 1797 the Grand Portage along the Pigeon River Route was the favoured route of the voyageurs. It bypasses Middle and High Falls on the south side of the Pigeon River. It was about 9 miles shorter than the Mountain Portage route. Following the establishment of the United States, tension arose between the Americans and the British colonies to the north. The voyageurs reverted to the Mountain Portage Route, despite its extra length, because it avoided entering American territory. The portages lost their economic importance as the route to the west when the transcontinental railway was built.

Beaver Hats and the Fur Trade

In the middle of the seventeenth century a new fashion emerged in England: beaver hats were suddenly much in demand, and were to remain so until the 1830s when they were replaced by silk hats. Although the actual styles of beaver hats changed over time, they remained popular because the felt created from the underhairs of the beaver pelt was very malleable and permitted creative designs. Beaver hair is the easiest hair to "carrot," that is, to curl and interlock with other hair to make felt. Carroting is produced by the effect of mercury on the hair. Beaver hair made a firm and rigid felt, permitting the wide-brimmed hats worn by the cavaliers to have brims that stayed flat. The demand for beaver pelts was the major impetus for the fur trade in North America. This quirk

"CONTINENTAL" COCKED HAT (1776)

"NAVY HAT" COCKED HAT (1800)

ARMY (1837)

CLERICAL (18TH CENTURY)

THE WELLINGTON (1812)

THE PARIS BEAU (1815)

THE D'ORSAY (1820)

THE REGENT (1825)

MODIFICATIONS OF THE BEAVER HATS

of fashion wear had devastating effects: the mercury used in making beaver hats caused madness among the hatters—hence the Mad Hatter in the Tea Party in *Alice in Wonderland*. The consequent economic changes imposed upon the Indians of North America led to the destruction of cultures that had lasted for millenia.

Things to do

1. Visit Old Fort William in Thunder Bay. In 1803 the British North West Company moved its headquarters from Grand Portage and established Fort William. The fort has been restored to what it might have been like in about 1815. There are over 40 historic buildings, with displays, and staff in period costume.

2. Cross the border and visit the Grand Portage National Monument in Minnesota. The 13.6-kilometre portage route is still maintained, so you may choose to hike along for awhile, and imagine that you are carrying a 90-pound pack or a 24-foot canoe.

3. Arrive at Fort William from the river, just as the voyageurs did. Take a cruise ship from the Thunder Bay North Marina on Water Street at Red River Road. The hour-and-a-half boat ride offers many amenities which the voyageurs did not have. Food and beverages are served, and the captain offers a commentary.

Things to eat

Since this is a voyageur picnic, we will supply some useful recipes, and a few that are more likely to be of historical interest than stimulants to a present-day appetite.

Pemmican

Making pemmican was the method used by the Indians for preserving and storing buffalo meat. Voyageurs purchased their pemmican from the Plains Indians and used it as a main source of protein on the voyage east.

Select cuts of:
> *buffalo sinew*
> *buffalo tallow*
> *dried berries*

Place hams, shoulders and sinews of buffalo in sun to dry for several days. When completely dry, pound until meat becomes a powder.

Melt the hard buffalo fat to form tallow, and pour into pounded meat powder. Mix well until meat is saturated. Add dried saskatoon berries or rose hips. Store in hide bags. (It is easier to store the pemmican bags if you knock them into square or rectangular shapes before the mixture has completely hardened.)

Voyageur Stew
(Serves 4 Voyageurs or 8-10 Picnickers)

On their trip between Montreal and Thunder Bay, the voyageurs would make a great pot of pea soup over their fire in the evening, and then place it in insulated wrappings for the next day. By the time they ate it, the consistency was more like stew than soup. It provided a hearty, nourishing diet for the long journey up the Ottawa River and through the lakes to Fort William.

1 pound salt pork
1 Tbsp. dry mustard
1 pound dry peas
8 cups cold water
1 Tbsp. coarse salt
1 clove garlic, minced
1 tin sweet corn kernels
1 tsp. summer savory, preferably fresh

Rub salt pork with the dry mustard. Cover and refrigerate for 12 hours. Cut into bite-sized pieces.

Sort, wash, and soak the peas in the cold water overnight.

In a soup kettle place all ingredients except the corn. Bring to a boil, and then reduce heat and simmer for about 5 hours. The stew consistency will be achieved by checking the mixture from time to time, and adding water to thin, or removing the lid to thicken. Fifteen minutes before serving, add the corn, stirring it into the mixture. This dish can easily be reheated at the picnic site.

Biscuits
(Makes 16)

Voyageurs carried flour with them, and often made biscuits to eat with their stew. Here is a slightly updated recipe, since it includes some spices which were not available to the men of the river.

2 cups whole wheat flour
4 tsp. baking powder
1/2 tsp. salt
1/2 tsp. cream of tartar
1 tsp. oregano
1 tsp. rosemary
1 tsp. thyme
1/2 cup shortening
2/3 cup milk

Sift the first four ingredients together, and then stir in the spices. Cut the shortening into the dry mixture until it resembles coarse crumbs. Make a well in the mixture and pour in the milk. Stir only until the dough follows the fork, then pat or roll the dough to 1/2" thickness. Cut with a glass or jar lid into rounds, and bake on an ungreased baking sheet for 10-12 minutes.

Wild Rice and Pork Casserole
(Serves 4)

Voyageurs who manned the canoes from Montreal to Fort William, without continuing on to the west, were called "pork eaters," while the others were considered more rugged, and were called "winterers." The pork eaters would add salt pork to their pea soup. They would purchase wild rice from the natives in the fall, after it had been dried. The following recipe is an adaptation of these foods. You can use bacon instead of salt pork, if you wish.

> 1 1/2 cups wild rice
> 2 1/2 cups cold water
> 2 1/2 tsp. salt
> 1 large onion, diced
> 1/2 lb. sliced fresh mushrooms (or 1 tin)
> 1/2 lb. salt pork, diced
> 1 cup grated carrots
> 1/2 cup milk
> 1 egg

Bring the cold water, rice and salt to a boil, and boil for 10 minutes. Cover and set aside for 30 minutes, or until the water has been completely absorbed.

Meanwhile, brown the salt pork. Add the onion and mushrooms, and brown them gently. Then add the carrots, mix well and heat through. Stir in the rice. Beat the egg, add the milk to the egg and mix well, and then add egg mixture to rice mixture and stir. Place in a casserole and bake covered, at 325°F for 45 minutes, stirring once with a fork after 20 minutes. You can either keep this warm until you reach the picnic site, or reheat it in a barbecue oven or cast iron frying pan.

Mad Hatter's Tea

The explorers and fur traders often drank Labrador tea, a plant that grows in most parts of Canada. You might find Labrador tea in the woods. It was often used by Indians and traders alike.

4 Wawa
Mr. Vallée's Picnic

Wawa is in the midst of the beautiful Algoma-Lake Superior country. The area abounds with scenic picnic places, some of which are listed here as things to do, because this beauty really should be seen and enjoyed. However, when we enquired of our Wawa friends where the best picnic spot is they told us the story of Mr. Vallée and the special place he has created.

How to get there

The trail to the picnic spot begins at the little footbridge just behind the Public Works shops. Turn east off Highway 101 (Mission Road). Turn right onto Magpie Road, then right again on Montreal Road. The shop is half a block along on your left. Park, and walk around to the back, where you will spot the footbridge which crosses Wawa Creek. A sign announces Vallée Park. The path is easy to follow, and in under 20 minutes you will reach Anderson Lake, and Mr. Vallée's picnic place.

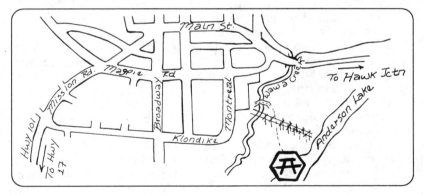

Mr. Vallée

Mr. Vallée had worked hard all his life, and enjoyed it. With retirement he found himself sitting around in the coffee shop, or reading, or walking the streets of Wawa—not pastimes that pleased him. The Wawa Creek was a particular eyesore. Old culverts and assorted garbage had accumulated there over the years, and so Mr. Vallée though he might as well tidy up the creek. One thing sort of led to another, and he thought a bridge might be nice. He scavenged some timber and concrete, built the little foot bridge, and then cleared a path to the ridge. And so it went. Just over the ridge was a pond in a muskeg bog, which he planned to skirt with his path.

One day Mr. Vallée was sitting on the point by Anderson's Lake when he noticed two children in the bog, about to go fishing. He stopped them, and explained about the danger of the muskeg, which can act like quicksand. He demonstrated the danger to the boys with a long stick,

The Canada Goose at Wawa

which he easily pushed into the sand at the edge of the bay. As it disappeared beneath the surface Mr. Vallée suddenly realized that he, too, was stuck. He managed to remove himself from the bog at the edge, but the demonstration was convincing. The children went away without any fish, but with Mr. Vallée's promise that he would make them a safe fishing spot.

He did. He started that fall digging a ditch to drain the bog. Working constantly (14 hours a day) with his pick and shovel he carved a ditch through the muskeg and down to the shore of Anderson Lake. It took four months to dig. That was five years ago. Mr. Vallée has cleared the brush, built the 20-minute trail which leads to the point, created a flat ledge overlooking the lake, and even built a 20-foot picnic table from old bridge timbers. He has planted grass and clover in his magic place in the woods, and he will tell you that there are lots of blueberries along the trail in August. This is the kind of swimming hole that kids dream about! It is on public land, for the use of everybody.

Mr. Vallée is over seventy now, but he still works 14 hours a day, year-round, maintaining and improving the little park he has built.

The two sets of staircases along the trail were also constructed by Mr. Vallée. He was chatting one day with some visitors to his park, and one of them mentioned that it was difficult to get over some of the rocks on the trail. That was enough for Mr. Vallée. The first staircase has 29 steps, and the second, incomplete at the time of writing, will likely be just as big.

Watch as you walk along the trail. If you see an old man with an axe or a wheelbarrow at work in the woods, that will be Mr. Vallée. He will be delighted to stop for a minute and tell you about his special picnic place. You'll bring a twinkle to his eye when you tell him that you are enjoying it

Things to do

1. Take a picture of the famous Wawa goose. The word Wawa is Ojibwa for wild goose. That big statue of a Canada Goose that you passed as you left the main highway is the well known symbol of Wawa, and of the Canadian north country. It weighs 4,400 pounds, and is 28 feet high.

2. Go fishing. The village is a centre for outfitting for hunting and fishing in the wilderness. If you want to be adventurous you can hire a guide and spend a weekend or a week at one of the remote fishing lodges. The best time for catching chinook, coho and pink salmon is in the fall.

3. Drive south along Highway 17 from Wawa and stop at any of the magnificent beaches along the coast of Lake Superior. One of the first you will come to is Old Woman Bay, about 22 kilometres south of Wawa, a favourite with Wawa residents.

4. Spend a day or a week in Lake Superior Provincial Park, an enormous area stretching along the splendid eastern coast of Lake Superior. The park includes 1,540 square kilometres of natural wilderness and serves every possible recreational activity.

5. If you are an amateur archaeologist, stop at Agawa Rock. It is part of a sheer cliff face in an especially rugged setting, a place considered sacred by native peoples for centuries. The rock features many pictographs—ancient symbolic drawings made by prehistoric Indian people, and is well worth a visit. Wear shoes with good treads, as the rock can be slippery.

6. Watch for merlins, birds of prey which have been nesting in the Agawa Bay area since 1966.

7. It is not necessary to spend a whole day to appreciate the beauty of Agawa Canyon. If your time is short you can still board the northbound train at Frater, south of Wawa, and ride for one stop into the canyon. Then, half an hour later, the southbound train will carry you back. Check with the Algoma Central Railway for the exact times and fares.

Merlins

Closely related to peregrine falcons, merlins nest in the eastern Lake Superior region. Their bodies are long and streamlined, with long, pointed wings. Hunting from very high altitudes they spot their prey, and swoop down in veering flights, diving at speeds of up to 165-330 kilometres per hour (100-200 m.p.h.). With this high speed, they overtake smaller birds. They also seek prey from the ground such as squirrels, mice, bats, toads, snakes, dragonflies, butterflies, grasshoppers and spiders.

In an unusual switch from most bird species, the female merlin is larger than the male, as is the case for all hawks and falcons. Pairs mate for life, returning to nest in the same place year after year. They are squatters; they don't build their own nests, but use an old crow's nest, or a hole in a hollow tree. In the fall they migrate south, sometimes as far as the northern regions of South America. They return to the Superior area in May to lay their eggs.

Things to eat

Since this is fishing territory, we will picnic accordingly.

Barbecued Salmon

There are two traditional ways to barbecue salmon. One employs a vertical spit, and the other a reflecting oven. The fish is mounted the same way in both cases.

Vertical spit:

Cut the fish alongside the backbone, open and lay flat. Lay six little sticks across the meat, pinioning each end slightly in the meat. Split one end of a small pole and slide the fish and sticks down the spit, head end first. Tie the split pole together above and below the fish. Push the other end of the pole into the sand in such a way that the fish is positioned above the hot coals of the campfire. Cook one side for 20 minutes, then rotate the pole and cook the other side.

Reflector oven:

The cooking can be made more efficient by constructing a log reflecting panel as follows: cut six green logs of equal diameter (about four to six inches) about four feet in length. Make a rack by placing two poles the same distance apart as the diameter of your logs. Place another two poles in the same fashion about three feet away, in such a way that sliding the six logs between them will result in a wall about a foot away from the fire. This log wall will reflect the heat back onto the salmon.

Alternatively, turn a large flat rock on its side by the edge of the fire, to serve as a reflector. Place the fish, mounted as above, between the fire and the reflecting surface.

Campfire Potatoes

Wrap medium-sized potatoes in foil, with a dab of butter in each. Wait till your fire has burned down to a bed of coals, and place the foil packages among the coals.

Campfire Vegetables

This dish can be cooked on a barbecue grill, or on a makeshift grill over a camp fire, or by placing the packages of vegetables right in the fire, as with the potatoes. Vegetables wrapped in pockets of heavy aluminum foil and baked on a barbecue grill are easy to prepare in advance, and scrumptious to eat.

Carrots:

Peel and cut to sticks. For each pound of carrots combine a Tbsp. brown sugar, 1 Tbsp. lemon juice, 1 tsp. salt, 2 tsp. powdered ginger, 1 Tbsp. melted butter. Mix together in a bowl, divide into four equal portions and wrap each loosely in aluminum foil, sealing the edges tightly. Cook for one hour.

Mushrooms:

Wrap one pound of large mushrooms in foil with butter, salt and pepper. Cook for 20-25 minutes.

Potatoes:

Brush each medium sized potato with oil and wrap in foil. Cook for 45-60 minutes.

5 Sault Ste Marie
An Entrepreneur's Picnic

The picnic spot is by the Historic Ship Canal on North St. Mary's Island. From this point you can see the great Algoma Steel Corp., the base of Sault Ste Marie's economy for decades—but only one of the many business ventures of Francis Hector Clergue.

How to get there

The main streets in central Sault Ste Marie are one-way streets. Queen Street East is the main westbound thoroughfare. Proceed west along Queen until just past the central business district and then turn left on Huron Street. Just before the castle-like stone building (which was Clergue's central office building) turn left onto Canal Drive. The drive then winds across the power canal by the Francis H. Clergue Generating Station, and onto North St. Mary's Island. Continue on Canal Drive past the Visitor Centre, the Lock, and the two swing

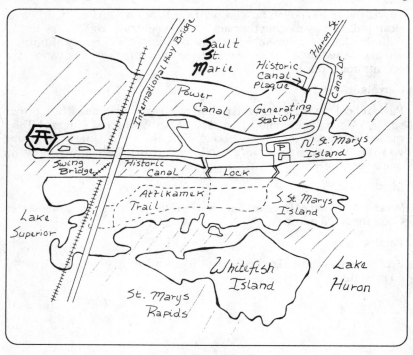

bridges to the extreme east end. Here you will find picnic tables and a panoramic view of Clergue's empire.

Francis Hector Clergue

Francis H. Clergue

Francis H. Clergue, dreamer, promoter, builder, entrepreneur, was fascinated by the power of the St. Mary's River, the only outlet of Lake Superior, the largest freshwater lake in the world. He felt that with such great power he could build an industrial empire.

He first gained control of the power rights of the river by taking over the town's defunct power company. Then, with the backing of Philadelphia and New York capitalists, he built a power plant with a capacity of 20,000 h.p.

Clergue needed customers for his power. Since none other than the small town itself was available, he began to create his own. Clergue obtained the timber rights to the large spruce stands north of the lake and built the Sault Ste Marie Pulp and Paper Company. Then, because it wasn't economical to ship wet pulp the great distance to market, he undertook to revolutionize the pulp industry by producing sheets of dry pulp. To do this he built a large machine shop and foundry to make the machinery, and a large laboratory to devise the processes. To further purify his pulp he needed to treat it with sulphur. His chemists told him that sulphuric acid could be produced from pyrrhotite ores, so he bought mines at Sudbury. Byproducts of this process could produce an alloy suitable for armour plating. Clergue had completed these projects in just three years. He had also established an alkali plant, a charcoal plant, a power plant across the river in Sault, Michigan, street railways on both sides of the river, and had started the Algoma Central Railway running northward into the pulp forests.

In 1897, a prospector, searching for gold around present-day Wawa, discovered a large deposit of siderite. He sold his claim to Clergue, who started the Helen Mine and used it as the basis to construct a Bessemer steel plant and rail mill at the Sault. To transport the ore, he developed Michipicoten Harbour and acquired a fleet of 16 steamships. All these enterprises were owned and controlled by Clergue's holding company, The Lake Superior Corporation.

Clergue's empire collapsed almost as quickly as it had been built. It was under-financed; it had grown too quickly; there were not enough trained managers. By 1903 Clergue could not pay his employees' wages.

Despite his losses at the Sault, Clergue continued to view Canada as a land of opportunity. In 1912 he actively promoted a northern railway across Canada. In 1915 he was in Tsarist Russia selling rails made at the Sault, and was trying to sell heavy gun turrets. In the 1920s he was lobbying for an improved St. Lawrence Seaway, and in the 1930s he was in Manchuria trying to sell railway equipment to the Japanese. His one successful venture during this time was his move to introduce Red Delicious Apples into Canada.

When Clergue died in 1939, he was described in the Montreal Gazette as the "Cecil Rhodes of Canada."

Things to do and see

1. Wander along the Historic Ship Canal. The canal beside the picnic spot was built in the 1890s. Prior to that, the only route had been via the American locks on the other side of the river. In 1870 the Americans refused passage to a Canadian military supply ship. This action prompted the Canadian government to build its own lock.

2. Go back to the castle-like office building on Huron Street. Beside it you will see a reconstruction of the very first lock at the Sault. It was part of a canal built in 1798 by the North West Company to move their canoes and bateaux around the rapids. The Americans destroyed the original in the War of 1812. Also, inside the paper mill grounds, there is an old blockhouse which Clergue restored and used as his personal residence.

3. Take a boat tour through and around the locks. The tour affords close views of Algoma Steel, and of the world's largest jack-knife railway bridge. Tour boats depart from the Norgoma Dock near the civic center.

4. Ride the Algoma Central Railway to Agawa Canyon. Clergue's railway, which for years tottered on the brink of bankruptcy, passes through some of the most rugged and most beautiful scenery in northern Ontario. Now it is possible to take a one-day excursion into the wilderness, with a two hour stop-over in beautiful Agawa Canyon.

Things to eat

For this picnic we are fortunate to have excerpts from the book, *Culinary Landmarks: Half-Hours with Sault Ste Marie Housewives*. The first edition came out during the heyday of Clergue's empire. All the recipes, except for the tea, are taken directly from that volume.

MENU

Mock Turtle Soup
Lobster Salad and Potato Salad
Peach Trifle
Sunshine Iced Tea

Mock Turtle Soup

"Take a shank of beef and two pigs' feet, put into half a gallon of water, boil till meat separates from the bones, remove the bones and add one pound of lean beef, boil well, then strain, add pepper and salt, a little mace or nutmeg. When serving, add about a teaspoonful of sherry and a few drops of lemon juice to each. Enough boiling water can be added to serve six or eight persons."

—A.J. Rodgers.

We suggest that you pour this into a Thermos and transport it hot to the picnic.

Lobster Salad

"Boil the lobster and cut into shreds. Place in a china bowl and mix with it one and a half tablespoons olive oil, one teaspoon salt, two tablespoons vinegar.

Dressing—One tablespoon of mustard, one tablespoon of sugar, a very little cayenne, one teaspoon salt, beaten very thoroughly with the yolks of three raw eggs. An egg beater must be used and the bowl of dressing should be placed in another container of ice-water during the entire process. After the ingredients already used are very light and thick one pint of olive oil should be added, a few drops at a time. When the dressing becomes very thick, add half cup vinegar in small quantities alternately with the remaining oil. When the process of beating is over, add the juice of half lemon and one cupful of whipped cream. When ready to serve mix half the dressing with lobster, then pour the remainder of dressing over prepared salad and garnish with the coral."

—Mrs. Kuderling

If this dressing sounds like a lot of work, you could substitute the Herb Mayonnaise in the Wasaga picnic. Also, refrigerate and keep this salad cool.

Mrs. Scherk's Potato Salad

"Take eight good-sized boiled potatoes, cut in dice, a small onion and small cucumber chopped fine. Pour over all the following dressing: Three eggs well beaten, butter size of an egg, two teaspoons sugar, one teaspoon salt, half a teaspoon pepper, half teaspoon mustard, three tablespoons vinegar. Put in a double boiler, and cook until thick. Add cream or rich milk until thin enough to pour over salad."

—Mrs. Scherk

Peach Trifle

"Line the bottom of a well-buttered pudding dish with stale sponge cake and cover with fresh peaches sliced and sugared (canned ones will do). To a cup of wine add a cup of water, and heat to boiling. Beat the yolks of three eggs with one-half cup of sugar and one teaspoon cornstarch. Pour over this gradually the hot wine and water. Cook over hot water until thick, stirring constantly, then pour over the fruit. Beat the whites of the eggs, add three tablespoons sugar and vanilla. Spread on top and brown in oven until firm to touch."

—Miss Luscombe

Chill in refrigerator, serve topped with fresh cream or ice-cream.

Sunshine Iced Tea

Avoid hard water (it makes murky tea) and China teas (which lack the requisite body). Consider using some of the tisanes or herbal teas for variety.

Combine:
> 4 teaspoons tea (or 8 teaspoons tisane)
> 1 L of cold water

Let sit in the sunshine all day, strain, and refrigerate overnight. Serve over ice cubes.

6 Midland
A Picnic Among the Hurons

In 1639 there were many villages near here, some of them home to the Huron Indians, and some centres for Jesuit missions. The villages vanished because the two societies could not co-exist. The Jesuit fathers withdrew, burning their settlement to the ground as they left, and taking with them some of the Huron people who had converted to Christianity. Today a reconstruction of the Jesuit mission of Sainte Marie Among the Hurons restores a time now past.

How to get there

The picnic site is southwest of the town of Midland, on a hill beside the Martyrs' Shrine. Drive east on Heritage Drive (Highway

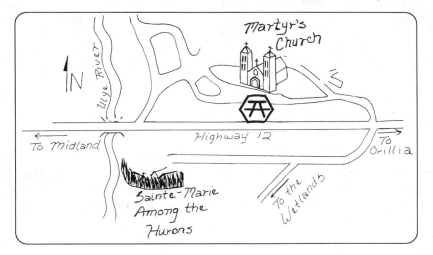

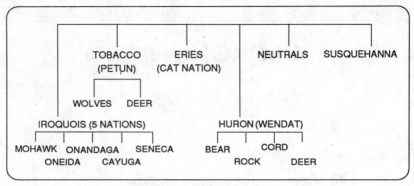

Descent of the Iroquoian Tribes

12), cross the river, climb the hill and turn left, following the sign to the Martyrs' Shrine. Drive to the top of the hill and park on the left by one of the picnic tables overlooking the mission site of Ste. Marie Among the Hurons.

The Indians

The Huron Confederacy was a loosely associated group of clans, the Bear, Rock, Cord, Deer and Swamp, each of which traced their heritage to a common ancestor. The Huron Confederacy was one of the Iroquoian tribes—peoples who shared a common language base and cultural characteristics. Traditional enemies for many generations, the Iroquois and Huron confederacies had continued a series of blood feuds which had become for them a way of life. Although they had long since become primarily agricultural people, warfare remained the primary source of prestige for young males.

In the early part of the seventeenth century the Huron served as middle men to the fur trade of Nouvelle France. The Five Nations Iroquois had become middle men for a company of Dutch traders to the south, and were beginning to encroach upon Huron territory.

The Missionaries

Sainte Marie Among the Hurons existed from 1639-1649, only 10 years. It was described in *The Jesuit Relations*, the reports written back to headquarters in Paris, as a pleasant place, and a successful mission in the beginning. But, although the Hurons nearby were somewhat amenable to the Christian teachings, and also attracted to the trade goods offered at the mission, the Iroquois were not. They saw the "black robes" as interlopers among the Indian tribes, dividing them against each other.

With the white men came the dreadful diseases of small pox and measles . . . the diseases that seemed to kill only the Indians, not the white people. Champlain estimated the population of the Huron people in the early 1600s as about 30,000. By 1635 epidemics had reduced that number to only about 18,000 people. We do not have estimates for the Iroquois tribe, who were in less frequent contact with the disease, but it is likely that they, too, suffered heavy losses. The social disruption caused by this drastic reduction in population can hardly be imagined.

The Mission of Sainte Marie Among the Hurons

The restored site illustrates the patterns of daily life of both the Jesuits and the Hurons in the middle of the seventeenth century. Central to the community were the *donnes*, white people who had given their skills and knowledge to the mission in exchange for food and lodging, and assured support upon retirement. In 1649 there were 14 donnes, 17 Jesuit priests, and various other tradesmen, for a total of 62 European residents. At that time this was one-fifth of the French population in Canada, since there were only about 200 others in Montreal. The Indian population in the mission, housed just outside the walls, varied with the season.

By 1649 three mission villages had been destroyed by Iroquois Five Nations warriors, and seven priests had been killed, including fathers Brebeuf and Lalement. The decision to leave the area was first made by the Huron peoples, and with reluctance, Father Ragenau decided to abandon Sainte Marie as well. The settlement was burned to the ground as they left, and the weeds soon hid the site from view. Interest in the site of the mission has been sustained over the centuries, but serious excavation did not begin until the 1940s. Reconstruction began in the '60s. The study of the life of the people who lived here so long ago continues today.

Things to do

1. Visit the Martyrs' Shrine, the Catholic Church beside the picnic spot. This shrine is dedicated to North America's first canonized saints, among them fathers Brebeuf and Lalement.

2. Explore the mission of Sainte Marie Among the Hurons. The reconstruction is extensive, and the staff are dressed in period costumes, and well versed in the history of the site. You can learn about the daily life of the Hurons, the Jesuits and the donnes. The museum has a fine collection of artifacts from the site, and excellent displays of historical and environmental interest.

Trumpeter Swans

Once thousands of trumpeter swans nested in southern Ontario. Then they vanished from their traditional nesting areas in Canada, and were thought to be almost extinct from over-hunting and trapping, and possibly from climatic changes. They are now being re-introduced to habitats such as the Wye Marsh. They are now fully protected from hunting. It is thought that there are presently about 9,000 birds throughout the world. Four of the major nesting areas are within Canada. They prefer shallow open water, and their long, graceful necks are well adapted for collecting plants from as much as one metre below the surface.

At the Wye Marsh Wildlife Centre the Trumpeter Swan Program began in 1988 with a male (a cob) and female (a pen), but the pen died over that winter. She has been replaced, and it is hoped that the new couple will produce cygnets in the spring of 1990. This family will be the base for a future population of wild trumpeter swans.

3. Visit the Wye Marsh Wildlife Centre, 1 km past Sainte Marie Among the Hurons. The nature centre features excellent displays, and an extensive collection of books on environmental topics. This is a year-round facility, with nature trails for hiking in the spring, summer and fall, and cross-country skiing and snowshoeing in the winter months. You can take a guided hike, and learn about the aquatic and mammalian inhabitants of the wetlands. Or you can pick up a checklist at the information desk, and record your own observations to help the naturalists keep track of the ever-changing population of the marshes. There are many exciting projects underway here, among them the efforts to re-introduce the trumpeter swan to the area. Check on the progress of the first family of swans and their cygnets. Telephone (705) 526-7809 for complete program details. Don't miss the highlight of the season, the annual Wye Marsh Festival of Conservation and Art, held on the third weekend in September.

Things to Eat

The following historical recipes appear with permission from Sainte Marie Among the Hurons.

Sunflower Soup
(Serves 6)

2 1/2 cups (625 ml) unsalted sunflower seeds, shelled
8 cups (2 L) chicken bouillon
6 green onions, or 1 medium onion, chopped
pinch of sea salt

Cook ingredients in a large saucepan over medium heat for 2 hours.

Rabbit Stew

1 rabbit, cut up
2 cups (500 ml) flour
4 Tbsp. (60 ml) lard or vegetable shortening
1 tsp. (5 ml) baking powder
1/2 tsp. (2.5 ml) salt
vegetables

Put meat, with bones, into a pot with enough water to cover. Make a dumpling dough of the remaining ingredients and add in spoonfuls to the stew. Cook over medium heat until meat is cooked and tender. Add spices to taste and any vegetables you have on hand.

Sagamite

2-3 handfuls of raw pounded corn
water
small quantity of fish (fresh or dried)
small quantity of pumpkin, cut up

Boil the corn meal and water in an earthen pot until very clear, stirring occasionally to prevent scorching. Add the fish and the pumpkin. When cooked, remove the fish, cool, pound very fine, and return to the pot. (In the bush, the fish was added bones, scales, entrails and all.)

Midland Corn Bread

1 egg
2 cups (500 ml) corn meal
1 1/2 tsp. (7.5 ml) sugar or maple syrup
3 Tbsp. (45 ml) melted butter or drippings
3/4 cup (180 ml) milk or water
3/4 tsp. (3 ml) salt

Generously grease a loaf pan and heat in a hot oven until the grease spits. Beat the egg in a bowl and add it, along with the milk, butter, sugar or syrup and salt, to the corn flour. Mix together fairly well. Pour into the pan and bake at 400°F (200°C) for about fifteen minutes or until done.

7 Wasaga Beach
A Picnic on the Nancy

For a short while in the War of 1812 the schooner *Nancy* was the only British naval vessel on the upper Great Lakes. As such she was the target in the battle for control of the western lakes; a battle in which the *Nancy* was lost but the British won. Today the hull of this ship rests in a museum on an island oasis in the Nottawasaga River, which is a beautiful spot for a picnic.

How to get there

Wasaga Beach is on Georgian Bay about 140 kilometres (90 miles) north of Toronto. Drive north on Highway 400 toward Barrie; signs to Wasaga Beach will direct you along Highway 27 to Highway 92. The Nancy Island Historic Site is on Mosley Street at Third Street (between Beach Areas 1 and 2 of Wasaga Beach Provincial Park). Note that the admission charge is for the parking lot; admission to Nancy Island and the exhibits is free. The place to picnic is on the Island, where you will find green grass, a cooling breeze, and picnic tables.

The *Nancy*

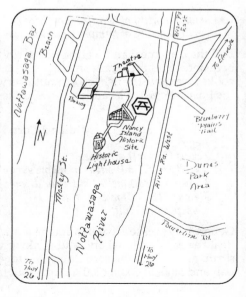

In the Battle of Lake Erie, September 10, 1813, the American Navy under Commodore Perry defeated and captured the entire British Upper Lakes Fleet. From that time, the continued existence of the British garrison at Fort Michilimackinac, which was the gateway to the west and the key to the lucrative fur trade, depended upon the supply schooner, the *HMS Nancy*.

In July of 1814 the Americans attacked the fort but were unable to overcome the defences. They moved to blockade the supply lines and starve the garrison into submission. The brig *Niagara* and the schooners, *Scorpion* and *Tigress*, went in search of the *Nancy*.

They found the *Nancy* hiding in the Nottawasaga River; in the resulting battle she was destroyed. However the detachment and crew—22 seamen, 23 Indians and 9 voyageurs—fled to the woods. There they had secreted two large bateaux, a large canoe, and one hundred barrels of flour. They then rowed and paddled the 360 miles along the north shore to Fort Michilimackinac to deliver the flour and report the loss of the *Nancy*.

Six days later, when they were almost at the fort, they sighted the American schooners, *Tigress* and *Scorpion*, blockading the route. Hiding the supplies and bateaux, all 54 men crammed into the canoe and slipped past the American boats under the cover of night.

Upon reaching Fort Michilimackinac they found the garrison on half-rations. They gathered reinforcements, fifty Newfoundland soldiers and

Replica of the Nancy's figurehead

two hundred Indians, and retraced their journey to capture the two American schooners. Thus the *Tigress* and the *Scorpion*, renamed the *Surprise* and the *Confiance*, joined the British Navy and protected the supply route to Fort Michilimackinac until the end of the war in 1814.

Meanwhile, the burnt hull of the *Nancy* lay at the bottom of the Nottawasaga River. Gradually the river currents deposited silt and sand about the hull and an island was formed. One hundred years later, public interest was such that the *Nancy* was raised and on August 14, 1928 the Nancy Museum was opened.

Things to See and Do

1. Enjoy the 14-kilometre expanse of Wasaga Beach Provincial Park. The water is shallow and warm, and inviting to swimmers and wind surfers.

2. Explore Nancy Island Historic Site. In the theatre, designed to suggest three sails straining against the wind, there is a movie on the battle. The museum encloses the hull of the *Nancy* together with a replica of the figurehead and other displays.

3. Hike the Blueberry Plains Trail. The trail winds through a complex parabolic sand dune system unlike any other in Ontario. An excellent pamphlet available at the Nancy Island office describes the geology and ecology of the area.

Things to eat

In 1813, the daily rations per man for British sailors consisted of a pound of salt pork or beef, some hard tack biscuits, peas, potatoes and rum.

The Blueberry Plains Trail was so named because of the abundant harvests of blueberries available there. In the spirit of these people and places we offer the following suggestions to you:

Corn Relish

kernels from 18 ears of corn
4 large onions, chopped
2 green peppers, chopped
1 sweet red pepper, chopped
1 lb. light brown sugar
1/4 cup salt
3 Tbsp. celery seed
4 Tbsp. dry mustard
2 qts. vinegar

Combine the ingredients in a large kettle, cook slowly for twenty minutes, pack in sterilized jars and seal at once. This spread is excellent with corned beef and rye!

Potato and Pea Salad

(Serves 4-6)

8 medium-sized new potatoes
500 ml bouillon
1 large red onion, chopped fine
4 stalks of celery, chopped
2 sweet red peppers, chopped
1 kg fresh or frozen peas
chopped parsley
salt and pepper
250 ml herb mayonnaise

Boil the potatoes in their skins until tender but firm (about 20 minutes). Drain, cool, and chop into cubes. Marinate the potatoes in the boullion for one hour. Drain the potatoes and combine them with all the remaining ingredients. Keep cool during transport to the picnic place.

Herb Mayonnaise

Mix together in a blender at medium speed for 70 seconds:
1 egg
50 ml lemon juice
2 ml salt
3 ml dry mustard.

Then add 250 ml olive oil in a slow, steady stream through the opening in the top of the blender cap, while the blender is running. Ingredients will emulsify while the oil is being added. If, however, the ingredients fail to emulsify, pour mixture into cup, rinse out blender with hot water, put a new egg and lemon juice into it, and repeat the process, using the mixture in place of the oil, and this time pouring in a slow, steady stream.

Blend in with a spatula:
1 clove of garlic, crushed
85 ml minced green herbs (parsley, chives, basil, marjoram, thyme)

Let stand in refrigerator overnight so that spice flavours permeate. Potato salad is always a dangerous food for picnics, since it has real eggs in it; botulism can develop if it is not kept well chilled until serving.

Aunt Nell's Pie Crust

4 cups flour
1 lb. lard
butter the size of an egg
4 Tbsp. sugar
salt
1 Tbsp. vinegar
water

Sift the flour and mix together the dry ingredients. Cut in lard with a pastry cutter until the mixture has the consistency of corn. Place the butter in a measuring cup, add the vinegar, and fill cup to 3/4 full with water. Add to first mixture. Mix well. Store in refrigerator until needed (can also be frozen). Makes 4 pie crusts.

Blueberry Pie

Fill an unbaked pie crust with blueberries. Sprinkle with 100 ml cornstarch and 200 ml of white sugar. Cover with a lattice pie crust. Bake in a 350 °F (180 °C) oven for 45 minutes. It is a good idea to sit the pie plate on a cookie sheet as the berries often boil over.

8 Wiarton
A Picnic at the McNeill Mansion

Alexander McNeill was the Conservative Member of Parliament from North Bruce riding from 1882 to 1903. He lived near Wiarton on an estate which he called The Corran after his family home in Ireland. The leaders of his time—even royalty—were guests in this stately old mansion with its circular carriageway. Although the mansion burned in 1976, enough remains to suggest its years of splendour, and of the gracious meals which must have been served here.

How to get there

Take Highway 6 north from Wiarton for 1 kilometre and turn east into the Spirit Rock Conservation Area. Follow the road around until you see the ruins of The Corran. Park and select a place in front of the old mansion to spread your picnic blanket.

The McNeill family

Born on the family estate in Ireland, The Corran, in 1842, Alexander McNeill practised law for awhile in Ireland, married Hester Law Howard, and came to Canada to farm. He brought with him to Canada his ardent Imperialism, a characteristic of his election campaigns and speeches throughout his career in parliament. He died at The Corran in Ontario in 1932 at the age of 90.

The majestic ruin of The Corran tell a story of their own. Once great stone gates opened on a half-mile of driveway, lying among three acres of lawns and flower gardens. From the porch the clear blue water of Georgian Bay could be seen.

Alexander and his wife, Hester, had come to Canada to develop a farm for Alex's uncle. Soon, however, he found the land upon which he could recreate his childhood home. The result was a 17-room mansion, the hollow walls of which surround our picnickers.

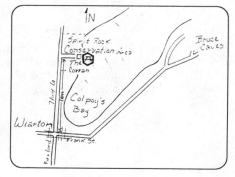

The vista is no longer clear, but if you follow the little path to the edge of the escarpment, you can imagine the splendid view the McNeills enjoyed from their verandah. McNeill settled in to be a gentleman farmer and a political leader in his new country.

Hester and Alexander had one child, a son, called Malcolm, who never married. He inherited the estate when his father died. Unfortunately for The Corran, Malcolm had never been taught how to run the estate, and the complexity of it was too much for the refined gentleman that he was. Malcolm remained in the mansion, but the house, gardens, and fortune that his father had left him were fast fading away. Some of the land was even sold for taxes. When Malcolm died in 1956 he left the estate to his housekeeper, but she, too, was unable to keep it up, and she sold it in 1960. The new owners chose not to live in The Corran, which, although a bit tatty now, still housed all the treasures of the McNeills.

And so the vandals came, hastening the tragic end of the once great residence. They smashed the oriental vases, slashed the beautiful oil paintings, broke all the windows, destroyed the walls and the light fixtures, and tore Alexander's precious volumes to shreds. The Corran was all but destroyed, and the job was finished by a fire in 1976.

The gardens are now filled with weeds and wildflowers. Trees have grown up inside the foundations of Alex's proud barns and obscure the once fine view of the bay far below. But if you stand well back, where you think the circular drive must have been, and then squint your eyes, you can almost see the lights twinkling from the windows and the carriages parked below. And perhaps you can hear in the distance the music of the fine musicians that Alex and Hester hired for the gala this evening in honour of a visiting prince.

The Remittance Man

Behind The Corran stood Escott's beautiful little cottage—not too far from the grape arbours. Escott was a remittance man with a delicate problem—he was prone to drink. His family in Ireland had sent him off to distant Canada, with the gentle but firm understanding that he was never to return and disgrace them. They sent enough money to permit Escott to live comfortably, and the McNeills made wine of a fine reputation in their vast cellars. The life of a remittance man was apparently tolerable.

At the turn of the century there were many such people in all parts of Canada—men who were second sons and could not inherit the family estate, or men who were an embarrassment to their family for one reason or another. Although these men were often maligned, they made a fair contribution to the Canadian economy with their remittances, which were spent lavishly in Canada.

The Corran

Things to do

1. The first week in February features the annual Wiarton Ground-hog Festival. On February 2nd Wiarton Willie, a very famous ground-hog, is observed by millions as he ventures out of his hole, stretching after a longish snooze underground. In his hands—or paws—lies the advent of spring. If Willie sees his own shadow, a seemingly innocu-ous occurrence, he runs back into his hole and Canadians, or at least the ones around and about Wiarton, will experience six more weeks of winter. If Willie doesn't see his shadow, presumably because of a cloudy day or his own stupidity, an early spring can be anticipated. Awesome responsibility for a groundhog.

2. This region is full of interesting legends and people. One of these was Robert Bruce, the hermit. He lived to an indeterminate age in the Wiarton area, having emigrated from the Orkney Islands. He worked at various jobs over the years, but he always spent his winters in what came to be known as Bruce's Caves. When he died in 1908 he owned 300 acres of land, and had several thousand dollars in the bank. To visit the caves, drive northeast from Wiarton on County Rd. 26 (Shore Drive). At 4.8 kilometres (3 miles) you will go through the village of Oxenden, and then pass by the entrance to a conservation area. About 1 kilometre farther you will see a small parking area, and

the head of a trail which leads to the caves. The woodland walk takes about 10 minutes.

3. Botanists will enjoy the woods near Bruce's Caves. In June they are festooned with white and purple trillium. The area is also renowned for the more than 40 varieties of ferns which grow here; more than perhaps anywhere else in the world. Some of the ferns are evergreen, and can be found in the winter.

4. Pick up a brochure at the Tourist Information Booth at the south end of Wiarton's main street and take a walking tour of the town. There are many fascinating historic Victorian structures to be enjoyed as you wander down the tree-lined streets.

Things to eat

This is a remittance man's picnic. Escott would undoubtedly have free-loaded (or rather, been invited to attend) the McNeill's parties, and so we offer an appropriate menu for the Laird's garden party. The menu should be accompanied by a bottle of fine Irish whiskey, from which you can sip, according to your predilection for the stuff. There are those who can even drink it straight.

MENU

Cauliflower and Leek Soup
A Tray of Sandwiches
Sweet Onion Pickles and Stuffed Olives
Orange and Lemon Ice
White Cake with White Icing
Earl Grey Tea

Cauliflower and Leek Soup

1 medium cauliflower, cut into florets
3 leeks, trimmed and thickly sliced
3 medium potatoes, peeled and chopped
1 quart stock or water
1 1/2 cups milk
salt and pepper to taste
1 Tbsp. fresh parsley, chopped fine
1/2 cup medium cheddar cheese, grated
dash nutmeg

Combine the vegetables and the stock in a pot and bring to a boil. Add the salt and pepper, and simmer while covered, until the vegetables are cooked, about 20 minutes. Cool a little, and put through a blender in batches. Replace in pot, stir in remaining ingredients, and heat, stirring constantly, until cheese has melted. Carry to the picnic in a Thermos.

Lemon and Orange Ice

Heat to a boil:
   2 tsp. grated orange rind
   2 cups sugar
   4 cups water
   1/4 tsp. salt

and simmer for about 5 minutes. Chill the mixture and add:
   2 cups fresh orange juice
   1/4 cup lemon juice

and churn-freeze the mixture in an ice cream churn.

White Cake

Preheat oven to 375°F. Have all ingredients at room temperature. Sift before measuring:
   1 3/4 cups white enriched flour

Resift with:
   1 cup sugar

Add:
   1/2 cup melted butter
   2 eggs
   1/2 cup milk
   1/2 tsp. salt
   2 tsp. double acting baking powder
   1 tsp. vanilla

Beat vigorously for 3 to 4 minutes. Bake in a greased pan for 30 minutes. Put on a rack to cool.

White Icing

Sift two cups icing sugar into a bowl. Add gradually to 1/4 lb. soft butter and beat until creamy. Add 2 tsp. vanilla. If icing is too thin, add more sugar; if too thick, add a little cream. Spread on a warm cake.

9 Manitoulin Island
An Island Picnic

This island has always been a sacred place for the Indian people, and a great intertribal pow wow is held here each summer. The beauty of the place has attracted white settlers over the last few centuries, too. This picnic emphasizes the mix of the two cultures.

How to get there

The site of this picnic is in the village of Manitowaning, on the grass beside the *SS Norisle*, the first Manitoulin ferry, which is permanently docked here. The dock is at the end of Queen Street. Park, and carry your picnic basket to the end of the point, just beyond the *Norisle*. There is a fine view of the lake.

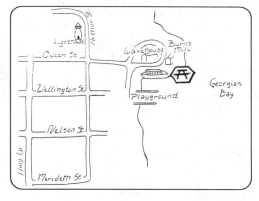

The Island

This is the largest freshwater island in the world, with an area of 2,766 square kilometres. It has been inhabited for centuries by Indian peoples, more recently tribes of the Algonquin nation, the Ojibway and the Odawa. The word Manitou is Algonkian for "mysterious being." It evokes the sense of mystery which underlies the powerful life force of the world and the universe. How appropriate that Manitoulin Island is thought to be the home of Gitchi Manitou, the greatest spirit of all.

The Ojibwa-Odawa People

The Ojibwa nation is a loose confederation of four tribes: the Ojibwa, the Mississaga, the Odawa and the Potawatomi. Each tribe is subdivided into a number of bands, which, in turn, are composed of clans. These smaller groupings trace their heritage back to a common ancestor, although sometimes this ancestor is so far back that he or

The Niagara Escarpment

As one approaches the Niagara Escarpment from any direction it is a bizarre vista. This very distinctive geological formation stretches for hundreds of kilometres diagonally bisecting southern Ontario. It was not caused by glaciers, earthquakes, or volcanoes; it was the abrupt termination of subterranean strata over 400 million years ago which caused the rise of a steep rock face. The embankment rises to heights of 335 metres, and stretches the 725 kilometres from Queenston Heights on the eastern edge of the Niagara Peninsula all the way to the fishing village of Tobermory at the northern tip of the Bruce Peninsula.

Spanning the length of the escarpment is the 720-kilometre Bruce Trail, Canada's longest hiking trail. It passes through an incredibly diverse range of environments and offers access to beautiful waterfalls, jagged bluffs, rich fauna and foliage, and more. One hundred and sixteen parks have been established along the escarpment to protect the delicate and precious environments.

she has become legendary. Each clan has its own totem, a spiritual symbol which binds everyone together, and provides a special link with the spirit world. Totems for the Ojibwe are usually animals, and this is reflected in paintings and other artifacts.

In August, 1836, in a typically generous gesture, the Ojibwe chiefs gave up their claim to the island so that it could become a reserve for all Indians, regardless of tribe, to settle here. This experiment failed, however, since few mainland Indians chose to come. The second treaty was signed in 1862 by the Indians living west of Manitowaning and South Bay, in which they relinquished their lands, with the exception of six small reserves. The Indians of Wikwemikong refused to sign the treaty, making the eastern part of Manitoulin the only unceded reserve in Canada.

Today the size of the bands on Manitoulin Island varies from 50 to several hundred. Each band is a distinct political unit with its own chief. The band is responsible for the well being of the members, and owns the land where the band lives. On Manitoulin each reserve community is a band. The band chief works closely with the provincial and federal government officials to ensure appropriate development for the reserve. Small businesses and shops as well as farms now contribute to the economic stability of the reserves.

Things to do

1. Tour the *SS Norisle* beside the picnic site, and the 105-year-old grist and flour mill beside it. The Manitowaning Roller Mill features agricultural displays. Both the boat and the mill are open only in the summer months.

2. Drive over to West Bay to see the Ojibwe and Odawa arts and crafts shops that line the main street. The people still honour traditional values, and this is reflected in the quality and originality of their designs.

3. Drive to the lookout at Ten Mile Point. The enormous panorama is so beautiful that one must stand silently for awhile to absorb

The SS Norisle

its majesty. This is the northern tip of the Niagara Escarpment, which crosses beneath Lake Huron from Tobermory. The day we stopped there, the panorama was further enhanced by the strains of Indian music issuing from the adjacent Ten Mile Trading Post. Here Charlotte and George Wigle display some of the finest examples of Ojibwe arts and crafts. Here, too, you can buy a painting by one of the great Ojibwe artists, or a tiny, perfect moose-hair embroidered picture. The store serves many purposes. We saw crafts from many distant Indian tribes, too, such as Iroquois soapstone carvings. Ask to see the excellent collection of peace pipes! And stop to smell the sweet grass—this, burned slowly, plays an important part in Ojibwe religious ceremonies, somewhat like incense.

4. Attend the annual Pow Wow on the August 1st long weekend at Wikwemikong. Native people from distant places arrive in the hundreds to attend this festival each year. There are dances, ceremonies and celebrations here in the presence of the manitous, or spirits, of the island. Manitoulin Island has been a summer gathering place for native people for centuries. The current series of annual gatherings has been continuous since 1960—now well into the second generation.

5. Take the 4-hour bus tour of the island. It leaves daily at 1:15 from the South Baymouth ferry dock, Monday through Saturday in

July and August. This is a fine way to get an overall perspective of the diversity of Manitoulin Island.

6. Take your diving gear and ride the ferry over to Tobermory. The only way to visit Fathom Five National Park is by diving—it is completely underwater. In the beautiful clear water you will see wondrous marine creatures, and even several old shipwrecks from a century or more ago. You can also see parts of the park on tours in glass-bottomed boats.

Things to eat

To get to Manitoulin Island from the north, you turn south from the town of Espanola, which is situated on the banks of the Spanish River. We found out that Espanola, meaning "Spanish woman," refers to a particular Spanish woman of a few centuries ago. It was the custom for Indian people to take prisoners in battle, and often women were taken as slaves or wives. A long time ago a tribe in the southern part of the United States captured a Spanish woman, a colonist from Spain. She was traded to a tribe which ranged further north. Ultimately, the group with whom she settled and had children chose to camp in northern Ontario. Imagine the astonishment of the explorers passing through this remote area, when they were greeted with Indians shouting "Buenas dias, Señor." It is recorded that they found a Spanish-speaking woman here, with a number of children who also spoke Spanish. Hence, our Spanish picnic.

Gazpacho
(serves 6)

3/4 kg tomatoes
1 cucumber, peeled and seeded
1 green pepper
100 g dry bread crumbs
1 clove garlic, peeled
1 medium onion, chopped
50 ml vinegar
7 ml olive oil
1 L water
salt

Reserve one tomato for garnish. Scald the rest of the tomatoes in boiling water for 1 minute, remove the skins and slice into quarters. Sauté the green pepper, cucumber and onion until soft. Sprinkle the bread crumbs with the vinegar and let stand for a few minutes. In a blender or food chopper grind all the vegetables. Add the bread crumbs and the garlic, with a little of the water. Slowly add the oil, stirring well, and then the rest of the water. Chill well, and serve cold at the picnic.

Paella
(serves 10)

1 1/2 kg rice
saffron
2 medium onions, chopped
4 cloves garlic, chopped
2 green peppers, cut into small pieces
2 large red peppers, cut into small pieces
1 tin tomatoes
1 tin peas
1/2 kg shrimp, unshelled
1 kg baby clams
1 kg mussels
5 chicken stock cubes
1 cooked chicken, chopped into pieces
oil
white wine

Put the saffron to soak in 1/2 cup water.

Build the fire up and let it burn until you have a good bed of coals. Scrub the clams and mussels and soak in cold water for 1 hour. Remove the heads from the shrimp and wash in cold water.

Smooth the coals out and place the paella pan directly on them (if you don't have a paella pan, 2 large shallow frying pans will do, and a wok won't—not enough bottom area). In the pan sauté the chicken pieces with the garlic in oil until they are brown, and set them aside. Next sauté the chopped onions and peppers, and set aside.

In a separate pot boil the clams and shrimps until the clams open.

Add more oil to the paella pan and add the rice to the oil. Sauté the rice until it is transparent, 2-3 minutes. Take the pan off the fire. Add to the rice the chicken, tomatoes, peppers, onions, clams, shrimp, 5 chicken stock cubes, the saffron liquid, and more liquid (roughly twice the volume of the rice). The liquid that was used to boil the clams is good, but so is water, and so is dry white wine, or chicken stock - or any combination of the above. Rake the coals down so that there is a level place for the pan; return the pan to the fire, and let simmer for 20 minutes. Resist the temptation to stir or cover, but do add more liquid if it seems to be boiling off too quickly.

In a separate pot boil the mussels until they open.

When the paella is cooked (liquid gone), remove it from the fire. Cover with a cloth and let stand for 5 minutes. Split the mussel shells, and arrange them on the half-shell as garnish just before serving.

10 London
The Sweetest Picnic This Side of Heaven

Millions of Americans, and even a few Canadians, think that Guy Lombardo, the band leader who brought in the New Year on the radio for over four decades and played at President Roosevelt's inaugural balls, was an American. Guy was born in London, Ontario, and throughout his life returned frequently to assist with local events, and to visit the haunts of his childhood, one of which is Springbank Park, the site of this picnic.

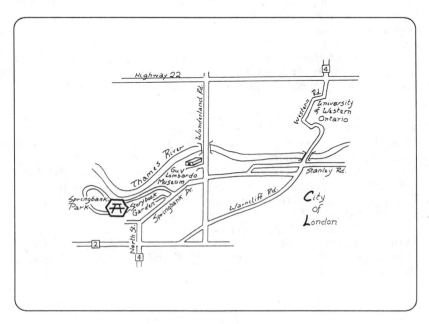

How to get there

Springbank Park is on the Thames River, just off Springbank Drive, on the west side of town. Pick any picnic place that suits you—this is a large park, and there are many. Our favourite spot is near the pavilion in Picnic Area #8.

The Guy Lombardo Story

Before the days of Guy Lombardo and the Royal Canadians, we didn't always sing *Auld Lang Syne* at midnight on New Year's Eve. Now it is a well established tradition. The song was written in 1778 by Robert Burns. It was always in the Lombardo band's repertoire because of the large Scottish population in their first London audiences. In 1929 the song became the theme of the New Year's Eve broadcasts, and an integral part of the New Year's Eve celebration for three generations. The tradition is still going strong.

It really all began with Papa Lombardo. He was born on the Italian island of Lipari. He wanted very much to be a tailor, and he got permission from his parents to emigrate when he was 14. He came to London, Ontario, because there were other relatives here, already established in the clothing trade. By the time he was 28 he had his own tailoring establishment, right on the main street of London. He soon married Angelina Paladino, and they had their first son, Gaetano (Guy) in 1902. Carmen, Lebert, Elaine, Joseph and Victor appeared in rapid succession, followed in 1925 by Rosemarie. Papa Lombardo believed that each of his children should "know a little bit of music—it's a light load to carry," and had the boys practising to play various instruments for at least three hours a day, before and after school. With that kind of practice, they became quite skilled, and when the older boys were still in high school, they were playing for parties, weddings and dances around the London area. Guy, the eldest, was the leader.

In 1923 Guy arranged for the band to play in Cleveland, and after a couple of engagements, he realized that the key to success was the radio. He convinced a local radio station to carry fifteen minutes of the band's music from the nightclub, and after the first broadcast the future was assured. The radio station was besieged with calls demanding more music from the band, and the program was expanded. From then on, Guy Lombardo and his Royal Canadians became known throughout the United States. Carmen wrote many of the songs—"Boo Hoo," "Don't Fence Me In," and others that became mainstream songs for several generations of sing-alongs. The easy-going style of the band was often criticized, but the public liked it, and the Guy Lombardo sound endured.

An Auld Acquaintance

The band left London in 1923 for the United States, but returned often to their home town to perform. When they heard of the London flood of 1937, Guy phoned the mayor of London immediately, and offered to play benefit concerts in London to help the victims. The offer was accepted, of course!

During the '30s and '40s most young writers wanted the Guy Lombardo Band to play their songs first—it was almost an assurance of a hit. Even Irving Berlin brought many of his songs to the Guy Lombardo Band first. For a long time the band played at every presidential inaugural ball, except John F. Kennedy's.

Guy was the leader of the band, and although every member was part of the rehearsal discussions of song selections and arrangements, Guy's word was final. The band was owned by Guy and his brothers, Lebert and Carmen. Lebert played the trumpet, and Carmen, who played the saxophone, was often also vocalist and song writer. The brothers tried many related enterprises such as a restaurant and a song publishing company, but the band was their security. They all enjoyed playing in it, and most of the players remained with the band throughout their careers. Nothing pleased the band more than to play before live audiences. Although there were some television series, they were short-lived, as they kept the band away from the audiences they loved.

Guy Lombardo died in 1977, but the band plays on. Led by Lebert's son, Bill, the band still tours for ten months of the year, and you can still catch Auld Lang Syne on your radio at midnight on New Year's Eve.

Things to do

1. Visit the Guy Lombardo Museum at 205 Wonderland Road, on the edge of Springbank Park. To get there, drive west on Dundas Street, cross Wharncliffe Road where Dundas becomes Riverside Drive, and continue to Wonderland Road. Turn south, and just after you cross the Guy Lombardo Bridge, turn right immediately, into the museum parking lot. There you will see a fine collection of photos of the band, a video which will bring back lots of old memories of your own New Year's Eves, and Guy's hydroplane, the Tempo VII.

2. Explore the many attractions of Springbank Park. The dance hall where the Guy Lombardo Band used to play every night is gone now, but there are the Rose Gardens, the collection of exotic animals, the carousel, and many walking trails. Canoe and boat rentals are available, and you can also take ferryboat rides on the Thames.

3. Visit Story Book Gardens, if there are those in your picnic crowd who don't remember Guy Lombardo. There is a castle, a gingerbread house, seals, beavers, bears and llamas to admire, and many other exhibits designed to satisfy the curiosity of the young. You can even rent a paddle boat for a ride on the Thames.

Things to eat

This is a New Year's Eve picnic, and so we suggest foods that you might find at the midnight buffet at a party at the Roosevelt Grill in New York, where Guy Lombardo played every New Year's Eve from 1929-1962. Haggis is for the purists, and those of Scottish descent. Everything on the menu should be accompanied by chilled, pink champagne, of course.

Quiche Lorraine

1 pie crust, partially baked   *1/4 lb. bacon, chopped*
6 large eggs   *2 cups milk or cream*
salt and pepper to taste   *dash freshly ground nutmeg*
1 tsp. chopped chives   *1/2 cup grated Swiss cheese*

Prick the pastry shell. Brown the bacon pieces in a heavy cast iron skillet until cooked, but not crisp. Drain the bacon on paper towelling, and arrange on the pastry shell. Beat the eggs, and stir in the cream or milk, salt and pepper, nutmeg and chives. Stir in most of the cheese. Pour mixture into pastry shell, and sprinkle remaining cheese on top. Bake for about 30 minutes at 300 °F.

Vol Au Vent
(Serves 6)

Dice:
> *1 cup cooked chicken*
> *1/2 cup tinned mushrooms*
> *1/4 cup tinned sweet pimento*

Melt:
> *3 Tbsp. butter*

and blend in:
> *3 Tbsp. flour*

Add while stirring:
> *1 1/2 cups chicken stock*

and when the sauce is smooth and boiling, add the chicken, mushrooms and pimento. Reduce heat and add:
> *the yolk of one egg.*

Stir until it has thickened slightly.

This can be prepared at home and reheated at the picnic table in a sterling silver chafing dish. Ladle onto puff pastries that you have bought at the bakery.

Green Bean Salad with Almonds
(Serves 4-6)

> *2 tins green beans*
> *or 2 cups fresh green beans, cooked, drained and cooled*
> *1/4 cup slivered almonds*
> *1/2 tsp. salt*
> *1/8 tsp. freshly ground pepper*
> *1/4 cup tarragon vinegar*
> *1/2 tsp. Dijon mustard*
> *3/4 cup olive oil*

Place all ingredients except the beans and almonds in a blender and mix. Toss the beans and almonds in the dressing, and chill.

Waldorf Salad
(Serves 4)

This is especially appropriate, since the Guy Lombardo Band often played at the Waldorf Astoria Hotel.

> *3 apples, cored and diced*   *1 cup celery, chopped*
> *1/2 cup walnuts, chopped*   *1/4 cup sultana raisins*
> *3/4 cup mayonnaise*

Toss apples, celery, nuts and raisins in mayonnaise, and chill.

11 Lucan
An Irish Picnic

Over 100 books have been written about the five people who were murdered in the early hours of February 4, 1880. Who were the Donnellys, and why does their story still cause some of the citizens of Lucan to change the subject a century later? Some say that the Donnellys were a bad crowd and deserved their fate, while others say that they were ill-fated Irish settlers who were poorly treated by their neighbours. This is the black part of the history of this region. But Lucan is, in spite of the infamous legend, a quiet little village on the banks of the Little Ausable River.

How to get there

From the village of Lucan, which is 17 miles north of London on Highway 4, turn west on William Street onto County Road 13. The road soon leaves the village and becomes a gravel road. Watch for a sign announcing the Little Ausable Conservation Area on your right. Drive along to the small parking area, and select a picnic table with a view of the Little Ausable River. The setting is charming, much like a nineteenth-century English landscape painting.

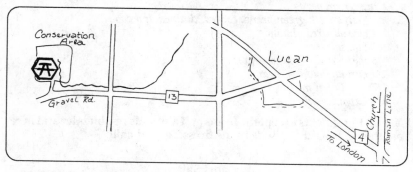

The Irish in Lucan

The Irish settlers carried their loyalties and traditions to their new homes in Canada. Those that came to this area hailed mostly from Tipperary. They renamed the place Lucan, after an Irish lord, the third earl of Lucan (who, incidentally, had transmitted the fateful order to "charge" to the commander of the Light Brigade). In Lucan the factional animosity was strong, and religion became the sole focus for differences, since land was no longer an issue. Each man was his own landlord now. The factions continued to exist well into the twentieth century in Ontario because they still united the working man to his peers, and provided a sense of belonging in a new world.

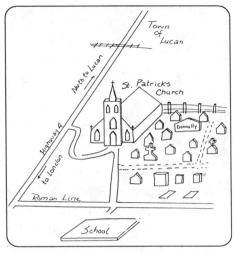

Several factions reappeared in Lucan. One group of Catholic people carried a grudge against Protestants because of their supposed support of the British government. This group tended to be very conservative. They were called the Whiteboys. Another Catholic group voted liberal, against the edicts of the traditionally conservative Catholic church. By their politics they aligned themselves with the Protestants, and their Catholic countrymen saw them as "black." There were also Protestant factions, but the two Catholic groups dominated the Donnellys' neighbourhood. The factions were also clustered geographically in Biddulph Township and Lucan, with the Catholics living along the Roman Line, and the Protestants living along other roads such as Swamp Line.

Johnny O'Connor's Story

He was only eleven years old in February, 1880. His father had been friends with Mr. Donnelly for a long time. That afternoon Mr. Donnelly had stopped by to take Johnny home with him for the night. The Donnellys were being called up in court the next day for yet another incendiary charge which they believed was unfair; but regardless, they would have to be away from the farm all day, and Johnny was a good hand with the animals, despite his youth. One member or another of the Donnelly family was always being charged with the crimes of the neighbourhood: arson, maiming farm animals, assault, even murder. There was no doubt that they were responsible for some of this—the Donnelly boys were a tough bunch. But they were blamed for far more than they did, from the fear and jealousy of their neighbours. There was definitely a faction in the community against them. The priest had even organized a vigilance committee to restore peace and order to his flock. Those who signed the priest's manifesto were those who killed the Donnellys.

The Donnelly Tombstone

On the night of February 3rd, Mrs. Donnelly put Johnny O'Connor to bed in Jim's big bed. Her premonitions served her well—she sensed that this would be a night of danger, so she sat up knitting. The vigilance committee arrived at the door after midnight. Some of them wore the white hoods of the Whiteboys. There were thirty men, all neighbours and members of the same small community as the Donnelly family. Johanna Donnelly greeted them from her rocking chair, showing no surprise or fear. Her husband Jim awoke, and so did their son, Tom. Young Johnny O'Connor was awake, but so frightened that he hid under Jim's bed.

With little preamble the men set about clubbing and shooting the Donnellys. All manner of weapon was used, including spades and pitchforks. Once the four were unconscious or dead, kerosene was poured about the house, and it was set alight.

The committee left quickly—there was more work to do. They went on to the home of Will Donnelly, the most feared of the brothers, and by mistake shot and killed his brother, John, who had the misfortune to answer Will's door that night.

Once the committee had left, young Johnny rushed from the burning house through the darkness to the Whelan's home, nearby. Johnny told his story many times over, to his parents, to the courts, to writers and reporters. Most people believed him. The story didn't change much for the many tellings. But Johnny's story wasn't enough to convict the vigilance committee members on trial for the murder of the Donnellys. To this day no one has been punished for these crimes.

Things to do

1. Go for a swim in the little river below the picnic site. It is a fine old-fashioned swimming hole. Just follow the little trail down the hill.

2. Wander along the main street of Lucan. You can pick out which buildings are old enough to have felt the footsteps of the Donnellys.

3. Visit the Donnelly family grave beside St. Patrick's Catholic Church. Drive south from Lucan for 1 km towards London, and you will see the church on the corner. Turn east—this road is known as The Roman Line. The graveyard is east of the church. The Donnelly marker is a large one toward the back, and is easily spotted. The original tombstone was replaced with the present one in 1964. The words "murdered February 4, 1880" beneath each name were removed.

4. Ride the Roman Line. This road runs east from the church through the Township of Biddulph. The Donnellys lived along this road, on Lot 18. The house was burned to the ground that night, but was rebuilt later by one of the surviving sons. This house, too, later burned.

5. Drive over to Goderich and take a tour of the historic Huron Gaol, where James Donnelly, father of the clan, was held until he was sentenced to seven years in Kingston Penitentiary for the murder of Pat Farrell, his neighbour. He had been sentenced to hang, but this was commuted thanks to a petition signed by over one hundred members of the Lucan community, who believed that he killed in self defense. James survived his years in prison, though he never regained his former vigour after he returned to Biddulph. You can enter the Gaol from Victoria Day to Labour Day, with shorter hours until November 30—and you are free to leave at the end of your tour.

Things to eat

Irish traditions are still honoured with pride in Lucan. So it's an Irish picnic we'll be havin', and God bless ye!

Potato Soup

(Serves 6)

1/4 cup butter
5 medium or 4 large potatoes
3 cups stock or water
1 tsp. salt
salt to taste
3 cups cream or whole milk

3 medium onions
1 Tbsp. flour
1 bay leaf
2 Tbsp. chopped parsley
dash fresh pepper

In a large pot melt the butter. Chop the onions and add them to the butter, cooking just until clear. Scrub, peel and cut the potatoes into small pieces. Add them to the onion mixture, stirring to coat. Turn the heat to medium low and continue cooking for about 5 minutes. Sprinkle the flour over the potato pieces, and stir well until flour is absorbed. Heat the stock separately, and slowly add to the potato mixture, stirring constantly. Now add the spices, and cover the pot. Cook at low heat for another 10-15 minutes, stirring occasionally. Scald the milk or cream and add to the soup. Adjust the seasoning. Blend the soup if you wish a smooth consistency. Carry to the picnic in a Thermos and serve garnished with fresh chives or more parsley.

Irish Stew

(Serves 6)

4 pounds stewing lamb
6 medium potatoes
6 medium onions
1 stalk celery
1/4 cup fresh parsley
1 bay leaf
1 tsp. thyme
1 tsp. rosemary
1 tsp. salt
pepper to taste

Cut the meat into bite-sized pieces, removing all fat. Peel and slice the onions and potatoes. In a casserole dish arrange a layer of lamb pieces, then a layer of onions, and a layer of potatoes. Season with salt and pepper. Repeat the layers with all of the meat, onions and potatoes. Make the last layer of lamb. Over it sprinkle the thyme, rosemary, and parsley. Add water just to cover. Bake covered at 350 °F for an hour and a half. If you have an old-fashioned Dutch oven or cast iron stewing pot, you can cook this on the top of the stove, or on a fire at the picnic. Prepare the stew as above, but simmer over low heat for 2-3 hours. Serve hot.

12 Stratford
A Shakespearian Picnic

Good picnic people all, we shall attempt
To honour William Shakespeare in his metre.
As simple swans their floating food enjoy
We sit on Avon's banks, most welcome eaters.

How to get there

The feast has been proclaimed! A sunfelt Sunday
Shall find us on the grass beyond midday
On Avon's silky banks, below the stage
Where rhymes well-writ are lifted from the page.
So rest awhile. Let Bacchus and his heirs
Deliver you of sorrows, woes and cares.

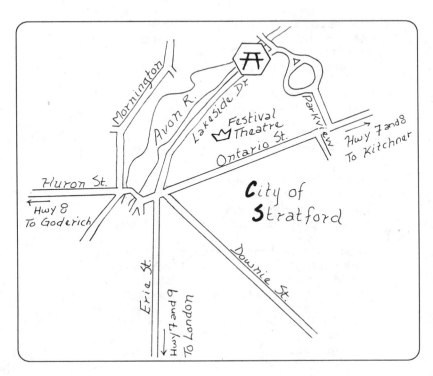

Stratford-Upon-Avon

Methought this spot reflects another place.
'Tis England's merry shore this place recalls;
Mirrored here is Stratford's stately town.
Tradition honoured echoes through the halls.

'Tis not the bard alone who walks this stage
But other scholars of an equal rank.
Plays drawn from both the past and present age
Give credence to this place. Those bards we thank.

Some play is work, but players must needs feed
On victuals plain, and swills of sweetened mead.
Our picnic theme reflects the past full well
'Tis present food and friendship casts the spell.

And here a merry afternoon we spend
Delightful feast and twice delightful friends
And aft a stroll, a ride upon the stream
Or read delicious verse, or seek a dream.

The fairies counsel those who wisely rest
On Avon's banks post-feast, and play at chess.
Players at the game with wit and wile
Cause kings and queens to leave their domicile.

O gentle reader, lest your patience fail
We'll onward move, reducing our travail.

Things to do

1. A little booklet filled with plays or sonnets
   Words ordered by the bard in times begone.
   'Tis balancing digestion for the mind
   An appropriate task for all, of course. Play on!

2. The saucy swans bear watching now, methinks.
   Pay heed should one approach. O curious birds!
   They'd steal your precious morsels fast away
   And leave thee with but few—the nasty finks.

3. Lose thyself and wander up and down
   To view the burg which holds our picnic day.
   A pamphlet boasting of fine shops and homes

Picknicking on the banks of the Avon

Will guide thy feet along the cobblestones.
Peruse the gifts most rare—perchance you'll buy.
'Tis their intent to tempt thy tasteful eye.
This paper can be had twixt eight and four
The Tourist Info. place has this and more.
The flavour of the town is from past tyme.
O gentle reader, do forgive the rhyme!

4. Shalt not thou look upon a play? Of course!
   Such is on stage most every day, oft twice.
   Applaud the ends of Shakespeare's honoured works
   As players play with life's most weighty quirks.
   From May until October's cooling light
   'Tis possible to visit every night.
   But Sunday players and directors rest—
   Hence picnicking and sport fill Sundays best.

5. Attend the artists. Twinkling stars are they
   Whose art embellishes your holiday.
   On Wednesday mornings at eleven sharp
   And Friday similarly for an hour
   Discuss, consider, question them and learn

About the plays throughout the summer term.
'Tis possible at eventide as well
To play amongst the players for a spell.
To know the days and times pray telephone
(519) 271-4040.

6. After picnic fever doth subside
   Obtain a boat and glide upon the stream.
   Rentals abound at number 40 York
   A chance to doze apace, perchance to dream.

Things to eat

Elizabethan feast, O rare event
That succours soul and gut in one accord
The courses gathered, delicately meant
To please full well, tho' simple to afford.

And so, dear reader, with this rhyme we break.
So that the fulsome feast with ease you'll make.

This meal is prepared in advance, and served cold at the picnic.
A minimum of implements should be used, and instead, meat should
be torn from the bone, and bread ripped into portions. Traditionally
you would throw the bones over your shoulder to the dogs, but this
behaviour is discouraged by the parks department.
'Tis simple fare but adequate for all!

Medieval Chicken and Ribs

2 or 3 beef ribs per person
1 medium-sized roasting chicken or capon
3 medium onions, peeled
2 cloves garlic, crushed
pepper
several sprigs of fresh rosemary, or 1 Tbsp. dried

Brown the ribs in hot fat, and set to one side. Wash the chicken carefully,
and place the onions in the cavity. Rub the chicken with rosemary,
pepper, and garlic. Put sprigs of rosemary, if you have some, in the cavity
with the onions. Place the ribs and chicken on a rack in a broiling pan and
bake covered until the ribs are done—they will take less time than the
chicken. Remove the ribs and continue cooking the chicken until almost
done. Remove the lid for the last half hour or so to brown the chicken. A
five-pound capon will take about 3 hours to cook at 325 °F.

Test your chicken for doneness by cutting into the thick breast meat to the bone. It should be white all the way through.

Chill the ribs and chicken and serve at the picnic with Tangy Tomato Dip.

Tangy Tomato Dip

1 cup tomato ketchup
1/4 cup cider vinegar
1 tsp. dry mustard
1 tsp. Worcestershire sauce
1 tsp. paprika
1 clove garlic, crushed
1/2 cup brown sugar

Mix ingredients together in a pot and simmer for 20 minutes. Cool and take to the picnic for dipping the meat. We leave it to you to buy a hearty bread. It should be whole grain, crusty, and unsliced so that you can tear it into chunks at the picnic. Serve it with real unsalted butter.

Trifle

This is truly an "olde Englysshe" recipe.

Remains of plain yellow, sponge or white layer cake
1/2 cup dark rum
2 cups raspberries
custard
thick cream

Place the pieces of cake in the bottom of a deep dish. Sprinkle with the rum, and then with the raspberries. Pour the custard over it all (you can make your own if you like, but we simply purchase a package of Bird's custard and follow the instructions—a more recent English tradition), and fold a few times. Chill, and serve with a pitcher of thick cream. There should be a large bowl of varied fruits in the centre of the picnic table, and a platter of old cheese beside it.

Like as the waves make towards the pebbled beach,
So doth our picnic hasten to its end.
All those who lasted to this distant reach
Are loyal souls and valu'd, trusty friends.

13 Kitchener-St. Jacobs
The Mennonite Picnic

One Mennonite custom is to drop in on each other on a Sunday after church to eat and talk together. The supplies in the farm larder can always accommodate as many as fifty unexpected guests. Mennonite food and hospitality are world-famous for both their quality, and their quantity. Here, in the village of St. Jacobs, by the Conestoga River behind the old mill, we can eat our fill of Mennonite food and reflect on this remarkable group of Christians.

How to get there

St. Jacobs (originally Jacobstettel, which translates as "Jacob's little town") is just a few minutes north of the twin cities of Kitchener and Waterloo. Leave the cities on the Conestoga Parkway, Highway 86, and the signs will direct you to St. Jacobs. The picnic site is on the river bank behind the old mill. There are no tables, so bring a blanket to sit on.

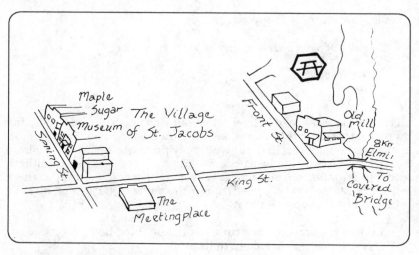

The Mennonites

The Mennonites belong to a Protestant Christian faith that started in Switzerland during the Protestant Reformation of the sixteenth century. The early founders believed that Martin Luther had not gone far enough and they sought to follow Christ using an almost literal interpretation of the Bible. They believed in a free, as opposed to a state, church made up of people who freely choose to become members. This led to the concept of adult rather than infant baptism, baptizing those who were old enough to commit themselves to the discipline and fellowship of the believers. This practice brought them the mocking label of re-baptizers, or Anabaptists.

A free church of people following the commandments of God was not welcomed by churches of the time. The Anabaptists were imprisoned and banished. When this failed to halt the movement, many Anabaptists were executed. Between 1527 and 1631 alone, over 5,000 were executed in the most cruel manner imaginable. The methods of execution included public drowning, beheading, torture, and burning at the stake. To escape persecution, the groups fled Switzerland to southern Germany and Moravia. In the seventeenth century they found their way to France and Holland, and thence to Russia and North America.

An early Dutch leader, Menno Simons, did much to strengthen the group. His writing, preaching and organization welded the Anabaptist movement into a strong socio-religious culture and the title Anabaptist was gradually replaced by Mennist or Mennonite.

While the more conservative members spurn electricity and technology, there are other Mennonites who feel that if God made man smart enough to build a machine, he intended for him to use it. Thus Mennonites started sawmills, breweries, furniture factories and hydro-electric plants and, with a thrift and dedication to hard work that was truly inspired by God, made the region a model of economic progress and prosperity.

Kitchener - Waterloo

In World War I, feelings ran high in the town as residents of English descent questioned the loyalty of their neighbours of German ancestry. The statue of the Kaiser was taken from the park and thrown into the lake, and German was no longer taught in the schools. But the loyalty and courage of a thousand Kitchener-Waterloo boys, who joined up to fight for Canada, at least half of them with German names, did much to heal the rift. The town of Berlin was renamed Kitchener.

Kitchener is now the most industrialized city in Canada, and Waterloo, with two universities and six major insurance companies, claims it has more money and brains than any other city of its size in Canada. Kitchener and Waterloo, founded and developed by Mennonites, are billed as two of the finest cities ever raised on "sauerkraut and enterprise."

The Covered Bridge at West Montrose

Things to do

1. Go to the Meetingplace in the village of St. Jacobs. In this unique visitor information centre you can see a multi-media presentation on the history and beliefs of the Mennonites. It includes a short feature film, a replica of a Swiss cave, and artifacts, photographs and brochures.

2. Drive, and/or stroll across the "kissing bridge" in West Montrose, the last remaining covered bridge in Ontario and the oldest one in Canada. West Montrose is northwest of St. Jacobs.

3. Visit the Seagram Museum at 57 Erb St. West in Waterloo. Operated by the Seagram Distillery, the museum provides a fascinating look at the history and technology of one of the world's oldest industries. Here you will find a 1919 Pierce Arrow barrel truck, a 35-foot-high still, and barrels of every shape and description. Also on the site is a special liquor store that sells all of Seagram's more than 200 products, many of which are not sold elsewhere in Canada. It is open during the afternoon, from Tuesday to Saturday.

4. Visit Brubacher House on the Waterloo University campus, open Wednesday to Saturday in the afternoon, from May until October, and learn first-hand about the life of a Pennsylvania German Mennonite family during the mid-nineteenth century.

Things to eat

Perhaps even more than for their sixteenth-century costumes and their religious beliefs, the Mennonites are known for their food. We suspect you probably have to grow up in a Mennonite farm kitchen to be able to produce all the incredible sausages, pickles, pies, cakes and puddings that characterize the Mennonite table, but here is a picnic menu that you can try.

Creamed Onion Soup

(Serves 4)

1 kg onions
60 ml butter
45 ml flour
400 ml milk
salt and pepper

Slice the onions and boil them until they are soft, about 20 minutes. Drain them and save the water. Make a cream sauce by melting the butter and stirring in the flour until uniformly mixed. Then slowly add 250 ml of the milk while heating the mixture, stirring until it is thick and creamy. Add the onions to the mixture, and the remaining milk, and sufficient water from the onions to make a smooth soup. Add salt and pepper to taste. Transport hot in a wide-mouthed Thermos.

Onion and Cucumber Salad With Sour Cream Dressing

(Serves 4-6)

2 large Spanish onions
2 large cucumbers
salt
250 ml sour cream
5 ml sugar
5 ml vinegar
pepper

Peel the onions and cut into several thin slices. Separate the rings and sprinkle all lightly with salt. Set aside and let stand for 15 minutes. Peel the cucumber and cut into thin slices. Sprinkle with salt, set aside, and let stand for 15 minutes. Stir the remaining ingredients together to make a dressing. Shake, then squeeze the excess moisture from the cucumbers and onions. Combine and pour the dressing over. Take to the picnic.

Shoo-Fly Pie

1 unbaked pie crust
125 ml molasses
5 ml soda
250 ml boiling water
a pinch of salt
375 ml flour
250 ml brown sugar
180 ml sugar
2 ml cinnamon

In a bowl dissolve the soda in the molasses and stir until foamy. Then stir in the boiling water. Pour one-third of this mixture into the pie crust. In a separate bowl combine the flour, cinnamon and sugar, and cut the butter into the dry ingredients until it forms crumbs. Sprinkle one-third of the crumbs over the molasses in the pie crust, and continue with alternating layers, finishing up with crumbs on top. Bake in a 375°F (190°C) oven for 30 minutes.

14 Elora
A Gorge-ous Picnic

Long ago the Indians knew that this was a sacred place, and frequently camped here. A legendary Indian maiden, bereaved by the death of her lover in a raid, threw herself off the cliff to join him in eternity. Our picnic is at Lover's Leap.

How to get there

The park overlooks Irving Creek, just before it joins the Grand River, near the mill. From Mill Street in the centre of the village, drive north on Price Street or Metcalfe Street, to James Street and turn left. The park entrance is just where James Street turns into Victoria Crescent.

The gorge

The concept of eons of time is almost impossible to grasp when we measure time in minutes and seconds on digital watches. To

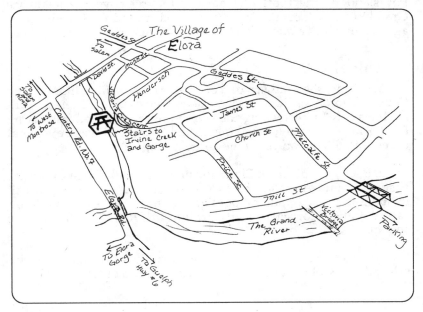

understand the formation of Elora Gorge you must be able to imagine a process that took place very gradually over 300 million years. Back in the past, much of central North America was covered by a great inland sea. The great inland sea vanished and was replaced by differing cycles of vegetation and animals. And then, about 12,000 years ago, during the last Ice Age, the Wisconsin Glacier covered the land. As this huge mass of ice slowly receded it caused enormous changes in the topography.

The Elora Mill

The vast amounts of water released by the glacier over the centuries cut through the rock in many places creating canyons, gorges, caves and waterfalls. The 23-metre (70-foot) Elora Gorge is one of the manifestations of this ancient glaciation. And it continues to change. All that is left of the thundering waterfall which cut the gorge in centuries past is the rapids at Islet Rock—also called Flower Pot Island, or The Tooth of Time. It is the tree-covered rock in the Grand River by the mill. The softer rock surrounding it eroded long ago, leaving it as a memorial to another time.

Things to do

1. Explore the southern part of the gorge by visiting Elora Gorge Conservation Area, just south of the village of Elora. There are full facilities here for picnicking and swimming, and several fascinating trails which take you to the Hole-in-the-Rock, the Cascade, several caves, and other features of the gorge geology.

2. Plan your picnic in Elora during the 3-week Three Centuries Festival in mid-August. This is a festival of classical music which includes the very popular moonlight "Concert in the Quarry." You can book ahead for that concert by calling (519) 846-0331. It is always sold out.

3. Get a brochure at the tourist information office and follow the self-guided walking tour of the historic sites and buildings in Elora.

4. Go swimming in the old quarry—it is thirty feet deep with cool, clear water. Although it has been recently developed as a recreation site, it has been the unofficial local swimming hole for several generations. The quarry was operated from 1900 to 1930, when the site was abandoned. You can explore the ruins of the old quarry operation. The Elora Quarry Conservation Area is on the outskirts of town, on County Road 18 (the Fergus-Elora Road).

Things to eat

Captain William Gilkinson, founder of the village of Elora, recognized the unusual combination of industrial potential and physical beauty of the gorge. Because of the caves on the rocky ledges he chose to name his village after the Ellora Caves of India. Thus we shall have an East Indian meal on this picnic.

Dhal

(Serves 4-6)

This is a staple, served daily in many Indian households. It is made by boiling lentils in water with various spices. We prefer the orange dhal for its colour.

1 1/2 cup lentils
3 cups water
1/4 tsp. cumin
1/4 tsp. coriander
1/2 tsp. salt
1 tsp. butter

Wash lentils in cold water. They will be more tender if soaked in water overnight. Place in a pot with the water and bring to a boil. Reduce heat, simmer and stir occasionally for 1 hour, adding water when necessary to keep lentils moist. Add salt and spices and continue cooking until water has almost evaporated. Lentils can take about 1 1/2 hours to cook. Dhal is easily reheated at the picnic site.

Curried Lamb

(Serves 4)

2 lbs. lamb shoulder
3 Tbsp. vegetable oil
1 medium onion, chopped
2 Tbsp. curry powder
1 cup stock or water

1/3 cup chopped celery
2 Tbsp. chopped fresh parsley
Remove the fat and cut the meat into one-inch cubes. Heat the fat in a heavy cast iron frying pan and cook the onions until just transparent. Add lamb, stir and sprinkle with the curry powder. When meat is browned, stir in the remaining ingredients. Cover and simmer until meat is tender, about one hour, stirring frequently. Reheat at picnic site.

Potato and Pea Curry

(Serves 4)

Peel and dice 5 potatoes.

Heat in a pot:
   3 Tbsp. oil

Add:
   1 tsp. salt
   1 tsp. cumin seed
   1 tsp. turmeric
   1 tsp. ground coriander
   1 tsp. mustard seeds
   1/2 tsp. cayenne pepper

Cook for 3-5 minutes. Add potatoes, stir until evenly covered with the spices, and cook until slightly crisp (5-10 minutes). Then cover the potatoes with water and simmer for 30 minutes.

Add:
   1 cup yogurt
   2 cups frozen peas

Continue cooking for another 5 minutes. Serve hot or cold.

Lhassi

Put some plain yogurt into a blender with an equal amount of cold water and a few ice cubes. Blend, leaving a few chunks of ice, and serve. Salt is sometimes added. We choose to add a few raspberries in the blender for colour and flavour. Put Lhassi in a Thermos and carry to the picnic site.

Mango Ice Cream

Select 3 or 4 ripe mangoes, or 1 tin of mangoes, drained. Purée the fruit in a blender. Thaw a container of vanilla ice cream until it can be stirred. Fold in the mango purée. Re-freeze the mixture. Keep frozen until serving.

15 Brantford
The Six Nations Picnic

Brant's Ford was named after the Iroquois Chief, Joseph Brant. He aligned his followers with the British in the American War of Independence and consequently the Iroquois lost all their land in the United States. In 1779, in recognition of their loyalty, the British government granted them a tract of land six miles deep on each side of the Grand River, from its mouth to its source, 570,000 acres in total. This has subsequently been reduced to a reserve of just 45,902, now called the Six Nations Reserve.

Another famous personage of the Six Nations Confederacy was Pauline Johnson, the Mohawk poet and theatrical performer.

These two supply the theme for our picnic.

How to get there

Leave the city of Brantford heading east on Colborne Street East (Highway 2), toward the 403 and Hamilton. Signs to the Mohawk Chapel will direct you down Locks Road and onto Mohawk Street. The picnic site is just beside the chapel, behind the concession stand.

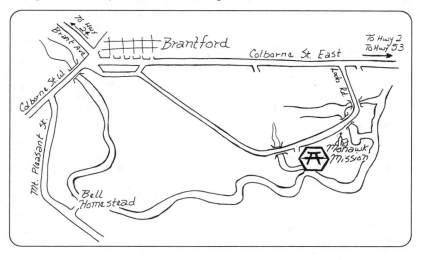

The Six Nations of the Iroquois

The Iroquois did not fit well into the "naked savage" stereotype of the North American Indian. When the white men came to this continent they found a settled people practising agriculture, who had developed a form of confederacy government so advanced that Jefferson was later to incorporate elements of it into the United States constitution.

It was the legendary warrior Hiawatha who proposed and developed the federation wherein each tribe managed its local affairs, with matters common to all being controlled by a permanent council or senate. The federation was open to all Indian nations and soon came to contain the Seneca, the Cayuga, the Onondaga, the Tuscarora, the Oneida, and the Mohawk, forming the Six Nations Confederacy.

The Mohawk Chapel

The Indians of the Six Nations welcomed the coming of the white men and taught the newcomers their farming methods. They readily converted to Christianity, and inter-marriage between the Indians and the whites was not uncommon.

One white man who was to have a major influence in the Indian's lives was a young Irishman, William Johnson. He became a major landholder in the Mohawk River valley and was liked and respected by the Indians. When his first wife died, he married a Mohawk girl, Molly Brant, and assumed responsibitlity for the education of her brother, future chief Joseph Brant. Johnson was made a baronet for leading the Mohawk Valley militia against the French, and in 1755 the British government appointed him superintendant of the Six Nations Iroquois.

It was a superintendant that he was attending the baptism of an Indian boy, during which the parents could not settle on a Christian surname for the child. Johnson volunteered his name and so the Indian boy, Tekahionwake, received the Christian name of Jacob Johnson. This boy would become the grandfather of Pauline Johnson.

The Indian Princess Poet

Emily Pauline Johnson, Tekahionwake as she liked to be called, was Canada's best known poet and most popular actress. The daughter of Mohawk Chief Henry Martin Johnson and Englishwoman Emily Howells, Pauline had an upbringing appropriate to a young

Victorian lady. However, her father's death, and the subsequent impoverishment of the family, brought Pauline to seek an independent life through writing and reciting poems which glamorized and romanticized her Indian heritage.

In the late 1800s and early 1900 she played to packed concert houses in Canada, the United States and England, always appearing in Indian dress. She appeared on public stages in every town and city between Halifax and Vancouver and crossed the Rocky Mountains nineteen times.

In 1908 she retired from the concert stage and settled in the city of Vancouver. There in 1911 she published *Legends of Vancouver*, a collection of mythological

E. Pauline Johnson

legends of the west coast Indians. When she died on March 10, 1913, flags all over Vancouver flew at half-mast and offices were closed. Such was the affection of the Vancouver public for their adopted Indian princess. She is buried at Siwash Rock in Vancouver's Stanley Park, beside the forest where she loved to wander.

Things to do

1. Visit the Mohawk Chapel. Her Majesty's Royal Chapel of the Mohawks was built in 1785 as the first Protestant church in Ontario, and has silver vessels donated by Queen Anne.

2. Visit Chiefswood, home of Mohawk Chief George Johnson and birthplace of Pauline Johnson. The house is now a literary shrine and museum.

3. Visit the Woodland Cultural Centre just down Mohawk Street from the Chapel. It features an ever-changing series of exhibitions of native art and culture.

4. Visit the home of Alexander Graham Bell in Brantford. Here the inventor conducted the first great experiments that proved that his telephone worked.

Things to Eat

It was on the west coast with the Capilano Indian Band that Pauline Johnson had some of her happiest times. Therefore it is the west coast, with its abundance of salmon and cranberries, that we look to for inspiration for picnic recipes.

Smoked Salmon Spread

250 g smoked salmon
125 ml melted butter
5 ml fresh dillweed

juice of one lemon
125 ml plain yogurt
50 ml white vermouth

Place the salmon and lemon juice in a blender and blend at low speed. Add the melted butter in a slow, steady stream. Mix the remaining ingredients together and add to the blender. Chill in a covered container and keep it chilled until serving. The bagels you buy at your favourite bagel emporium, and for the cheese we recommend Winnipeg Cream Cheese.

Harvest Salad
(Serves 4-6)

4 ripe tomatoes, diced
1 green pepper, diced
1/2 sweet onion, diced, or 4 green onions chopped fine
1 large cucumber, peeled, seeded and diced
5 ml ground rosemary
olive oil
red wine vinegar
salt and pepper

Mix the vegetables together in a bowl, sprinkle with rosemary and dress with olive oil and red wine vinegar. Add salt and pepper to taste and chill for at least 1 hour before serving.

Cranberry Pie

2 pastry shells (see Aunt Nell's Pastry)
1 L fresh cranberries, washed and chopped
375 ml sugar
25 ml flour
50 ml cold water
1 ml salt
15 ml melted butter

Preheat the oven to 450 °F (230 °C). Combine the ingredients in a bowl, mix well and pour into the two pie shells. Cover with a lattice top. Bake at 450 °F (230 °C) for 15 minutes. Reduce heat to 350 °F (180 °C) and continue baking for 30 minutes. Serve cold topped with vanilla ice cream.

16 Petrolia
An Oil Field Picnic

The very first commercial oil field in North America is still producing at Oil Springs. At nearby Petrolia the jerker rods still stretch across the fields, driving the pumps that pull the oil from the ground. This picnic takes place at Bridgeview Park near the Petrolia discovery field.

How to get there

Petrolia and Oil Springs are about 20 km southeast of Sarnia. From Sarnia proceed east on either Highway 7 or 402. About 20 km out of the city, turn south onto Highway 21. Petrolia is 10 km south of the turn-off. Oil Springs is a further 10 km along the highway. The picnic site is in Petrolia which you enter on County Road 4. The entrance to Bridgeview Park is on the left, south, immediately after crossing the bridge. See the map for directions to the museums and oil fields.

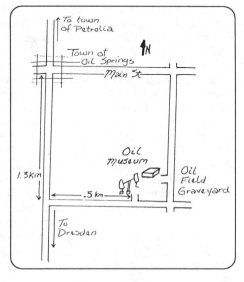

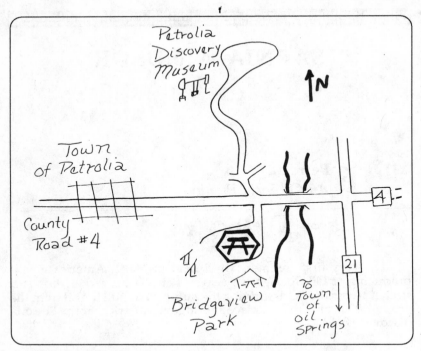

The birth of the petroleum industry

Even the Indians could find little use for the sticky black goo that oozed from the ground near Black Creek. They did use it occasionally for medical treatments but generally it seemed of questionalble utility.

But in the middle of the 1800s, the western world was looking for ways to lengthen the work day through artificial illumination. A Nova Scotian, Dr. Abraham Gesner, invented kerosene in 1846. This clear oil, which he distilled from coal, burned with a bright yellow flame, and provided a satisfactory means of interior lighting. Gesner demonstrated this by using the oil in lamps to illuminate a Prince Edward Island hall during lectures. Then, in 1854, he developed a process for distilling kerosene from petroleum, or "earth oil" as it was then called.

Earth oil was first found in a mixture with soil, called gumbo. The gumbo was mined like peat, and then primitive distillation methods were used to extract bitumen. The resulting asphalt made from the bitumen was used to waterproof ship bottoms and to burn as fuel.

Carriage builder and entrepreneur James Williams brought in the world's first oil well in late 1857 or early 1858. The oil boom was on!

Initially, refined earth oil sold for $1 a gallon, and this produced frantic activity around the discovery site. By 1960, there were over 100 wells producing over 300,000 gallons, but the price of refined oil had dropped to 70 cents. The drop was such that the owners of companies digging for oil attempted to establish a price-fixing cartel (an early version of OPEC). The cartel collapsed because the members were unable to enforce the prices in view of the increasing oil glut. The next five years saw the price of oil fluctuate between 28 and 60 cents.

Contributing to the oil glut was the discovery of rivers of oil running deep below the earth's surface.

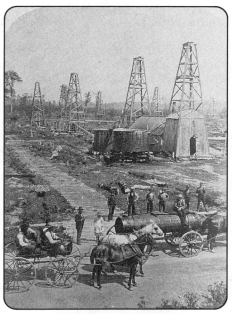

Oil Springs , circa 1870

Hugh Nixon Shaw, a near penniless entrepreneur, borrowed heavily to finance the drilling of a well into the bedrock at Oil Springs, in spite of the derision of his contemporaries. At a depth of 208 feet, 158 into the bedrock, a pressurized reservoir of oil was encountered, and the world's first gusher spewed oil 20 feet into the air. The subsequent discovery of oil at nearby Petrolia sparked another oil production boom.

Among the hopefuls attracted by the lure of oil was nineteen-year-old Jacob Englehart. He came to Petrolia in 1866, and by 1869, Englehart and Co. was one of the most successful oil producers. In 1880, Englehart united with 16 other operators to form the Imperial Oil Company. In 1898, the controlling interest in Imperial Oil was sold to John Rockefeller, and Imperial Oil became the Canadian branch of the Standard Oil Company (now Exxon).

The Englehart mansion in Petrolia is now the Charlotte Eleanor Englehart Hospital.

Things to do and see

1. Visit the Oil Museum of Canada at Oil Springs and see how oil was discovered at the world's first commercial oil well.

2. Visit the Petrolia Discovery Park, Canada's historic oil field. To get there follow signs from Bridgeview Park in Petrolia.

3. Walk the streets of Victorian Petrolia and look at the mansions that oil money built. A brochure outlining the walking tour is available at the Discovery Centre.

Things to eat

Canadian oil men went on from southern Ontario to discover most of the major oil fields in the world. They went to Cuba, and Persia, the Gobi desert and Russia, Indonesia and Australia—87 countries in all. Thus a picnic menu with an international flair seems appropriate.

Mulligatawny Soup
(Serves 6)

1 finely chopped onion	2 apples, peeled, cored and diced
1 diced carrot	125 ml cooked rice
2 diced celery stalks	125 ml diced cooked chicken
50 ml butter	5 ml salt
25 ml flour	1 ml pepper
10 ml curry powder	dash of thyme
1 L chicken broth	2 ml lemon peel, grated
1 bay leaf	125 ml yogurt

Sauté onions, carrots and celery in butter until onions are transparent. Stir in the flour and curry powder and cook for about 3 minutes. Add the broth and bay leaf and simmer for about 15 minutes. Add all the remaining ingredients except the yogurt and simmer for one hour. Transport to picnic in a Thermos. Stir in the yogurt just before serving, and garnish with slices of lemon.

Gado-Gado
(Serves 6)

This is a spicy Indonesian peanut sauce that is poured over a salad of raw and cooked vegetables.

1 medium onion, chopped	1 bay leaf
2 cloves garlic, crushed	15 ml cider vinegar
250 ml smooth peanut butter	750 ml water

2 ml cayenne pepper	5 ml salt
juice of 1 lemon	dash of soy sauce
3 cm of ginger root, grated	butter

Sauté the onion in the butter until transparent. Add garlic, bay leaf and ginger and continue cooking for 3 minutes. Add all remaining ingredients and simmer for 30 minutes, stirring occasionally. Transport to the picnic and reheat at the picnic table. Pour it over the salad vegetables.

Toss together:
    4 carrots sliced
    6 stalks chopped celery
    6 sliced hard-boiled eggs
    500 ml bean sprouts
    250 ml broccoli spears, steamed or microwaved until tender

Take to the picnic, pour the sauce over it, and garnish with raisins and chopped apples.

Baklava

(Serves 10)

250 ml chopped hazelnuts	500 g phyllo pastry (24 sheets)
250 ml chopped walnuts	500 ml melted butter
150 ml slivered almonds	500 ml water
250 ml sugar	500 ml honey
5 ml allspice	10 ml vanilla extract
5 ml cinnamon	1 ml rosewater
dash of ground cloves	

Stir together the nuts, half of the sugar, and the allspice, cinnamon, and cloves. Set aside. Place one sheet of phyllo pastry in an 11 x 15 inch buttered baking pan. Brush generously with melted butter. Repeat this with 11 more sheets. Spread the filling on the pastry and cover by layering with the remaining 12 sheets, buttered between as before. Cut the top layered sheets and the filling into 5-cm (2-inch) diamonds. Bake in a preheated 150°C (300°F) oven for 1 hour. Boil together the remaining sugar and water until the sugar is dissolved. Add the honey, vanilla and rosewater, and simmer until a syrup is formed. When the baklava is removed from the oven, pour this syrup over the puffed dough. Cool for 5 to 6 hours before serving.

The Underground Railroad carried thousands of Black Americans from the slavery of the American South to the freedom of Canada. Josiah Henson, a freed slave himself, established a terminus here which became a settlement for fugitive slaves.

How to get there

The picnic is in the town of Dresden, in the Dresden Conservation Area on the banks of the Sydenham River. From North Street proceed west on Brown Street or Queen Street to the parking area. Our favourite spot is on the river bank beside the boat launch.

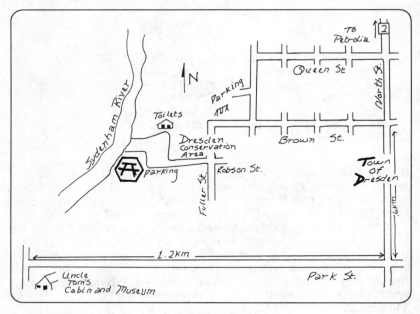

The Underground Railroad

The Underground Railroad was a network of pathways, roads, rivers and trails which led to safety in the north. A runaway slave was conducted along this railroad by a series of courageous men and women who provided safe passage from one "station" to the next, and hiding places along the way. The railway ended at "terminals" where the fugitives could settle. They were often agricultural communities such as Josiah Henson's establishment, near what is now Dresden. There are no accurate figures, but it is estimated that 60,000 to 75,000 people travelled by underground railroad to Canada in the mid-nineteenth century.

Josiah Henson

Born in Maryland in 1789, Henson spent the first 41 years of his life in slavery on a New England farm. On a dark night in 1830 he took his family by boat across the Ohio River, and they walked for six weeks until they reached friends in Cincinnati. From here they travelled by boat to Buffalo, and then to Canada.

They settled in the Niagara peninsula, and Henson soon became a leader of the black immigrant community. He was charged with the task of finding a suitable site for an all-black community venture. In 1842 he and Hiram Wilson, a white abolitionist from Ohio, established "Dawn," one of the several all-black communities which sprang up in southern Ontario. The base of the settlement was a trade school which taught the new arrivals skills suited to this agricultural setting.

In 1848 Henson published a short book about his experiences as a slave. This book came to

Josiah Henson's Chapel

Harriet Beecher Stowe's attention, and she invited Henson to visit her. Her novel, *Uncle Tom's Cabin* was based in part on the story Henson told her. As a result, he is better known today as Uncle Tom, and not as the Reverend Josiah Henson. Henson became very well known, partly because of the success of Dawn, and partly because of the publicity from Harriet Beecher Stowe's novel, and he made several trips to England to address audiences of abolitionists there. He even met Queen Victoria. He is buried in the family plot nearby.

Things to do

1. Visit the home of Josiah Henson and his family, now called "Uncle Tom's Cabin Historic Site." Leave the town on Park Street, driving southwest for 0.6 km. The turn-off north onto Park Street is well marked, and the museum is about 1 km farther. It is open daily mid-May to October.

2. Visit the graves of Josiah Henson and his family, and the graveyard across the street, which is the first graveyard of the British American Institute.

Things to eat

Baked Sweet Potatoes

Select enough sweet potatoes for your picnic crowd. Bake and cool. Peel, and slice lengthways. Place in a baking dish, and sprinkle with brown sugar. Dot with butter, and bake for 20 minutes at 350 °F. Wrap dish in newspapers to keep food warm, and convey to picnic.

Hush Puppy Fried Chicken
(Serves 4)

Traditional hush puppies were lumps of cornmeal batter fried in fat after the chicken was removed from the pan. Legend has it that this was then thrown to the dogs to "hush the puppies."

125 ml sour cream	1 ml nutmeg
1 ml cayenne pepper	1 ml salt
a 2-kg chicken	black pepper
3 strips bacon	a pinch of paprika
50 ml cornmeal	50 ml unsalted butter
50 ml flour	

Cut the chicken into pieces. Mix together the sour cream and cayenne in a large bowl. Toss the chicken pieces in the mixture until coated. Set aside for 20 minutes. Sauté the bacon strips in a heavy cast iron skillet until crisp. Drain, cool and crumble. Reserve the drippings. Combine the cornmeal, flour and spices in another large bowl, and drag the chicken pieces through. Add the butter to the bacon drippings in the frying pan, and sauté the chicken pieces a few at a time until golden. This dish will take about 10 minutes per side. This can be prepared at the picnic site if the sour cream/cayenne mixture, and the cornmeal/flour/spice mixture are pre-mixed. Alternatively, prepare it at home and serve cold at the picnic.

Hominy Grits

This is made of corn kernels that have been dried, and then soaked so that the skins split and come off. The kernels are then dried again, and ground. In case you don't feel like doing this all yourself, hominy grits can be bought in most grocery stores. To prepare this grain, bring water to a boil, and stir in the grits with a wire whisk to prevent clumping. Reduce heat and cook for about 10 minutes, stirring often. Consistency should be quite smooth, but this will vary according to the type of grits you buy.

18 Fort Malden
The Invasion Picnic

Two Shawnee brothers ought to be in Canadian school history books along with Champlain, Wolfe and our other founding fathers. Tecumseh and Tenskwatawa led the Northwestern Indians in that crucial period around 1800. They were heroic figures in a losing cause, for in that period of American expansion the Indians were attacked, harassed, murdered, driven from their lands, and devastated by famine and white men's diseases. However, because of these American actions the Indians chose to become allies of the British and provided General Brock with much of the military support he needed to block the American invasion of Canada in 1812. It was at Fort Malden that Tecumseh and General Brock met, and so this will be our site for this picnic.

How to get there

Fort Malden is in Amherstburg, 32 km south of Windsor on Highway 18. In Amherstburg you will see signs showing the way to the fort. There is adequate parking by the Orientation Centre. The official picnic area with tables is beside the parking lot, but we prefer to picnic on the grass beside the Detroit River.

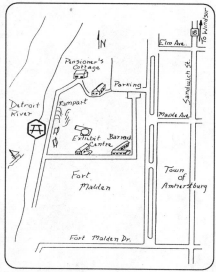

The Shawnee Prophet and the Shooting Star

In 1791 the American government sent out 2,000 troops under the command of Governor St. Clair with the object of defeating the Indians. The result was the exact opposite; an Indian war party of Shawnees, Miamis, Potawatomis, Delawares and other tribes met St. Clair's forces at the Wabash River and routed them, killing over one third of the troops. Leading one of the war parties was a young Shawnee war chief called Tecumseh, or Shooting Star. Wabash was a great victory for the Indians but only a minor setback for the white forces.

In 1804 Tecumseh's younger brother went into a coma for two days, and emerged to tell his people about his vision of the paradise awaiting them. Preaching such things as respect for elders, the brotherhood of the tribe, and a return to the food, implements and dress of their ancestors, the Shawnee Prophet—for such he was now called—soon gained a large following among these unhappy, beleaguered aboriginals. A holy man had arisen from the dead to lead his people!

The meeting of Brock and Tecumseh

The Prophet's influence spread through the tribes of the Northwest. In 1807 he established Prophetstown at the confluence of the Wabash River and the Tippecanoe River, about 480 km south of Fort Malden. Soon there were many Indians at the settlement: Shawnees, Kickapoos, Wyandots, Chippewas, Ottawas, Sacs, and Potawatomis. It was not just a religious gathering however, for Tecumseh was now a highly respected war chief, and he was building a military federation. The Prophet's call to the soul was mixed with Tecumseh's appeal to unite and resist the white men—together these messages were a powerful force for the Indians.

Unfortunately the Prophet was a better preacher than administrator. The Indians prepared their resistance, but neglected their crops, and famine and disease swept through Prophetstown in the severe winter of 1808-09. But despite the famines and disorganization, the confederacy continued to grow.

In the fall of 1811, William Henry Harrison, Governor of Indiana, moved toward Prophetstown with a force of 1,000 officers and men.

Tecumseh was away in the south recruiting more followers. Before leaving he had cautioned the Prophet to avoid a confrontation with Harrison. When it seemed obvious that Harrison was going to attack, the Prophet promised his followers that he had a magic spell that would stop the "Long Knives'" bullets, and he encouraged his braves to attack. In the resulting Battle of Tippecanoe, Harrison was successful in defeating and dispersing the Indians, and in sacking and burning Prophetstown. The Prophet was discredited among the Indians because his magic had failed and the leadership shifted to Tecumseh.

Tecumseh set about rebuilding the confederacy, and sought aid from the British who at that time had just started to fight the Americans. Tecumseh met the British Commander, General Brock and the two men instantly liked and respected each other. In return for the Indians' support, Brock offered them land. Tecumseh and the Prophet gathered over 1,200 Indian warriors to fight alongside General Brock and the British. Together they occupied Fort Malden and then captured Detroit.

Brock was killed on Queenston Heights, and his successor, Proctor, was not respected by Tecumseh and his braves. The likened him to a dog with his tail between his legs and were very disgruntled when he choose to retreat rather than face the advancing American forces. Following the defeat of the British fleet in Lake Erie, Proctor abandoned Fort Malden and prepared to retreat, pursued by Harrison and his reinforced American army. At Tecumseh's urging, Proctor stopped and fought the Americans at Moraviantown, on the Thames River. Here the British forces were routed, Tecumseh was killed, and the American forces took control of the Northwest. Proctor and the Prophet managed to escape from the battlefield; Tecumseh's body vanished.

Things to do

1. When one of us (Nancy) was a little girl growing up in Detroit, the Sunday outing consisted of driving across the Ambassador Bridge to Canada, and then returning via the tunnel under the river. This international outing is still an interesting round trip.

2. Wander about Fort Malden Historic Park. The costumed interpreters are well informed and help make history come alive.

3. Tour the bottling area of the Seagram's Distillery at 110 St. Arnaud, Amherstburg.

4. The North American Black Historical Museum, at 277 King St. in Amherstburg, houses artifacts depicting the history of the blacks' transition from slavery to freedom.

Things to eat

The story with this picnic was one of an unsuccessful American invasion of Canada. Now we acknowledge the recent American invasion of Canada—a successful campaign mounted and conducted by the fast and convenience food outlets. Therefore we suggest that before getting to Fort Malden you stop at a fast food outlet and pick up the following menu. To be truly authentic, you really should buy the food in Detroit and carry it across the border.

MENU

Big Macs or TeenBurgers or Kentucky Fried Chicken
McDonald's Fries
Milkshakes or Cokes
Hostess Twinkies

It is hard to say whether it was A&W, McDonald's, or "the Colonel" who made the major impression on the Canadian psyche. We could not hazard a guess and an informal poll of our children indicated that the jury is still out. Thus we feel that the safest course is to offer a choice of entrées. Of course, late arrivals such as Chicken McNuggets or Tacos are not considered eligible because they were not the shock troops of the invasion. Actually Chicken McNuggets were test marketed first in Canada so they partially represent a counterattack. The fries, however, can only be McDonald's.

Through extensive field trials—leaving them out on the pavement for an hour in July—we have determined that most modern soft ice cream cones and milkshakes do not melt. We are not quite sure of the scientific explanation for this phenomenon but we recognize that it simplifies the process of transporting them to the picnic site.

The only suitable end to such a meal has to be that triumph of food and taste technology, the Hostess Twinkie, which is mostly sugar and air and contains almost nothing that your mother would claim is good for you.

19 Point Pelee
The Naturalist's Picnic

Point Pelee National Park is as far south as mainland Canada goes. It is at the same latitude as northern California; but more relevant to this picnic, it is also the same latitude as Rome. We'll have an Italian menu for this picnic.

How to get there

Jutting out into Lake Erie, the Point Pelee National Park is just a couple of kilometres southeast of Leamington on Highway 33. Follow the signs until you have entered the park, and then watch for the Sanctuary Picnic Area on your right. It is one of the first that you will encounter, and our favourite.

Geology and Climate

Point Pelee is part of a series of islands which serve as stepping stones across Lake Erie to the south. For centuries the islands were safe stopping places for Indians canoeing across the lake. Sudden storms could be waited out in the shelter of the bays and beaches. The Indians already knew of the dangerous shoals which border the shores of the peninsula; the French explorers found out the hard way. They named the place Point Pelee, meaning bald point. More than forty ships lie at the bottom of the lake near the tip of the point.

In this tiny, twenty-square-kilometre park there

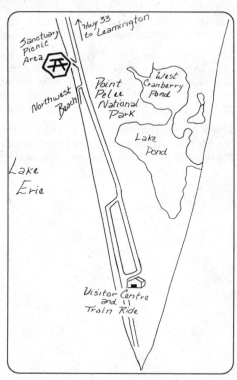

are four distinct climatic zones: marsh, forest, old fields and beach. There are, of course, fascinating transition zones between, displaying some of the characteristics of each of the bordering environments. The park is arranged to make it easy for day visitors to explore these zones. At the Visitor Centre there are maps describing trails through the various zones, with information regarding what to watch for in each. You can wander along the marsh boardwalk; the Delaurier Trail leads past an old log cabin and through fields and woods once inhabited by settlers in the nineteenth century; there are also two woodland trails, Tilden's and the Woodland Nature Trail. Finally, there is the Tip Trail through the most fragile of the park's environments. You can ride on the Tip Train which departs regularly from the Visitor Centre, or walk along the trail. There are also 22 kilometres of beaches and to explore these you need no trail or guide.

The Birds

The total number of bird species recorded at Point Pelee is 347, of which 328 species have been recorded for the spring migration period. Because of the relatively short flights necessary for migration from island to island, Point Pelee is an important migratory route for the small songbirds. They pass through quickly, their numbers peaking in mid-May, with as many as 350 species. Some, like the geese, swans, ducks and blackbirds, arrive even before the ice and snow have melted.

Yellow Warbler

In the fall the birds stay here for a little longer. Now there is time to watch the golden eagle, peregrine falcon, merlin, northern saw-whet owl, red-necked phalarope and buff-breasted sandpiper, among many others. For information on which birds are being sighted, call the park at (519) 322-2365 or listen to the information tape at (519) 322-2371. The bookstore at the Visitor Centre has a variety of books about birds.

The Butterflies

Butterflies migrate, too. The life cycle of the millions of monarch butterflies of southern Ontario includes a trip south to Mexico and back every year. They always travel through Point Pelee, which serves as a mustering point before the crossing of Lake Erie. Here for a few days in the fall the evergreen trees are covered with an orange blanket of butterflies.

Plants

Even the vegetation on Point Pelee is unusual. The tulip tree, black oak, blue ash, red mulberry, white sassafras, black walnut, sycamore and chestnut oak occur in Canada only in the Carolinian forest of southern Ontario. There are characteristic shrubs, such as climbing bittersweet, and the most extensive stand of hop-tree in Canada. Rare plants such as the prickly pear, which flowers in July, and the swamp rose, can be found here. For a detailed list of trees and plants, ask at the Visitor Centre. More than 700 different species of plants are found in this tiny park—an astonishing variety for an area this size.

Things to do

1. Spend some time in the Visitor Centre, 7 kilometres south of the park entrance. Naturalists are available to answer your questions, and brochures and checklists for birds and plants can be obtained.

2. Wander some of the trails in the park, especially the prickly pear cactus viewing-station, and the tip trail. Bring along your binoculars for sighting birds and butterflies.

3. Swim on the many beaches, but remember that swimming is prohibited at the tip of the peninsula because of the dangerous currents.

4. From Leamington take a ferry to Pelee Island which has many of the same natural features as the park, with some extras, such as a wider variety of reptiles.

5. Tour the Pelee Island Winery, and purchase a bottle of full-bodied red to accompany your Italian picnic. The winery is in Kingsville, just west of Leamington on Highway 18. Tours are offered daily.

6. Serious birders will want to spend a few hours at Jack Miner's Bird Sanctuary. Established in 1904 by this early Canadian conservationist, the centre attracts many migrating birds. Here they are

banded and studied as they pass through. Miner began banding birds long before the practice was regulated in Canada. Into his bands he inserted biblical verses reflecting his personal commitment to religion, as well as to conservation. National Wildlife Week was declared in his honour. He was issuing warnings about the danger of polluting the great lakes as early as 1927. The centre is open year round from 8 a.m. to 5 p.m., except on Sundays. It is 3 miles north of Kingsville, off Division County Rd. #29.

Things to eat

Our picnic includes a number of Italian-style recipes which can be made ahead for your picnic. Don't forget the bottle of wine from the Pelee Island Winery.

Antipasto

Traditionally, antipasto is a platter spread with little nibbles and nice tasty bits. Some items are suggested here—select the ones that please your group:

> *marinated mushrooms*
> *slices of prosciutto*
> *sliced tomatoes with herbs*
> *anchovies*
> *olives*
> *pickled beets*
> *gherkins*
> *caviar*
> *melon balls*
> *green pepper slices*
> *Fontina cheese*
> *Serve the antipasto with a basket of thinly sliced Italian bread, or buns.*

Pepperoni Salad

(Serves 6-8)

In a large salad bowl, combine:
> *1 head lettuce, torn into pieces*
> *2 tomatoes, cut into wedges*
> *1 cup mozzarella cheese, cubed*
> *1 tin drained garbanzo beans*
> *1/2 lb. thinly sliced pepperoni*
> *1/4 cup sliced green onion*

Toss with Italian salad dressing, sprinkle with salt and pepper, serve.

Italian Salad Dressing

1 cup salad oil
1/4 cup vinegar
1 tsp. crushed garlic
1 tsp. salt
1/2 tsp. white pepper
1/2 tsp. celery salt
1/4 tsp. cayenne
1/4 tsp. dry mustard

Combine ingredients. Shake or beat well, refrigerate until serving.

Torta Fregolotti

1 cup almonds
2 2/3 cups all-purpose flour
1 cup sugar
pinch of salt
1 tsp. grated lemon peel
1 cup and 2 Tbsp. butter or margarine, softened
2 Tbsp. lemon juice
1 Tbsp. brandy or water

In a blender or food processor, whirl almonds until finely ground. In a bowl, combine ground almonds, flour, sugar, salt, and lemon peel. With a pastry blender or 2 knives, cut butter into flour mixture until it resembles coarse crumbs. Sprinkle with lemon juice and brandy and mix lightly with a fork until blended.

Spread mixture (it should be crumbly) in a greased and floured 12-inch pizza pan (do not press into pan). Bake in a 350°F oven for 50 to 60 minutes or until browned. Let cool on a rack. When thoroughly cooled, wrap well and let stand for at least a day. To serve, break into chunks.

THE GOLDEN HORSESHOE

20 Kleinburg
An Artistic Picnic

Kleinburg, a sleepy little village just north of Toronto, houses a precious legacy of Canadian art—the McMichael Canadian Art Collection. Our picnic takes place beside the Gallery.

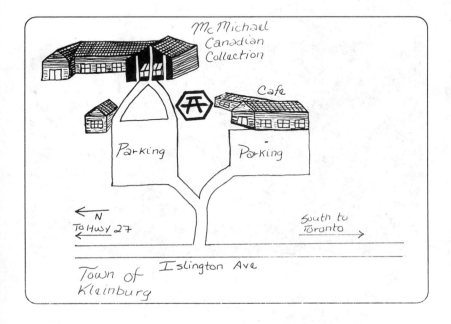

How to get there

Drive north approximately 35 minutes from downtown Toronto on Highway 27 (Islington Avenue) for about 40 km (25 miles). Exit east on Major MacKenzie Drive, and drive north for 1 km on Islington Avenue to the gallery entrance. Alternatively, drive north on Highway 400 to Major MacKenzie Drive, and west for 6 km to Islington. Turn north and drive for 1 km to the entrance. Once you have parked in one of the lots you will have passed several picnic tables on the approach to the main gallery. Pick any one.

The Group of Seven

The founding members of the group in 1920 were Frank Carmichael, Lawren Harris, A.Y. Jackson, Frank Johnston, Arthur Lismer, J.E.H. MacDonald and F.H. Varley. These artists were living and working in Toronto, and many of them were employed as commercial artists at Grip Ltd.

It wasn't until 1920 that the group took on their official name, and held their first exhibition. Their influence remained strong within Canadian art circles for some years.

The composition of the group changed over the years. Johnston left after the first exhibition. A.J. Casson, Edwin Holgate and L. Fitzgerald joined in 1926, 1931 and 1932 respectively. The group dominated the Canadian art scene for over a decade. By 1930 they realized that they were not representative of all Canadian artists,

The Group of Seven

based as they were in Toronto, so they expanded their membership to include artists from other parts of Canada. The group officially disbanded in 1933, but their legacy is legendary.

The Gallery

The McMichaels purchased this lovely property on the banks of the Humber River in 1952, and built a family home of old timbers which suited the landscape perfectly. They called it Tapawingo, an Indian word which means "place of joy." They chose to decorate the walls with paintings done by members of the Group of Seven. Their collection became well known, and in 1965 they donated their home and collection to the province of Ontario. The McMichaels continued to serve as curators in the gallery until 1981. Today they still serve on the board of trustees.

The collection has expanded over the years to include many donated works and some purchased through revenue earned in the gallery gift shop. The total number of works has swelled to over 5,000, all by Canadian artists. Several members of the Group of Seven are buried on the property.

Things to do

1. Tour the galleries of the McMichael Canadian Collection. Allow a couple of hours to do this—the collection is extensive, and the paintings worthy of study and reflection.

2. If possible, attend the Binder Twine Festival, which brings about 30,000 people to Kleinburg every September, on the first Saturday following Labour Day.

3. Visit the Kortright Centre for Conservation, also in Kleinburg, 3 km east of Major Mackenzie Drive on Pine Valley Drive. The site offers demonstrations at a sawmill, beehouse, maple syrup building, and wildlife pond.

4. Visit the Kleinburg Doll Museum, featuring a collection of 165 antique and character dolls. The museum is on the main street of Kleinburg, at 10489 Islington Avenue.

Things to eat

This artistic picnic features pretty things to eat that are brightly coloured, like the thick, rich colours in the paintings of the Group of Seven.

Impressionist Soup

(Serves 4)

This delicate soup is meant as an appetizer, and has just a few tidbits of vegetable for colour, artfully shaped.

  2 cups clear broth or stock
  1 carrot
  1/2 red pepper
  1 stalk celery
  1 green onion
  1/2 tsp. tarragon
  1/4 tsp. freshly ground pepper
  2 Tbsp. dry sherry
  1 cucumber

Prepare the vegetables as follows:

Carrot: peel, cut in half crossways, then cut into thin strips lengthways (julienne style).

Celery: cut into 3-inch lengths, then cut into thin lengthways strips (matchstick diameter).

Red pepper: blanch in boiling water for 2-3 minutes, then peel. Cut into thin 1/4-inch strips, then into 1-inch lengths.

Cucumber: Score the outside of an unpeeled cucumber with a fork by forcing the fork tines down the length of the cucumber. Repeat all around the cucumber—it will have a striped appearance. Thinly slice the cucumber. Slices will have an attractive serrated edge.

Green onion: Remove outer layers. Slice very thinly.

Bring the broth or stock to a boil. Reduce the heat and add all ingredients except the cucumber and the sherry. Cook for five minutes without boiling, or until vegetables are just tender. Add the sherry, and cook for 2 more minutes. Pour soup into Thermos. Place 8 of the cucumber slices in a moisture-proof container and transport to the picnic site. Serve the soup in white or glass bowls, and garnish each one with two slices of cucumber.

Pasta Pastiche

(Serves 6)

This is a colourful collection of pasta and vegetables which can be served hot or cold. Prepare ahead, and bring along to the picnic.

  4 cups broccoli florets
  1 cup baby peas
  12 stalks asparagus, diagonally sliced (optional)
  1 cup diagonally sliced celery

2 cups diagonally sliced zucchini
2 Tbsp. vegetable oil
12 cherry tomatoes, cut in half
2 tsp. minced garlic
1/2 cup pine nuts
1/4 cup chopped parsley
1/3 cup butter
1 cup whipping cream
1/2 cup grated parmesan cheese
2 Tbsp. dried basil
10 large mushrooms, quartered
1 lb. vermicelli noodles

Blanch broccoli, peas and asparagus in boiling salted water just until crisp, about 1 to 2 minutes. Rinse under cold water and drain. Set aside with celery and zucchini.

In skillet, heat oil. Sauté tomatoes, garlic, pine nuts and parsley for a few seconds. Season with salt and pepper to taste. Remove from heat. In large, heavy casserole, melt butter. Stir in cream, parmesan cheese, basil and mushrooms. Heat through, stirring occasionally.

In large pot of boiling salted water, cook vermicelli until tender but firm, about 4 to 6 minutes; drain well. Add pasta to cheese-cream mixture in casserole. Toss to coat. Add tomato mixture and vegetables. Reheat and toss lightly. Taste and adjust seasoning.

If you are serving the dish cold, skip the last reheat step; instead, toss lightly, taste and adjust the seasoning, and keep chilled until you are ready to serve.

Still Life With Fruit

On a large platter arrange a variety of fresh fruit. Garnish with fresh mint leaves. If you need inspiration, you can always run to the library and look up some of Cezanne's work.

21 Toronto City Hall
The Yuppie Picnic

This picnic is based on several assumptions and outrageous generalizations. We assume that lots of Yuppies (Young Upwardly mobile Professional People) live and work in Toronto; that lots of them are influenced directly or indirectly by the Toronto Stock Exchange on Bay Street; and that when they picnic Yuppies spend lots of the money that they earned on the stock exchange. For example, they will, of course, have their own portable picnic table, and will know just the right deli to cater the food.

How to get there

There is an ideal spot on a tiny patch of grass in Nathan Phillips Square in the shadow of the new City Hall. The City Hall is at the intersection of Queen Street West and Bay Street. If you can manage to approach it driving west on Queen Street, you will find an underground parking entrance just past the City Hall building, on the right. The stairs from this underground parkade will bring you up to

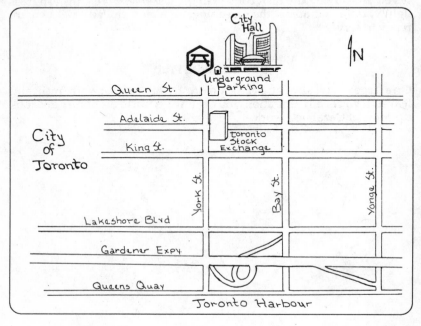

the middle of a pleasant lawn, immediately west of the fountain plaza with the reflecting pool. On this tranquil oasis you can erect your picnic table, and munch your delicacies while watching Torontonians hurtle by on their way to somewhere important.

Toronto

It is almost impossible for Canadians to be neutral about Toronto. They either love it or hate it.

Nathan Phillips Square

Those who love it regard it as the closest possible thing to a perfect city, where everything new and exciting happens first. They feel it is Canada's centre for culture, art and finance. Those who dislike Toronto feel that it is singularly responsible for everything bland and innocuous in Canadian temperament and character.

Both sides tell part of the story, but there is a lot more to Toronto. In many ways, it is the archetypal Canadian city.

Toronto has introduced Canadians to: the tallest structure in the world (the CN Tower), the busiest stock market, a covered football field, American League Baseball, the functioning of the Canadian cultural mosaic, the most expensive real estate in Canada, competitive conspicuous consumption, and that distinctive North American invention, the homogeneous planned suburb.

General Simcoe and the Loyalists (see Morrisburg Picnic) started it all by choosing Fort York (Toronto) as the capital of Upper Canada. (Note Lieutenant General John Graves Simcoe was never a lord—that is, until someone mistakenly named the Lord Simcoe Hotel.) From then on through much of the nineteenth century, Toronto was the destination of choice for British and Irish immigrants. The Protestant ascendency of the Family Compact was reinforced and sustained by the Irish Orange Order. The pervading attitudes were strong on church life; Sunday was regarded as a day of rest, when no other activities were permitted, and intemperance was considered the major social problem. This was Toronto the Good, a reputation that lasted for several decades.

In 1941, Toronto was 80 per cent Anglo-Saxon, but immigration after the Second World War radically changed the cultural makeup of the city. First came the European refugees, followed by the West Indians, and then the Asians. Each brought their own distictive character. Now it is possible to shop and eat in a variety of ethnic neighbourhoods. These new groups have added to the city's diversity, and Toronto the Good has become Toronto the Cosmopolitan.

Things to do

1. The new City Hall, built in 1965, was the result of an international design competition. The winning architect was Viljo Revell of Finland. The oyster between the curved buildings is the council chamber and is open to the public. The bronze to the west of the main doors is *The Archer* by Henry Moore. Inside, the first two floors are filled with works of art focusing on Toronto and its history. There are frequent guided tours of the public areas.

2. Across Bay Street is the old City Hall, the result of a 1890s design competition won by E.J. Lennox. Now a courthouse, it is also open to the public. Inside are some fine woodwork, stained glass, and pre-Raphaelite paintings. The architect Lennox was no shrinking violet and spelled out his name in the exterior ornamentation just under the eaves. It starts in the northwest corner and the letters are interspersed with the designs. The letter O is just to the west of the clock tower.

3. Get lost in the Eaton Centre, which stretches for blocks along Yonge Street. The gigantic glass and steel arched roof is reminiscent of the great European exhibition structures of the nineteenth century.

4. Tour the towers of Canada's financial centre. Immediately south of the picnic site is the King and Bay Street area known as Canada's Wall Street. Wander in and through the buildings. Many house interesting displays of art; and the Toronto Dominion Tower (the Black One) has an observation gallery on the 55th floor.

5. Ascend the CN Tower. There is a restaurant, cafeteria and gift shop up there, and from the Space Deck, 447 metres (1,465 ft.) above street level, on a clear day, you can see Niagara Falls, 75 miles away. Unfortunately the smog rarely clears.

Things to eat

There is no suggested menu here because Toronto is a place where one should sample the local fare. Toronto has become a city of infinite variety and the choice of eatables is constrained only by your imagination and your budget. However, sometimes a budget can be quite a constraint. We have assembled gourmet feasts from the exquisite delicatessens and catering outfits found along Bloor Street. We have enquired at several, and found all would happily cater a picnic at any location, especially Nathan Phillips Square. For general variety, reasonable cost, and a lot of fun in the bargain, a morning can be spent at the Kensington Market garnering an eclectic basket of eatables. To reach the market go to the corner of Dundas Street and Spadina Avenue, then head north along the west side of Spadina. The market is tucked into the streets immediately west of Spadina.

If your taste or inclination runs to ethnic foods, the following locations indicate where different communities are centred.

Chinese	Dundas Street West near Spadina Avenue
Caribbean	The Kensington Market
Greek	Danforth Avenue at Pape Avenue
Italian	Street Clair Avenue and Dufferin Street.
Jewish	Lawrence Avenue and Bathurst Street
Polish	Roncesvalles Avenue, north from Queen Street
Portuguese	College Street at Ossington Avenue
South Asian	Gerrard Street, west of Coxwell Avenue

The islands are the traditional haven for the city folk across the bay. Every weekend hundreds of Torontonians go downtown, catch the ferry, and spend the afternoon on the island. We suggest you do the same, although in the summer it is much less crowded on a weekday afternoon!

How to get there

Ferries leave regularly from the Bay Street ferry dock behind the Harbour Castle Westin Hotel. For this picnic you want a ferry that takes you to Ward's Island. Once you land on the island, take the little train (free), walk, or ride your bicycle to the lighthouse at Gibraltar Point on the western side of the island. There is a picnic place near the water, across the road from the lighthouse.

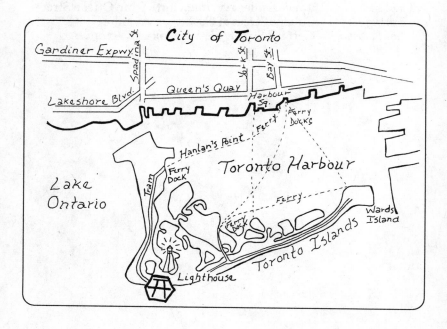

The Islands

Toronto Island is now several islands, but it was not really an island to begin with. It was a peninsula until an unusual storm in the 1850s caused the land linking the peninsula to the mainland to vanish. Since then a variety of ferries, some horse-drawn in the early days when the water was still quite shallow, have carried city-worn

Torontonians to the peacefulness of the park. In the 1950s the water level of the lake rose several feet, some say due to the inauguration of the seaway. It was then that the Metro Toronto government bought the land from the city, razed many of the wonderful old buildings, and declared it a park for all to enjoy.

The halcyon days of the islands were at the turn of the century. Much of the land was still Crown property, and it was an ideal place for a summer cottage. (A few of these still stand on Ward's Island.) Amusement parks sprang up, and the boardwalk along the beach was built. Gracious homes and several hotels appeared—one on the western point of Ward's Island was built and operated by the Hanlon family—hence Hanlon's Point. There were baseball diamonds, one of which was where Babe Ruth hit his first home run. There were forested areas and sand dunes. And there were many large, well organized picnics: Sunday school picnics, company picnics, family reunion picnics, community picnics and club picnics.

The Legend of the Lighthouse

Built in 1808, the lighthouse is one of the oldest buildings still standing in Toronto. It stood on the coast of the island in those days—decades of wind and silt have extended the coastline considerably since then, as you can see. Gibraltar Point was known to navigators of the lake as very dangerous because of underwater shoals.

The lighthouse was built to guide them through this treacherous passage to Toronto Harbour. It was built just before the War of 1812, and because of its strategic location, a blockhouse was built next to it to guard the entrance to the harbour from invasion. The blockhouse was destroyed during the war. During the early years of its operation the lighthouse was operated by one J. P. Rademueller. Because the keeper was well known for his hospitality and his generosity with his home-brew, the lighthouse was frequently visited by the soldiers.

His generosity must eventually have threatened Rademueller's personal supply of whiskey, because there came an evening when Mr. Rademueller no longer welcomed the soldiers. His refusal angered them, and a struggle ensued. Mr. Rademueller was killed, but his murderer was never charged or punished. And so, the ghost of J.P. Rademueller never rests; instead, it is seen walking the steps of the lighthouse at night, holding a candle, still seeking justice for an ancient crime.

Things to do

1. Wander around the lighthouse, and try to imagine it situated on the shore, on a point, as once it was. And if you find yourself there after dark, beware of Rademueller's ghost on the stairway.

2. Baseball fans will insist on continuing on to the northwestern tip of the island. Here, in this hallowed spot, Babe Ruth hit his first professional home run. The ball is still out there, somewhere, underwater.

3. Rent a bicycle and tour the island. If you can find a copy of Gary Horner's *Bicycle Guide to Southwestern Ontario*, you will find several routes described, and you'll learn much detailed history along the way.

4. Rent a canoe or paddle boat and explore the shoreline of the islands.

5. Swim, but check first to make sure that the water is safe. If the pollution level is too high, signs are put out to warn swimmers.

Things to eat

Since traditionally the island was the preferred site for group picnics, and remains so today, this is the place for a few recipes for 40 people. If you anticipate a lot more, see the chapter at the end of the book, "Loaves and Fishes," for recipes for 100.

The baseball game and the hot dog are the mainstays of the North American picnic. Here we dress up the hot dog a bit, and incorporate it into a German menu in honour of Rademueller.

For 40 picnickers you will need to buy:
60 frankfurters
5 dozen hot dog buns
4 Black Forest cakes
several cases of beer

German Potato Salad

(serves 40)

12 pounds potatoes
4 dozen eggs (hard-boiled)
2 cups finely chopped onions
1 cup finely chopped dill pickles
1/2 cup chopped pimento
1 cup chopped green pepper

Boil and cool potatoes. Peel and dice into a large bowl. Slice the eggs, and add remaining ingredients. Mix well.

To make the dressing, combine:
2 cups mayonnaise
1 cup hot bouillon
1 cup white vinegar
1/2 cup salad oil
1 Tbsp. dry mustard
salt & pepper to taste

Mix into the salad thoroughly, but gently. Let stand in refrigerator for at least 12 hours. Keep chilled until serving.

Cucumber Salad

(serves 40)

Place 16 large or 20 medium cucumbers, peeled and sliced thinly, in a bowl with 6 tsp. salt, and let stand for 2 hours.

Make a sauce:
3 cups sour cream
4 Tbsp. sugar
4 Tbsp. vinegar
1/4 cup chopped green onion
pepper to taste
Mix gently with cucumbers and chill.

Sauerkraut

(Serves more than 40 - take what you need)

Sauerkraut is the traditional way of pickling and preserving cabbage. Nowadays people buy it ready-made from their grocery store or deli. In case, however, your garden produced too many cabbages this year, the following recipe, adapted from the *Canadian Homestead Cookbook* by Jean Scargall, follows:

25 lb. cabbage
1/2 large onion
3/4 cup salt
1/4 cup red pepper for colour

Slice, chop and dice all ingredients and press lightly into a crock. Fill to cover with lukewarm water. Set in a warm place, cover with cloth and plate and leave for 5 days. Bottle.

23 Milton
An Archaeologist's Picnic

Here archaeologists have discovered evidence of human occupation as far back as 11,000 years ago—about the same time that Stonehenge was built. Based on the archaeological evidence, part of the site has been reconstructed as it might have been in the 1300s when it was occupied by the Neutral Indians (so called, because they assiduously avoided involvement in the continual warfare between the Hurons and the Iroquois).

How to get there

This picnic site is about a 45-minute drive from Toronto. Leave Highway 401 at the Guelph Line, and drive south to Steeles Avenue. Turn east to the Crawford Lake Conservation Area. From the parking area walk along the road past the Conservation Centre to the picnic area.

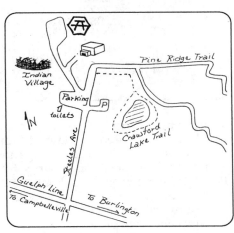

The Lake

Crawford Lake is a meromictic varved lake. "A what!" you say? Meromictic means that there is an incomplete turnover of oxygen, and the bottom half of the lake supports no life. There are thought to be only three such lakes in Ontario. Varved means that this lake, created by a past glaciation, retains clearly defined layers of sediment on the bottom, undisturbed because the lake is meromictic. Each varve is really a double line in the sediment, a light layer of calcium and lime from spring runoff, and a dark layer of organic material from twigs and leaves which fall into the lake in autumn. These layers have been accurately dated to over a thousand years ago.

The Indians

It is thought that there were at least three villages near the lake, judging from the concentrations of pollen. From artifacts associated

Part of A PALISADED HURON-IROQUOIS VILLAGE

with this time period, archaeologists conclude that one of the villages was likely populated by Neutral Indians living in about ten long-houses. The reconstructed village includes a palisade, partly for educational purposes, and partly to increase security of the site. Palisades were used as lookouts, and for storing rocks to drop on marauding enemies, and clay pots of water for putting out fires started by the enemy.

A major form of recreation here in the village was lacrosse. As played by the Neutrals, a game could last for several days, and involve several villages, with a hundred or more players on each team. The Iroquois word for the game is *bagotae*.

Things to do

1. Pass through the palisade and visit the Indian village. Interpreters are on site, and demonstrate aspects of fifteenth-century Indian life.

2. Visit the conservation centre and ask to see some of the films on the history and ecology of the area. The centre also features historic and wildlife exhibits.

3. Take a half-hour walk around the Crawford Lake Trail. It is 1.4 km long, and is well marked with self-guiding interpretive signs. You

can also pick up a brochure at the centre which will help identify some of the unusual wildflowers near by. Guided wildflower hikes are offered in the spring.

4. If you have a little more time, take the 2.6 km loop trail to the Niagara Escarpment. The 50-minute walk features fine views of the Nassagaweya Canyon.

Things to eat

Corn Soup

(Serves 6)

2 medium onions, chopped
1 garlic clove, minced
80 ml olive oil
6 ears of corn, shucked, with the kernels cut off the cobs, and the cobs reserved
1 L canned chicken broth
125 ml heavy cream
a large handful fresh basil leaves, rinsed and spun dry
2 ml salt
dash of white pepper
750 ml water

In a kettle cook the onions and the garlic in 30 ml of the oil over moderate heat, stirring, until the onions are transparent. Add the reserved corn cobs, the broth and the water, bring the liquid to a boil, and simmer the mixture for 10 minutes. Add the corn kernels, simmer the mixture for 15 minutes, and discard the corn cobs. Stir in the cream, white pepper, and salt and simmer for 5 minutes. In a blender or food processor purée the mixture in batches and transfer the soup to a bowl and chill. In the food processor purée the basil leaves and the remaining 50 ml oil with salt to taste until the purée is smooth. Divide the soup among chilled bowls and swirl some of the basil purée into each serving.

Squash Canoes

(Serves 8)

3 large handfuls fresh coriander, rinsed and spun dry
2 to 3 garlic cloves
180 ml walnut pieces
80 ml freshly grated Parmesan

200 ml olive oil
500 ml fresh corn (cut from 4-6 ears of corn)
2 tomatoes, seeded and chopped
4 zucchini squash (each about 1/2 pound), scrubbed

In a food processor create a concentrated mix of spices, by making a purée with the coriander, garlic, walnuts, Parmesan, and salt to taste. With the motor running, add 160 ml of the oil in a stream, and blend the pesto, scraping down the sides, until it is smooth. Transfer the pesto to a bowl, cover with plastic wrap, and chill. The pesto may be made in advance, kept covered and chilled.

In a large heavy skillet sauté the corn in the remaining 40 ml of oil over moderately high heat, stirring, for 2 to 3 minutes, or until it is just tender. Stir in the tomatoes with salt and pepper to taste, transfer the mixture to a bowl, and let it cool. Trim the stem end of each zucchini, halve each zucchini lengthwise, and with a melon baller scoop out the insides, leaving a 1-cm-thick shell. Arrange the shells with cut sides up on a steaming rack set over simmering water, partially cover the pot, and steam the zucchini for 3 to 5 minutes, or until they are just tender. Transfer the shells with cut sides down to paper towels to drain and cool.

Spread a heaping tablespoon of the pesto in each shell, top it with some of the corn mixture, and top the corn mixture with 3 1-cm stripes of the pesto. Serve the squash canoes at room temperature with the remaining pesto.

Corn Bread

1 cup yellow cornmeal
1 tsp. salt
1/2 tsp. baking soda
3/4 cup milk
1/3 cup vegetable oil
2 eggs, beaten
2 cups cream-style corn
1/4 cup chopped mild chili peppers
1 1/2 cup grated Monterey Jack cheese

Mix the first three ingredients, stir in the milk and oil and mix well. Add the eggs and corn. Spoon half the mixture into a pan, and sprinkle with half the chilis and half the cheese. Pour on the rest of the batter, and top with the rest of the chilis and cheese. Bake for 45 minutes at 350°F.

24 Hamilton
A Family Compact Picnic

The group of families who controlled much of Ontario at the turn of the century lived well. Sir Allan Napier MacNab was among them. He built Dundurn Castle for his family in 1832-35. It is a somewhat ostentatious dwelling, in the gardens of which our picnic takes place.

How to get there

Dundurn Castle is in the city of Hamilton, on York Boulevard between Dundurn and Highway 403.

It is on the northern tip of the city and overlooks Hamilton Harbour. Signs indicating the directions to the castle are on all the major thoroughfares.

The picnic spot is on the lawn behind the castle. This area is reached by walking around the south end of the castle (the right end as you face the entrance).

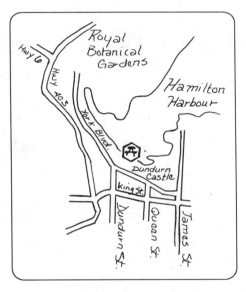

Allan Napier MacNab and the Family Compact

The Family Compact was the disparaging name given to the ruling elite that dominated and controlled Upper Canada in the early 1800s. They were a small group of friends and relatives who were fiercely loyal to Britain and things British, and who collectively controlled most of the government posts and patronage, including the lucrative granting of land.

It was probably started in 1792 by Upper Canada's first lieutenant governor, John Graves Simcoe. In order to create a local aristocracy he appointed his loyalist friends to government posts and gave them large land grants. However, the man who developed the Compact to a refined form was John Strachan, the penniless son of a Scottish quarryman.

Dundurn Castle

Because his mother hoped he might one day be a clergyman, John was sent to school and learned to read and write. In 1799, at the age of 21, he came to Canada to work as a tutor to some loyalist children.

The young colony seemed to agree with Strachan for he quickly rose through the social classes, becoming a missionary, then a rector, then a school master, founder of King's College (now University of Toronto), member of the governor's executive council, founder of Trinity College, and by 1839, bishop of Toronto and ruler of the Anglican Church in Upper Canada. His mother must have been proud of him.

John Strachan was the undisputed leader of the Family Compact and his former students filled many of the key government posts. Strachan's house was the first brick residence in Toronto. Built in 1818, it was two stories high, had shade trees and a carriageway, and was appropriately called the Palace.

However, the Palace was surpassed in elegance by Sir Allan Napier Macnab's Dundurn Castle. MacNab combined law with a lucrative real estate practice, married a Boulton, and started construction of his mansion, which he named Dundurn after the ancestral home of the MacNab clan. It was his intent to create a house grander and more elegant than those that Strachan, the Boultons and others had built. It is reported that at the time Mrs. Henry John Boulton, disturbed that MacNab's Castle would surpass her house, had her own residence totally rebuilt. Nevertheless she was unsuccessful at having the most elegant home, for Dundurn Castle outshone them all, and so did the subsequent career of Allan MacNab.

The Mackenzie Rebellion of 1837 shook the power of the Family Compact. The removal of 2.2 million acres of church lands from Bishop Strachan's control, and other reforms, further weakened their influence. By 1854, reformers dominated the Legislative Assembly and the power of the Compact was broken.

MacNab, however continued on. He and James FitzGibbons (see Queenston Picnic) were solely responsible for putting down the 1837 Rebellion and it was on MacNab's orders that the Caroline was sunk (see Niagara Falls Picnic). He was knighted by Queen Victoria, he was responsible for the Great Western Railway, and he capped his political career by becoming prime minister of Upper Canada. He was also the founder of the Canadian Imperial Bank of Commerce. Not bad for a boy of humble origin.

Things to do

1. Tour Dundurn Castle. The 35-room mansion has been restored to its 1855 appearance and is run as a living history site with talented interpreters costumed in the clothes of the period. The castle is open daily June to Labour Day from 11 a.m. to 4 p.m. From Labour Day to May it is open at 1 p.m. until 4 p.m.

2. Visit the Hamilton Museum of Steam and Technology. The museum is housed in an 1859 waterworks pumping station. The pumping station has two five-storey-high walking beam engines and is a civil engineering landmark. It is at 900 Woodward Avenue, and is open daily from June until Labour Day at 11 a.m. until 4 p.m. From Labour Day until May its hours are 1 p.m. to 4 p.m.

3. The Royal Botanical Gardens offer 1,000 hectares of gardens and woodlands to explore, with the largest collection of lilacs in the world. The gardens, just north of Dundurn Castle, are open year-round. Follow the signs on York Boulevard.

Things to eat

Mrs. Beeton's Book of Household Management, originally published in 1859, suggests that a bill of fare for a plain family dinner for a Sunday in June should include: salmon with parsley and butter, new potatoes, roast fillet of veal, boiled bacon-cheek and spinach, vegetables, gooseberry tarts and custards. It seems that even ordinary families ate well, or at least a lot, in 1859. Scaling this down to a picnic, we get:

MENU

Baked Salmon with Parsley and Lemon
New Potato Salad with Spinach and Bacon Bits
Gooseberry Tarts
Nice Cup of Tea

Baked Salmon

(allow 1/3 kg cleaned fish per person)

Preheat the oven to 325 °F. Scale the salmon, remove its entrails, and clean it. Stuff with your favourite breadcrumb or rice stuffing. Place on thick foil, dot with butter and arrange thin slices of lemon on the salmon. Wrap the foil around the fish and seal. Bake for 30 minutes, or until a thermometer inserted in the thickest part of the flesh, just behind the gills, reads 145 °F. Cool and keep chilled until the picnic. Serve with lemon wedges and parsley.

New Potato Salad

(6 servings)

6 medium new potatoes	*1 clove of garlic*
60 ml wine vinegar	*60 ml stock*
3 tomatoes	*fresh spinach leaves*
parsley	*capers*
black olives	*bacon bits*

Boil the potatoes together with the garlic until they are tender but not mushy, about 20 minutes. Drain, peel, slice while still warm. Combine vinegar and stock and sprinkle over the potatoes. Let stand at room temperature for about one hour, then chill. Keep chilled until the picnic, then serve on a bed of spinach leaves garnished with parsley, olives, capers and bacon bits.

Gooseberry Tarts

Combine:

4 cups fresh gooseberries	*1 1/2 cups sugar*
1/4 cup flour	*2 Tbsp. lemon juice*

Stir until well blended. Let stand for 15 minutes.

Preheat oven to 450 °F. Using Aunt Nell's pie crust recipe (see Wasaga Beach) shape dough into 12 tart shells. Bake the shells for about 15 minutes. Remove from oven and reduce heat to 375 °F. Fill the tarts with the gooseberry mixture. Return to oven and bake for about 15 minutes.

It is not because she made fine chocolates that we remember Laura Secord here, but for her courageous 19-mile trek to warn Lieutenant FitzGibbon of an impending attack by the American army during the War of 1812. There is a link with chocolates, though, for it is the Laura Secord Chocolate Company which restored the home of James and Laura Secord, furnished it and staffed it as an historical home. So, of course, we will feature a few chocolate recipes which you can eat near the Laura Secord statue in Queenston Heights Park.

How to get there

Queenston Heights Park is just north of the junction of the Queensway and the Niagara Parkway. Although there are tables in the park, we chose to have a blanket picnic on the grassy hill just behind Brock's Monument and the Laura Secord monument.

Laura Ingersoll Secord

This is a tale that was heroic enough on its own, but was embellished over the years with the addition of a cow. But that comes later; suffice it to say that despite her heroism, Laura's contribution to the war was not recognized by the British until many years later, when she was an old woman living in retirement down the road in Chippewa.

Laura Secord was born in Massachusetts in 1775. Her father chose to bring his family to Canada, and settled first at Queenston, where Laura met her James. Laura and James were married in 1797, and had five children. They moved into their house (recently restored) in Queenston in about 1803.

This house was close enough to the battlefield for Laura to hear the gunfire of the American attacks in 1812. When the fighting came too close she took her children and sought safety at a neighbouring farm. Returning from just such a flight one October day Laura heard that James was missing in battle. She rushed to the battlefield where she found her husband alive but seriously wounded. She took him home and nursed him through a prolonged convalescence.

And so the war continued. A year later, in June of 1813, the Americans held Fort George at the northeast corner of the Niagara Peninsula and the lowlands around Queenston. The British held the land to the west. The De Cew house along the escarpment was one of four important British outposts.

According to the usual practice, several American soldiers commandeered Laura's home one day for a meal. While serving them, Laura overheard their plan for a surprise attack on the De Cew house and Lieutenant FitzGibbon's troops stationed there. Laura finished serving the men, holding herself in check until she could slip away to tell James what she had heard. James, still crippled from his wound, could not make the dangerous journey through enemy-held territory to warn Fitzgibbon, so Laura decided to go herself.

She left home on the morning of June 22, 1813. For the sake of appearances, she visited relatives along the way, and her niece joined her on the mission. The niece, lacking her aunt's stamina and determination, did not complete the journey. Laura stopped at an Indian encampment and convinced the chief that she had important

Laura Secord's house in Queenston

news for Fitzgibbon. The chief accompanied Laura to Fitzgibbons' headquarters at the De Cew house. She had walked nineteen miles over rough terrain. Heeding her timely warning, the Colonel surprised the Americans and defeated them. This came to be known as the Battle of Beaver Dams.

Feelings after the war were such that Laura did not tell her story. People on both sides of the Niagara River wanted to forget that friends and relatives had fought on opposite sides. Not until she was in her eighties did Laura relate her tale. Then the Prince of Wales rewarded her with recognition and 100 gold sovereigns. (After all, it has been said that if it weren't for Laura Secord, Canadians would be eating Fanny Farmer chocolates.) Her monument on Queenston Heights was not erected by the Canadian government until 1910.

The tribute of the chocolate company is by far her greatest recognition. The name of Laura Secord is known internationally now, but those who know it think of candy and ice cream cones, and not of the bravery of a pioneer mother so long ago. What would Mrs. Secord think of this?

The legend

We did ask several children if they knew anything about Laura Secord other than the association with treats. Those that had any knowledge at all invariably mentioned a trek with a cow. As you know from reading the above, there was no cow. Laura made most of her journey alone, though her niece, Elizabeth Secord, was along for a few miles.

By 1864 the story of Laura had crept into a few Upper Canada school textbooks. One biographer, W.C. Coffin, found the original story lacking in drama and interest for his junior readers, introduced the cow, and the story stuck. Many still believe that Laura bluffed her way through the American lines by posing as a farmer's wife delivering a cow to a relative. What would Elizabeth make of this unflattering substitution?

Things to do

1. Stop at Brock's Monument after your picnic and ask for the brochure with the self-guiding tour of the battlefield. For the healthy, there are only 235 narrow winding steps to the top of the monument, and a fine view of the battlefield. There are guided tours as well, during high season.

2. If you choose to have your picnic on a Sunday afternoon in July or August, you can listen to the Queenston Heights Concert Band. They perform pop concerts at 3 p.m.

3. While you rest in the grass after your picnic, read some of Pierre Berton's two-volume study of the War of 1812. It is available in paperback. The first volume, covering 1812, is called *The Invasion of Canada*, and the second, covering 1813-1814, *Flames Across the Border*.

4. Visit the homestead of Laura and James Secord, carefully restored by Laura Secord Candy Shops. To get there, drive north from Brock's Monument on the Parkway to Partition Street, and turn east. You can park beside the site. The house was purchased in 1969—much changed in a century and a half. But beneath the additions and the renovations of the many residents was the structure of the original homestead built by James for his family. The restoration reflects how the place might have looked in 1812. The tools used were fashioned from models of the period, and the furnishings selected were used by an Upper Canada family of the time. The guided tour is well worth your time, as the explanations of the artifacts and the period are carefully researched. Next to the house is an interpretive display and, of course, a candy shop!

5. Drive over to the site of the De Cew house, the other end of Mrs. Secord's journey. The ruins of the house remain, and there is an historical marker on the site. Ask at the shop for explicit directions. Or you can walk, as Laura did—it is only 19 miles.

6. Drive farther north along the Parkway to the restored Fort George. You can wander among the barracks and other buildings of this once-important bastion.

7. Not far to the west of Fort George is the little village of Niagara-on-the-Lake. Settled by Loyalists, it was the first capital of Upper Canada. Americans burned it to the ground during the later stages of the War of 1812. The main street is now a shopper's dream, with fascinating stores in century-old buildings. You can buy some English chutney at Crabtree and Evelyn for your picnic, and then go for tea and scones at the Prince of Wales Hotel.

8. Niagara-on-the-Lake is also famous for the annual Shaw Theatre Festival held here in a variety of venues from late April to mid-October. As well as several plays by George Bernard Shaw, each season offers a rich variety of theatre and musical presentations to suit every taste. Program information can be acquired from The Shaw Festival Office, P.O. Box 774, Niagara-on-the-Lake, Ontario L0S 1J0, or by phoning (416) 468-2172, or 361-1544 direct from Toronto. Discounts are often available.

9. Tour one of the wineries in the region, and purchase a sample for your picnic. Inniskillin Wines can be reached at (416) 468-2187, and Hillebrand Estate Winery at (416) 468-7123 for times of tours.

Things to eat

This meal includes dishes appropriate to the early nineteenth century, as well as a few chocolate treats.

Dandelion Salad

(Serves 4-6)

Dandelions, as you may recall, were not always a weed. In fact, they were brought to this continent by early British settlers so that this important vegetable would not be lost to them. And indeed, it flourished.

2 cups tender young dandelion greens
1/4 cup chopped fresh parsley
3 green onions, chopped
1 apple, chopped
2 carrots, grated
1 small, sweet onion, thinly sliced

Combine ingredients and toss with olive oil and vinegar.

Potted Beef

(Serves 6)

2 pounds stewing beef
3 cups water
1 large onion
1 carrot
1 tsp. salt
1 envelope unflavoured gelatin
1/4 cup dry white wine
1 bouquet garni (see Ottawa-Rideau Falls picnic)
3 hard-boiled eggs
1/4 cup pimentos or tinned sweet red peppers

Bring the water to a boil. Cut the meat into one-inch chunks and add to the water with the salt, carrot, onion and bouquet garni. Cover and cook over medium heat until meat is tender. Remove the meat from the pot and cool. Strain the liquid and return to the pot. Put the meat through a meat grinder.

Meanwhile, soak the gelatin in a little cold water for five minutes. Stir it into the broth and heat until gelatin is completely dissolved. Correct the seasoning. Cool and remove fat. Stir in the meat and chopped pimento or red pepper. Slice the eggs and line a loaf pan with them. You may use a few cooked peas, asparagus spears, more pimento, or whatever else to create an attractive design. Then carefully pour in the meat-broth mixture, pressing it down firmly to remove all air. Chill for several hours or overnight. Turn out onto a platter. Keep chilled until you reach the picnic site. Garnish with parsley or watercress before serving. Slice this fine-looking loaf for your picnickers and accompany it with a bowl of chutney.

This sort of "potted meat" was a common way to store meat for special occasions in the nineteenth century. The finished dish would be kept in the loaf pan, and the top sealed in with a layer of melted lard. Thus protected from the air, it would not easily spoil—hence the name "potted" or "jugged" beef or hare.

Chocolate Mousse

(Serves 4)

4 eggs
150 g fine chocolate
150 g butter
250 ml whipping cream
1 ounce brandy

Melt the butter and chocolate in the top of the double boiler, stirring constantly. When it forms a cream, remove it from the heat. Separate the eggs, and stir in the four egg yolks. Beat the whites until they stand in stiff peaks, and fold into the chocolate cream. Pour the mixture into a serving bowl. Chill thoroughly. Top with whipping cream with a dash of brandy gently folded into it, and garnish with lots of grated chocolate. Supreme decadence!

The platter of assorted chocolates should be purchased from the shop by the Laura Secord Homestead, and the wine should be a dry white selected from your winery tour. Bring along a Thermos of hot chocolate for the children or non-drinkers in the crowd. Finish the wine before you get to the chocolate course. You can top the meal off with a chocolate liqueur, if you can stand it, and even more sweets.

26 Niagara Falls
The Honeymoon Picnic

Niagara Falls has long been advertised as a honeymoon haven—the place to visit on the trip of a lifetime. Perhaps the most bizarre honeymoon the area had was its brief flirtation with Canadian rebel William Lyon Mackenzie.

In mid-December of 1837 Mackenzie, along with several hundred followers, occupied Navy Island above the falls. There he established a republic, and declared the island as having seceded from Canada.

On December 29, 1837, the British captured Mackenzie's supply ship, the *Caroline*, set her on fire, and sent her toward the falls. This marked the end of the unsuccessful rebellion.

Our picnic is upstream from the falls, towards Navy Island. It is also near an island which is most definitely a Canadian one.

How to get there

Yes, it is possible to find a tranquil spot for a picnic amongst the hubbub of the tourist trade at Niagara Falls. After you have seen the magnificent torrent and ridden on the *Maid of the Mist*, you can relax by the little inlet on Dufferin Islands Nature Area.

You can reach the nature area by travelling south along the Parkway about 1 kilometre above the falls. Cross the second bridge and drive into the Nature Area. Our favourite table is about three quarters of the way around the U (see map). If you cannot find a parking spot, unload your picnic at the table and then, leaving some of the party to set up the picnic, drive further south on the Parkway to the large public parking lot. It is just 500 metres past the Niagara Parks Greenhouse, which is just 500 metres above the falls.

Early picnickers at Niagara Falls

Today a quiet nature area, this island has been in the past the site of a sawmill and grist mill, and an iron foundry.

Rebellion in Upper Canada

On December 5, 1837, several hundred men gathered at Montgomery's Tavern in what is now north Toronto. Led by William Lyon Mackenzie, inspired by his rhetoric, and fortified by ale, these would-be revolutionaries planned to seize Toronto, displace the ruling elite, and bring responsible government to Upper Canada.

It was early in the afternoon that their challenge was met. Colonel James FitzGibbon (see Queenston Picnic) and Colonel Allan MacNab (See Hamilton Picnic), accompanied by Lieutenant-Governor Sir Francis Bond Head and two bands playing Yankee Doodle, arrived at the tavern with 600 militia men and two artillery pieces.

Within half an hour the rebellion was over and the rebels were fleeing across the fields. Mackenzie jumped upon a horse and fled. Four days later he reached Buffalo, New York, and was greeted as a hero by the Americans.

With American aid Mackenzie set up a republic on Navy Island in the Niagara River (British territory three miles above the Niagara Falls). He created his own flag—red, white and blue with stars and stripes—and promised land and money to new recruits. Soon Mackenzie had a considerable garrison which was supplied from the

United States side by the paddle steamer, *Caroline*.

The British responded by grouping 2,500 militia men on the Canadian side of the river at Chippawa. There they set up batteries and proceeded to bombard the rebels with artillery fire. The river is narrow enough here that the soldiers could stand on the banks and make rude gestures at each other.

On December 29, Mackenzie's wife arrived on the *Caroline*. She was a great inspiration to the troops and had been spending her time, in keeping with revolutionary traditions, sewing cartridge bags from flannel. However, she proved not to be inspiration enough, as that same evening 50 British militia men managed to board the *Caroline*, set her on fire, and send her steaming toward the falls. The ship did not actually go over, but ran aground above the Horseshoe Falls and burned.

The sinking of the *Caroline* was effectively the end of the rebellion. American authorities, not wishing to antagonize the British, generally discouraged further support for the rebels. Mackenzie's recruits drifted away and by mid-January they abandoned Navy Island.

Mackenzie lived in exile in the United States for 11 years before he was permitted to return to Canada. His grandson, William Lyon Mackenzie King, was Canada's longest serving prime minister.

Dufferin Park

Things to do

1. Rent a paddleboat and/or play in the waters of the Dufferin Islands Nature Area.

2. Visit the Niagara Parks Greenhouse, 500 metres north of the picnic site. This popular attraction provides the 135,000 bedding plants that fill the colourful parks of Niagara. The greenhouse is open year-round at 9:30 a.m. and there is always a seasonal display such as easter lilies, Christmas poinsettias, and spring daffodils. On the north side of the greenhouse is the delightfully aromatic Fragrance Garden for the visually handicapped, complete with braille labels.

3. Travel behind the falls via the Table Rock Scenic Tunnels. Entrance is within the Table Rock Gift Shop, and protective rain gear comes with the price of admission.

4. Ride a *Maid of the Mist* right to the foot of the thundering Horseshoe Falls. The boats operate from mid-May until October.

5. Check the Queenston Heights and Welland Canal picnics for other activities in the immediate area.

Things to eat

It would be possible to pattern the picnic menu after the food that Mackenzie and the recruits ate, except that their fare was quite crude and ghastly. Therefore we think it more appropriate to acknowledge the other Niagara tradition, that the falls is a great destination for that trip of a lifetime, the honeymoon. We have devised a romantic picnic for two.

MENU

Avocado Soup
Ham Mousse on Crackers
Asparagus with Herbed Mayonnaise
Marinated Artichokes
Olives
Chocolate Fondue
Pink Champagne

Avocado Soup

(Serves 2)

2 medium avocados
juice of 1 lemon
15 ml butter
15 ml flour
500 ml jellied chicken stock
125 ml yogurt
salt and pepper

Purée the avocados with the lemon juice in a blender. Melt the butter in a saucepan and blend in the flour. Add the stock, stirring constantly until thickened and smooth. Remove from heat and add the avocado and yogurt. Season with salt and pepper and chill in refrigerator. Transport to the picnic in a wide-mouthed Thermos bottle.

Ham Mousse

(Serves 2-4)

500 g ham
1 carrot, sliced
1 onion, chopped
celery leaves
parsley stalks
pepper
30 ml butter
30 ml flour
125 ml dry white wine
125 ml stock
100 g Gruyère cheese, grated
2 eggs, separated
nutmeg

Poach the ham in water with the carrot, onion, celery leaves, parsley and pepper for about one hour. Chop the cooked ham finely.

In a saucepan melt the butter and blend in the flour. Gradually add the stock and wine, and stir until the mixture thickens. Then add the ham, cheese, egg yolks and nutmeg and stir well.

Beat the egg whites until thick and fold them into the sauce. Butter a bowl deep enough for the mousse to rise and pour the mixture in. Bake in a 150°C (300°F) oven for one hour. Cool, chill in the refrigerator and carry to the picnic. Provide a selection of crackers, flatbreads, and thins.

Buy the artichokes and olives at a deli.

Asparagus

(allow about six stalks per person)

Wash the asparagus stalks, snap off and discard the tough ends. Simmer the stalks in a pot of boiling water until tender, about 6 to 8 minutes. Rinse under cold water, cool, cover and refrigerate. Serve with herbed mayonnaise (See Jones Falls picnic).

Chocolate Fondue

(Serves 2)

It seems that newlyweds always receive several fondue pots as wedding gifts. Usually, they keep one, return the rest, or give them to other friends for wedding presents. A fondue pot with heater is an ideal picnic utensil. If you have difficulty making the alcohol burner behave, substitute a tin of canned heat (available at any camping store) and you will have worry-free chocolate fondues.

Prepare an assortment of fruit in bite-sized pieces. Possibilities include: strawberries, pineapple, banana, pears, and orange segments. Sprinkle lemon juice on the fruit to prevent discolouration. Remember to bring fondue forks or spears to hold the fruit while dipping into the chocolate sauce.

To make the sauce, combine in a blender:
4 squares semisweet chocolate pieces
125 ml either warm milk, cream, coffee, or a coffee or chocolate liqueur
2 ml vanilla or rum

Blend until smooth, and heat in fondue pot at picnic table, and stir until smooth and thick. Then dip the fruit into the chocolate and indulge.

This is a slow process during which you are expected to gaze lovingly across the pot at your companion. If successfully done, conversation is unnecessary.

27 Welland Canal
A Seaway Picnic

From the observation balcony you can almost touch the great freighters as they pass through the Welland Canal. These locks of the Welland Canal, which lift ships up over the Niagara Escarpment, are the key link in the St. Lawrence Seaway that stretches from the Atlantic Ocean 3,700 kilometres into the heart of the North American continent. This picnic is set at Lock 3 at the Welland Canal Viewing Centre.

How to get there

From the Queen Elizabeth Way take the Glendale exit and turn left onto Glendale Avenue. Immediately after crossing the bridge, turn right onto Canal Road. The viewing centre is along on the right and is clearly marked.

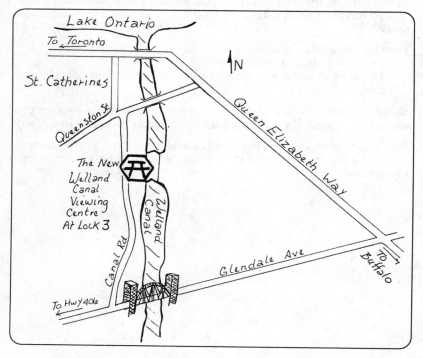

From Highway 406 take the Glendale East exit. Jog to the right at the corner of Merrit Road and Glendale Avenue and continue along Glendale until you can see the canal. Turn left onto Canal Road at the stop lights just before the canal.

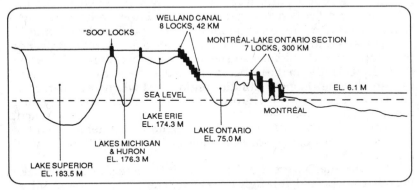

The St. Lawrence Seaway

The St. Lawrence Seaway

The great seaway—the linkage of lakes and rivers and canals that permits ocean-going vessels to sail to the ports of Lake Superior and into the industrial heartland of Michigan and Illinois—was not completed until 1957. The barrier to its completion was not the drop of 99.5 m (326.5 ft.) of the Niagara Escarpment between Lake Erie and Lake Ontario, for this had already been bridged by the first Welland Canal in 1829. Rather, the barriers were political ones, erected by economic interests that might have suffered should a seaway have been completed.

It was in 1895 that the governments of Canada and the United States jointly established a Deep Waterway Commission to investigate the feasibility of a route up the St. Lawrence River into the Great Lakes. At that time there were two shallow water routes from the sea to the lakes. One was the Hudson River-Erie Canal route from New York to Lake Erie. It had been built in 1817-1825 as a barge canal. It saw active use and in 1918 was improved, rebuilt and deepened so that its locks were 328 ft. long and 45 ft. wide with a 12 ft. depth of water over the sills. The other route was via the Canadian canals up the St. Lawrence from Montreal to Prescott. The locks in this system were 270 ft. by 45 ft. with a 14 ft. depth. This depth limited the draft of a ship that could travel from Montreal into the Great Lakes and was referred to as the 14 ft. barrier.

The Deep Waterway Commission recommended the construction of a deep waterway up the St. Lawrence, and by 1932 a treaty was signed by the prime minister of Canada and the president of the United States. However, strong opposition was mounted and the U.S. Senate failed to ratify this treaty. The opposition came from Atlantic coast ports, ports in Texas, some midwestern cities, and the railways. They formed an organization called the National St. Lawrence Project Conference, and lobbied hard to defeat the scheme.

It wasn't until the 1950s when the need to develop the power of the International Rapids section near Montreal became crucial, when the U.S. steel mills on the upper lakes needed the iron ore that was to be mined in the Quebec-Labrador region, and when Canada threatened to build a seaway on its own totally in Canadian territory, that the American opposition was overcome and an agreement reached.

The 1932 reconstruction of the Welland Canal determined the final size for the seaway locks, namely 800 ft. long, 80 ft. wide, with a depth of 30 ft.

In 1988 there were 1,060 ocean-going vessels and 2,849 lake vessels transported through the canal. The cargo tonnage transported through the canal in 1988 was 43,536,000 metric tonnes. Wheat, iron ore and coal are the three most important cargoes carried through the canal.

Things to do

1. Climb the observation platform and watch the ships locking through. They can tell you at the centre when the next ships are due. It is especially interesting to watch the big ships in the flight locks, numbers 4, 5 and 6. Bring your binoculars and your camera.

2. Cruise through the locks yourself on the motor vessel *Garden City*. Phone (416) 646-2234 for fares and schedules.

3. Hike, or bike, the Merritt Trail. William Hamilton Merritt conceived and promoted the first Welland Canal in 1829. The current canal is actually the fourth one constructed. The first canal used forty locks to surmount the escarpment, while the current canal uses eight. The Merritt Trail takes you past earlier canals, including a reconstruction of original lock 24. Trail maps are available at the viewing centre.

Things to eat

As you lean out from the observation platform and gaze into the lock below there is the ever-present thought—what if someone stumbled and went "into the soup?" Thus the picnic should start with a little cold soup. The principal commodities that move through the canal are wheat going down, and iron ore going up. This leads us to suggest a wheat (Tabbouli) salad, and kabobs (on steel). The huge ships crammed into the locks reminds us of watermelon, so the menu is:

MENU

Vichyssoise
Shish Kebabs
Tabbouli
Watermelon Boat

Vichyssoise

(Serves 8)

6 medium leeks, chopped
2 medium onions, chopped
1/4 cup melted butter
8 medium potatoes, peeled and chopped
8 cups chicken stock
1 1/2 cups yogurt
salt and pepper to taste

Sauté the leeks and onions in the melted butter. Add all the vegetables to the stock and simmer for 15 minutes. Purée the mixture in a blender. Add the yogurt, season to taste and refrigerate. Serve garnished with chopped chives.

Lamb Shish Kebabs

Buy 1/2 pound lamb per person. Cut lamb into one-inch cubes and marinate in a covered non-metalic container in the refrigerator overnight.

Prepare the following marinade:
3/4 cup dry red wine
1/4 cup lemon juice
3 Tbsp. olive oil
1 tsp. salt
freshly ground pepper
2 garlic cloves, minced
1 onion, minced
1 bay leaf
2 Tbsp. oregano

At the picnic thread the lamb onto skewers, alternating with chunks of green pepper, cherry tomatoes, small onions, and mushroom caps. Broil on your portable barbecue, turning as needed. Baste with the marinade several times during broiling.

Tabbouli

(Serves 6)

375 ml bulgur wheat
2 L boiling water
250 ml parsley chopped fine
50 ml fresh mint, minced
6 green onions, chopped
2 large tomatoes, chopped
1 green pepper, chopped
125 ml lemon juice
125 ml olive oil
30 ml salt
pepper to taste

Put the bulgur wheat in a bowl and pour the boiling water over it. Cover and let stand for several hours or until the wheat is tender and fluffy. Drain off any excess water and stir in the remaining ingredients. Chill in the refrigerator for several hours before serving. Serve cold.

Watermelon Boat

(Serves 6)

The idea is to make the melon serve as the transporting and serving container. Cut the top quarter off the melon in a single piece. Scoop out the melon's pulp with a melon baller. Refill the shell with the melon balls plus any other fruit that is in season. Sprinkle lemon juice over the fruit to prevent discoloration, replace the top shell, and wrap in foil. Store in the refrigerator until departure. At the picnic site pour the following dressing over the fruit and toss.

Fruit Salad Dressing

250 ml yogurt
15 ml lemon juice
100 ml olive oil
pinch of tarragon

Combine the ingredients and put into a jar. Chill in refrigerator.

COTTAGE COUNTRY

28 Gravenhurst
A Chinese Picnic

Revered by the Chinese people; quoted by Chairman Mao; remembered by Spaniards for his heroism and determination in the Spanish Civil War; ostracized by Canadians for joining the Communist Party; introvert, surgeon, artist, humanitarian; this was Norman Bethune. He was born in the Presbyterian manse at Gravenhurst in 1890, and lived there for the first three years of his life. He died in China in 1939, a revolutionary hero.

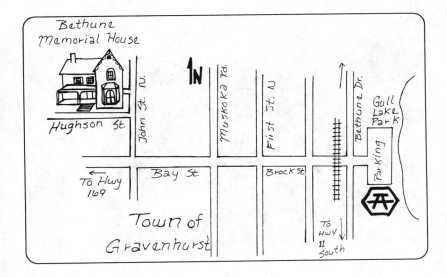

How to get there

The picnic is at Gull Lake Park in Gravenhurst. The parking lot is at the east end of Brock Street (Bay Street) just east of Bethune Drive.

Norman Bethune

By the age of 40, Norman Bethune was a well-respected Canadian thoracic surgeon whose innovative techniques and personally designed surgical instruments were widely emulated. He had contracted tuberculosis in the days when this frequently meant impending death. Fully expecting to die, he nevertheless insisted upon undergoing a risky new surgical technique for collapsing the diseased lung. Bethune survived the surgery and recovered from TB. The new surgical technique, re-designed by Dr. Bethune, was used widely for many years until it was replaced by the discovery of safer chemotherapy.

Early in his career Bethune began to question the morality of medicine as it was then practised in Canada. He came to believe that medicine should be equally available to everyone, regardless of

Norman Bethune in China

income, and that it should be paid for by the state. In the early part of the century, the days of capitalist individualism and the great entrepreneurs, this was heresy. Bethune tried lobbying the medical associations, but to no avail. A few joined his cause, but the mainstream practitioners began to shun him.

Canada

By 1935 the Depression had all of North America in its grasp. The government of R.B. Bennett was losing popularity daily as it failed to come to grips with the unemployment sweeping the country. Most disillusioned was the working class, many of whom were housed in labour camps—artificial work camps which were meant to isolate the men and occupy their time, to prevent their discontent from boiling over into riots. The men were paid $7.50 a week plus food and lodging, and given irrelevant work to do. They were ready to listen to representatives from the relatively new Communist Party when they spoke of jobs for all, universal brotherhood among the working class, and freedom from the tyranny of the rich capitalists who were profiting from the Great Depression.

In June of 1935 a great freedom march was organized. Because many of the workers had found that local and provincial governments could or would not help them, it was time to approach the federal government. Masses of men rode the trains from Vancouver towards the east. Most stopped in Regina when they learned that the government officials had refused to see their leaders in Ottawa. There was a riot, though its size has been exaggerated over the years. It was put down by the police. Many of those who took part in what became known as the "On to Ottawa" march went to join the international brigades that were forming in France and Spain to fight against Franco's fascism. Spain provided the answer for those whose frustration drove them to fight.

This was the climate of the mid-thirties when Bethune, by profession a member of the upper class, announced his espousal of Communism. Bethune was one of many intellectuals who joined the cause of the workers in the early 1930s. All of them suffered as a result of their choice, and the stigma, though less poisonous than it was, remains today.

The ideology of the Communist Party of Canada was attractive to Bethune. Here was a group of people working for the same goals he had come to support. He joined and the die was cast. Becoming a communist led him to the liberation wars of Spain and China.

Spain

The Communist Party, which was born from the writings of Karl Marx, had become an international force since the Russian Revolution in 1917. It was in the Spanish Civil War that the forces of communism and fascism first confronted each other militarily. Many leftist thinkers from around the world—people like Hemingway and Orwell—joined the Spaniards to fight against fascism.

In 1937 it was against the law for Canadians to join the military forces of another country not allied with Canada. Despite this Canadian leftists formed a special brigade. The Mackenzie-Papineau Battalion took its name from the two leaders of the 1837 rebellion. The many Canadians who fought in the Spanish Civil War were uncertain whether they would be fined or imprisoned upon their return home. Nevertheless, they went to the battlefields.

Norman Bethune also went to Spain, but as a doctor. It occurred to him, based on his experience in the Medical Corps in France in World War I, that many wounded soldiers could be saved if they could only receive fresh blood at the front. Without it, many would die while being transported to the field hospitals behind the front lines. Bethune initiated the world's first mobile blood transfusion unit, and proved its effectiveness by saving hundreds of Spanish soldiers. This revolutionary idea had not met with universal support; as with many of his beliefs, Bethune had to fight to get approval for a project which was outside the bounds of ordinary practice. Although still quite a new concept, blood transfusions had been done before, but always in the controlled setting of a hospital, complete with laboratories for cross-matching, and refrigerators for keeping the blood chilled. Willing to risk failure, and to adapt to extraordinary circumstances, Bethune delivered fresh blood to the Spanish soldiers, often stopping by streams to chill it when the refrigeration in his van failed. His success made him one of the heroes of the Spanish Civil War.

He returned to Canada in May 1937, a changed man. Gone were his old tastes for high living and expensive luxuries. Once a well-to-do doctor who moved with the rich and famous of his era, he now spoke of liberty for the working class, of his doubts about the morality of capitalism, and about state-supported medicine. The deeper his commitment to freedom became, the more he saw its antithesis everywhere. He was drawn inexorably to China just a few months after his return from Spain.

The Government of Canada refused to acknowledge the part played by Canadians in this foreign battle, although the times had changed by the end of the Spanish Civil War such that the men were welcomed home with no reprisals. In fact, their return was overshadowed by the first rumblings of World War II; another fascist leader was gathering strength.

China

China was torn by internal strife, as Communist revolutionaries fought to throw off the corrupt government of Chiang Kai-shek, while also fighting the Japanese, who had invaded China to establish more markets. Mao Tse-tung, a leader among the revolutionaries, was mustering resources as best he could, but the poverty of the peasants was abysmal, and the resources minimal. Outside help was not forthcoming. Freedom was a misty dream for the Chinese worker.

Norman Bethune arrived in China in 1938, and was immediately asked by Mao to serve as a medical officer with one of the battalions at the Japanese front. Bethune soon saw that he could best serve the soldiers, whom he saw as workers in uniform, by providing fresh blood at the front just as he had in Spain. This he did, despite continuous blocking from the nationalist government of Chiang Kaishek, whose officials often prevented delivery of essential supplies from North America to Bethune's camps. But the daunting conditions were, to Bethune, just challenges to be overcome. He managed to establish hospitals, schools, training facilities for field doctors, and the ubiquitous mobile blood banks at the front. Bethune believed in Mao's goals for his people, just as Mao saw Bethune as the ideal communist citizen. They both fought for freedom from the traditional tyranny which had dogged the Chinese peasant and worker for centuries.

Bethune died in China in 1939, tended by those who had worked with him under the Japanese guns, and who loved him fiercely, knowing him as no Canadians ever did. To them he was—and is—Pai Ch'iu-en. He died of blood poisoning which began in his hand from operating on an infected wound without rubber gloves—the supply had once more failed to appear. As the infection grew Bethune recognized his fate. Disinfectants and sulfa drugs had run out long before. The infection ran its full course; it became septicemia, and his exhausted body succumbed. He was forty-nine. But some months earlier he had been heard to say, "I am content; I am doing what I want to do."

Upon hearing of Bethune's passing, Mao Tse-tung observed:

Dr. Bethune's devotion to the common people is a lesson for all. The manner in which we commemorate his death indicates how deep an imprint his personality made on us. All of us should emulate his unselfish spirit. It should become a starting point for us to become individuals useful to the people. An individual may have great or little ability, but with such a spirit he can become a man of importance, of integrity, of virtue who forsakes self-interest for the interest of the people. (Allan and Gordon 1974:317)

Long after Bethune's death his name was the cry which spurred the Chinese revolutionary soldiers on to fight for the freedom of China, and of working people everywhere. "Pai Ch'iu-en is with us!" they shouted, as they rushed forward towards death—and freedom.

There was victory in China, and Mao's leadership triumphed. This would have pleased Bethune. In 1952 Bethune's body was moved from a rural valley to the Mausoleum of Martyrs, in the city of Shijiazhuang, southeast of Peking. Nearby is the Norman Bethune International Peace Hospital, and one of the many museums in China honouring his memory.

Canada

Bethune's death caused no great stir back in Canada. For decades he was all but ignored, except by a few friends and colleagues, who attempted to have him recognized as a national hero. It was not until international politics took another turn in 1972, and the Government of Canada officially recognized the People's Republic of China, that it also began to recognize Norman Bethune. In 1973 his birthplace in Gravenhurst was purchased by the government. It is now part of the historic sites system operated by the Canadian Parks Service. Bethune is still honoured far more in China than in Canada, but this Canadian attitude is changing slowly according to the winds of politics and the attendant labels. Ideologies, like fashions, come and go, but greatness such as that of Norman Bethune supersedes them all.

Things to do

1. Visit Bethune Memorial House. From the picnic site, drive west on Brock Street, which becomes Bay Street. Turn north on John Street. The house is one block farther, on the west side of the street. The visitor centre is in the building to the north. The house, birthplace of Norman Bethune in 1890, is restored to a Victorian style typical of the time. Tours are available regularly. At the Visitor Centre there are several videos about Bethune, and various gifts from the People's Republic of China to honour his memory. The display on the second floor of the historic house chronicles the major events of his life. This museum is twin to the Bethune Memorial Museum in China.

2. See the major film based on Roderick Stewart's biography, starring Donald Sutherland, called *Bethune*. Alternatively, borrow the film or video that the National Film Board made about Bethune's

life. There is a National Film Board office in most towns and cities in Canada, and they will mail the film to you upon request. The NFB film was made in the mid-1960s, and resulted in much criticism for the Canadian government for having publicized a communist.

3. Take a cruise on the historic *RMS Segwun*. For over a century this steamship has cruised the Muskoka Lakes. She was launched in 1887 as a sidewheel paddle steamer, a working ship serving the many ports along the coast of the lakes. Now, as a pleasure ship, she serves those who want a relaxing cruise during the months of June to October. Check at the Lake Muskoka harbour in Gravenhurst for the variety of cruises, and select one that suits your interest.

Things to eat

Since Norman Bethune is more honoured in China than in Canada, this must be a feast of Chinese food. If you're feeling a bit lazy, stop at a Chinese restaurant and get the combination plate to go. Purists will use the recipes below, and for this you will need to bring a wok and your portable stove. We leave the making of the bean sprout salad and the purchase of a tin of lichee nuts to you. The beverage we suggest is a bottle of chilled Muskoka Dry Ginger Ale, produced since 1873 at Brown's Beverages, next door to the Bethune house. The Bethune family undoubtedly enjoyed this beverage often.

MENU

Hot and Sour Soup
Bean Sprout Salad
Green Onion Cake
Fried Rice
Sweet and Sour Fish
Lichee Nuts

Hot and Sour Soup

(Serves 4)

Soak 4 dried Chinese mushrooms for 1/2 hour.

Heat a wok, and add
   1 Tbsp. cooking oil
   1/3 pound chicken, cut into narrow strips and soaked in beaten egg
      white
   the soaked mushrooms, cut into strips

1/2 cup bamboo shoots
1/2 tsp. chili oil (ah kee)

Stir for 1 minute.

Add:
5 cups chicken broth
2 Tbsp. rice vinegar
2 Tbsp. corn starch mixed with 4 Tbsp. hot water
1 Tbsp. soy sauce

Let thicken.

Remove the wok from the heat.

Beat 2 eggs lightly. Add them to the mixture in a thin stream. Sprinkle with 2 Tbsp. chopped scallions, and serve.

Sweet and Sour Fish

1 pound fish fillets

Combine the following in a jar at home:
1/2 cup lemon juice
1/2 tsp. salt
1/4 cup salad oil
1/4 tsp. black pepper
2 Tbsp. minced onion
1 tsp. dry mustard
2 Tbsp. brown sugar
1 tsp. soy sauce
1/2 tsp. powdered ginger

At the picnic, wrap the fish in serving sized packages, basted with the sauce. Bake in a barbecue oven about 20 minutes, depending on the heat of the coals.

Green Onion Cakes

These delicious cakes are well worth the trouble to prepare, and can be made well in advance and even frozen, and warmed up in the frying pan at the picnic. They are best served hot.
1 1/3 cup pre-sifted flour
1/2 cup warm water
4 stalks green onions, chopped
1/2 cup fresh onion, finely minced
shortening
1/2 tsp. chili powder
1/4 tsp. salt
dash white pepper

Mix:
  chopped green onions and minced onion together

Mix flour with water, and knead the dough for 5 minutes.

Separate into 8 to 10 parts and roll each into a flat four-inch circle. Spread a thin layer of shortening on each, and sprinkle with spices and 1 Tbsp. of the onion mixture. Roll up jelly roll style, then coil it around in a snail fashion, tucking ends under. Roll out again to a four-inch circle.

Store, chilled, with layers of waxed paper between the cakes, until you reach the picnic site.

Cook in a hot frying pan in oil, until golden brown on both sides.

(after Stephen Leacock's *Sunshine Sketches of a Little Town*)

I, Stephen Leacock, have been famous, and occasionally infamous, for my apparent skill as a humourist (which means that the things I take terribly seriously are seen as amusements to others) and for being an economist. I am never sure if the latter is because I think economically, or because those who read my writings on the subject find the price of my books economical. In any case, I have not yet been duly recognized by my public (a word which conjures up a crowd of country folk at a local fair) for my most remarkable skill: picnicking. Not just any picnic, where you spend half an hour on the damp lawn with Aunt Ethel eating peanut butter sandwiches which were squished in the bag, but a real picnic. Utopian picnics occur in places with familiar magic, like my garden at Old Brewery Bay. Every year we hold a remarkable picnic here. You might as well come—everyone else will.

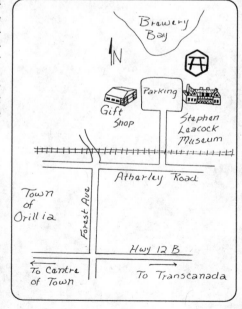

How to get there

Stephen Leacock's summer home is now a museum at Old Brewery Bay. It is on the eastern edge of Orillia just off Highway 12B. Spread your picnic blanket on the lawn in the garden on a sunny summer afternoon, and keep your eye on the lake, in case the *Mariposa Belle* goes by.

Leacock home at Old Brewery Bay

My Most Remarkable Picnic

The rain didn't spoil it, but Dean Drone's relentless grace almost did. It wasn't sacrilegious, or even disrespectful. The reverend simply grasped the opportunity to invoke the blessings of the deity on the assembled multitude—one by one. You have to understand, of course, the Dean of our Anglican church rarely gets a chance to bless everyone in town at once. But before he blessed us, following the usual course of such things, he had to forgive us for our sins—at least the ones he knew about. Individually, again. He had us bunched together under the big umbrellas like mushrooms in a manure patch.

He started off with some of the more important folks, likely so that we ordinary mortals wouldn't feel singled out. He scolded Mr. Smith for serving liquor after hours at the bar in his hotel, and then he scolded Judge Pepperleigh for being at Josh Smith's bar instead of the one in the court room. All of this was impersonal, of course. The Dean asked the Lord's forgiveness for a certain hotel owner, and then a certain judge...but since we only have one of each in Mariposa, we all knew who he meant. He mentioned that a certain young engaged couple were about to sin by being married by a justice of the peace instead of in the eyes of God and the Dean in God's proper church. We all knew that he meant Zena Pepperleigh and Peter Pupkin since they were the only engaged couple hereabouts. The Dean even mentioned a certain barber who tended to gossip. We all thought that was unkind, since Jefferson Thorpe was not only the Dean's and everyone else's barber, but also the source of most of the Dean's information about us sinners. It seems to me that the only person who got off unscathed was Mr. Golgotha Gingham, the undertaker, who was dressed in his usual moribund black suit and gloves. I suppose the Dean considers Gingham's work to be sufficiently close to that of the reverend himself as to be free of sin.

Some of us were doing some praying of our own, or at least I was, seeking a little divine intervention as regards to the simultaneous termination of the rain shower and the invocation. It worked. And you never heard such a chatter as sprang up amongst those neighbours as they explained away their sins to each other!

The rest of the picnic rolled along just as it should have, with the judge's wife pouring tea, since she had a silver tea service which she proudly offered to such community events. She always generously insisted on officiating, as the judge's wife should, being the most important wife in town.

So by the time it was three o'clock, the sun was shining, and the *Mariposa Belle* arrived at the dock at the foot of the garden, just as the organizing committee had planned. The ride back to town on that distinguished vessel was a fitting end to the excursion to Old Brewery Bay. I don't need to tell you that by the time everyone got back to Mariposa the sins of the multitude had all been forgotten, even by Dean Drone, who gave his benediction from an unsteady perch on the bow as the *Mariposa Belle* docked safely once more at the town harbour.

Things to do

1. Tour the Stephen Leacock Memorial Home. It is open daily from April 15 to December 15. The house was built in 1928 to replace a smaller cottage that Leacock had built in 1908. He spent his summers here, and his winters teaching economics at McGill University. He did much of his writing at a table upstairs in a boat house which used to sit on the point below the house. He wrote in the early morning, from 5 a.m. to 9 a.m. Part of his collection of books is still in the library, and his favourite chair is in the livingroom.

2. Take a boat cruise on Lake Couchiching. A two-hour cruise will take you past the Leacock home, so that you can see the gardens from the lake. Leacock spent part of most summer days on his boat.

3. Bring along your copy of *Sunshine Sketches of a Little Town* by Stephen Leacock and read a few of the chapters from the real thing as you relax on the lawn after your picnic.

4. Take along a notebook, and write a sunshine sketch about your own remarkable picnic.

Things to eat

This is a good old-fashioned garden party. Bring lots of iced tea with slices of lemon, and a pretty picnic cloth or blanket to set on the grass.

```
╭──────────────────────╮
│   ┌────────────┐      │
│   │   MENU     │      │
│   └────────────┘      │
╰──────────────────────╯
```

Chilled Cucumber Soup
Baked Ham
Vegetable Platter with Dip
Potato Salad
Peach Pie
Iced Tea with Lemon

Chilled Cucumber Soup

(Serves 4-6)

2 Tbsp. butter
1/2 onion, finely chopped
1 clove garlic finely chopped
3 large cucumbers, peeled, halved lengthwise, seeded and chopped
3 Tbsp. unbleached white flour
2 cups chicken broth
1 tsp. sea salt
3/4 cup sour cream or yogurt
1 Tbsp. snipped fresh dill weed
1 tsp. grated lemon rind
1/8 tsp. mace

Heat the butter in a heavy skillet and sauté the onion, garlic and cucumbers in it until onion is tender, about 10 minutes. Sprinkle with flour; stir well. Gradually stir in the broth. Add the salt and bring to a boil. Cover and simmer until the cucumber is tender. Cool. Purée the mixture in batches in a blender. Stir in the sour cream or yogurt, the dill, lemon rind and mace. Chill several hours, and pack in wide-mouthed Thermos for transport to picnic site.

Baked Ham

Select a precooked or ready-to-eat ham that is a suitable size for your group. Allow about one third of a pound per person. Preheat the oven to 300 °F and cook the ham uncovered in a roasting pan. Allow about 20 minutes per pound. When the ham is done, remove it from the oven and with a sharp knife, cut off the rind. Score the fat in diagonal slashes in both directions about one inch apart to make a diamond pattern in the fat. Stud the fat with whole cloves. Mix 1/2 cup of maple sugar with 1/2 cup of brown sugar and a tablespoon of dry mustard. Spread the glaze mixture over the ham and return to the oven. Increase the heat to 400 °F and bake until the sugar has glazed, about 25 minutes. Cool then chill. Transport cold and slice at the picnic.

Vegetables with Dip

Arrange on a large platter a variety of fresh, clean vegetables, cut into finger pieces. Some suggestions are:

carrot sticks	*celery sticks*
radishes	*broccoli*
cauliflower florettes	*cucumber spears*
turnip slices	*green onions*
mushrooms	*cherry tomatoes*

Dip

1/2 cup plain yogurt
1/2 cup sour cream
dash of tabasco sauce
1 tsp. curry powder
dash cayenne
Mix together and garnish with fresh coriander leaves.

Potato Salad

(Serves 10)

Combine in a bowl:

10 medium cooked, diced potatoes
1 peeled, diced cucumber
1 medium onion, chopped (red, if possible)
1 green pepper, chopped
2 eggs, hard-boiled and coarsely chopped
1 small tin pimento, chopped
1 1/2 tsp. salt
3/4 tsp. celery seed

1/4 tsp. pepper
1 tsp. fresh summer savory
4 leaves fresh basil, snipped
Mix well and chill.

Prepare a dressing of:
1/2 cup whipping cream
1/2 cup mayonnaise
1/4 cup vinegar
1 Tbsp. prepared mustard

Shake well in a sealed jar and carry to the picnic site. Toss with potato mixture 1/2 hour before serving. Garnish with raw, unsalted sunflower seeds and fresh, snipped parsley.

Peach Pie

No garden party is complete without a fruit pie.
1 unbaked pie shell (see Aunt Nell's pie crust recipe)
5 fresh, firm peaches, peeled and sliced
3/4 cup sugar
2 Tbsp. flour
1 tsp. cinnamon
1/4 tsp. allspice
2 Tbsp. butter
2 eggs, beaten
1 tsp. vanilla

Arrange the peaches in the pie shell. Mix together the flour, sugar, cinnamon and allspice, and sprinkle over the fruit. Cut the butter into the flour mixture until it is the consistency of crumbs. Sprinkle evenly over the peaches.

Mix together the eggs and vanilla, and pour over the pie. Bake at 400 °F for 15 minutes, then reduce the heat to 325 °F and bake 40 minutes more, until topping is browned. Cool, and serve with whipped cream.

30 Lakefield
A Writer's Picnic

Margaret Laurence chose to live and write here for many years. A century earlier, Catharine Parr Traill and her sister, Susanna Moodie, followed their husbands here from England to establish homesteads in the bush, whence both women continued to follow their propensity for writing. And long before any of these writers, unknown artists left a timeless message written in stone near by.

How to get there

The picnic site is in Lakefield Park, a large recreational facility on the edge of the village, on the west side of the Otonabee River. From Highway 28 (Bridge Street) drive north on Clement Street for three blocks, and turn east on Deyncourt Street. The entrance to the park is well marked. You can select a picnic table in the woods or on the beach.

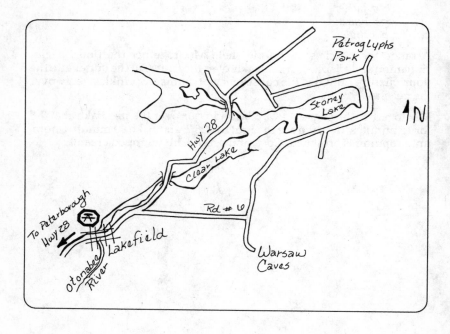

Margaret Laurence

One of the outstanding novelists of this century, Margaret Laurence wrote several of her books in Lakefield. From 1971-73 she spent her summers at a cottage on the Otanabee River, and in 1974 she bought a home in Lakefield. Here she lived and wrote until her death in 1987.

Margaret Laurence focuses on experiences and issues which are common to most people. Her popularity as a Canadian writer arises from her ability to achieve this common acknowledgement of a shared perspective with her reader, together with her remarkable skill as an artist. Laurence's stories are executed with brutal honesty and tempered with sympathy, understanding and acceptance which extend beyond her characters to her readers. It is this acceptance of the well-intentioned failures and small triumphs that account for Margaret Laurence's popularity as an author.

Readers readily accept and identify with the pioneering past of Laurence's central characters. Canadians have an ambivalent attitude toward their ancestors, and their ethnic traditions. On one side is pride in their accomplishments, and on the other is embarrassment or even shame because of their uniqueness. Overriding and unifying this ambivalence is the search for identity carried on by each individual. Personal maturity is represented by Margaret Laurence as an effort to come to terms with these contradictory elements as they exist in each person, and externally within society.

Catharine Parr Traill

Mrs. Traill is, to many of her readers today, a paragon of courage and fortitude, the exemplary settler. She came to Upper Canada in 1832. She set up a home in a log cabin in the bush, raised nine children, gardened, canned and preserved food for her family, collected wild herbs with nutritional and medicinal value, and wrote several books about these experiences. One of these, *The Canadian Settler's Guide*, is a comprehensive compendium of information for the new wife arriving from Europe and confronting life in the bushlands of Upper Canada. This book covers

Catherine Parr Traill with Susanna Moodie

Catherine Parr Traill's house

everything from making your own furniture to caring for your orchards, keeping bees, making bread, and knitting. Her advice extends as far as careful borrowing from neighbours, and cautions against intemperance. A redoubtable lady, indeed! She is truly an ancestor one can be proud of, but her accomplishments can intimidate the most determined contemporary back-to-the-lander.

Susanna Moodie

Mrs. Moodie was Mrs. Traill's younger sister. Their brother, Samuel Strickland, was also a writer in Canada, and their sister Agnes an accomplished historian and writer in England. Like Catherine, Susanna Moodie accompanied her young military husband to the bush and also wrote about her experiences. But Susanna saw things a little differently. For example, logging bees, which have been mythologized in our heritage as happy, cooperative occasions in pioneer communities, did not impress Mrs. Moodie.

"... to me, they present the most disgusting picture of bush life. They are noisy, riotous, drunken meetings, often terminating in violent quarrels, sometimes even in bloodshed. Accidents of the most serious nature often occur, and very little work is done when we consider the number of hands employed, and the great consumption of food and liquor" (Moodie 1962:156).

She describes her early "love for Canada [as] a feeling very nearly allied to that which the condemned criminal entertains for his cell— his only hope of escape being through the portals of the grave" (Moodie 1962:100). Two of her books, *Roughing it in the Bush* and *Life in the Clearings*, are replete with examples of her emotional response to her new homeland. She expresses anger, discouragement, amusement and joy, as she adjusts to the demands of her new life. She is somewhat intimidated by her sister's natural cheerfulness, yet the two were close friends and neighbours for six years until the Moodies moved to Belleville in 1840. Mrs. Moodie continued to write, and her works were published in Canada and England. She died in 1885 in Toronto.

And long before . . .

Margaret Laurence undoubtedly read the Strickland sisters' books. However, it is uncertain whether any of the three visited the petroglyph site nearby, but this is probably the earliest writing in the Lakefield area. On a large outcrop of marble, part of the Canadian Shield, a few miles from where the settlements are now, native people carved hundreds of symbols. Believed to be created by Algonkian-speaking Indians, they date from 500 to 1,000 years ago. They had survived the weathering of the centuries because of a thick covering of moss, and the protection of the forest. Today the site is protected from the elements and from vandalism by a seven-sided building with railed walkways from which the figures can be studied. The structure has been acclaimed by the academic community to be the most rational, scientific approach to preservation of a rock art site in the world. This is still a sacred place where tobacco and other offerings are made to the spirits by the native people. The more than 900 figures of animals, birds and other supernatural powers are probably the work of shamans, to facilitate communication with the supernatural. The oral history of the Ojibway people has traditionally referred to this site as *Kinomagewapkong*, the rocks that teach.

The images here speak to us mysteriously centuries later, a part of the artistic heritage to which other artists, Catharine Parr Traill, Susanna Moodie and Margaret Laurence, also contributed.

Things to do

1. Walk or drive by Catharine Parr Traill's house, at 16 Smith Street, just east of Clement Street. There is a historical marker outside, but the house is privately owned and occupied. Mrs. Traill lived here after her husband's death, until she died in 1899.

2. Drive to Petroglyphs Provincial Park and see the "Teaching Rock," the largest concentration of native rock-carving in Canada. Drive north from Lakefield on Highway 28 to Woodview, about 30 km. Turn onto Northey's Bay Road and follow the signs to the park. You will drive along the north side of Stony Lake for about 12 km, before reaching the park. The petroglyph site is about 8 km down the park road.

3. Ask for a trail brochure at the desk at the petroglyph site, and follow the 3 km self-guiding Nanabush trail. One of the legends told is of Nanabush, the teacher sent to the people by the Creator. You will also learn many other fascinating things about the natural features of the region as you wander around Minnow Lake. The walk will take about 1 1/2 hours. Watch for the large turtles that live in the woods nearby.

4. Visit the Warsaw Caves Conservation Area and climb down into the caves and caverns in the rock. Sturdy shoes, long sleeves and long pants are advisable here. You will need a flashlight, too. The more accessible caves are well marked along a trail. There is also a beach and picnic area. (This park is a bonanza for the amateur geologist, with its pots and kettles). There is also a beach and picnic area. To get there you leave Lakefield driving north on Highway 28 for 3 km. Turn right on County Road 6, turn right on County Road 4 after about 7 km, and follow the signs to the park. The trail leaves from the parking lot.

Things to eat

For this picnic we offer a menu of hearty but simple food, like that which the settler families such as the Traills and the Moodies might have enjoyed. There are several recipes, but we expect you to collect or buy the new potatoes and boil them up on your own. We suggest marble cake for dessert, in association with the Canadian marble upon which the petroglyphs are carved.

MENU

Mrs. Traill's Brown Fricassee of Venison
Boiled New Potatoes
Settlers' Salad
Marble Cake
Mrs. Moodie's Dandelion Root Coffee

Mrs. Traill's Brown Fricassee of Venison

This recipe is adapted from *The Canadian Settler's Guide.*

1 steak for each person
beef drippings, lard, or butter
water
1/2 tsp. each basil, thyme, rosemary
1 small onion
2 cloves garlic, minced
salt and pepper to taste
flour
1 Tbsp. catsup
1 tsp. vinegar

Brown the steaks in hot drippings; add a little water, the spices, garlic, salt and pepper. Cover and bring to a boil. Roll a bit of butter in flour, with a tablespoonful of catsup or tomato sauce, and a teaspoonful of vinegar; stir this into the fricassee. Reduce heat and let simmer for about 10 minutes, or until tender. Serve hot. This dish can be made before-hand, or right at the picnic.

Settlers' Salad

The settlers brought with them seeds for their gardens. One of the seeds the British brought was the dandelion—a salad delicacy at the time, and not a weed at all.

a handful of young dandelion leaves
several leaves of freshly picked lettuce
3 spring onions, fine chopped
1/2 cup fresh peas
2 vine-ripened tomatoes, chopped
1/4 cup chopped fresh parsley
1/4 cup dried, hulled sunflower seeds
1 tsp. each of fresh oregano, summer savory, thyme

Tear lettuce and dandelion leaves, and toss with next five ingredients. Chop the herbs and sprinkle over the salad. (Mrs. Traill was an enthusiastic botanist, and published several books on the topic. Undoubtedly she had a herb garden.)

Settler's Salad Dressing

Since there was no oil, butter was used in making salad dressing. The following recipe is adapted from one that was widely used in the nineteenth century.

1 cup cider vinegar
2/3 cup sugar
4 tsp. flour

2 tsp. dry mustard
2 eggs
salt and pepper to taste
1 Tbsp. butter

Heat the vinegar, and while it is heating, mix together the sugar, flour and mustard. Beat the eggs until smooth, and blend in a little of the hot vinegar. Add the egg mixture to the hot vinegar, stirring until smooth and thickened. Stir in the butter, and add salt and pepper to taste. Cool and dress your salad.

Mrs. Moodie's Dandelion Root Coffee

This recipe also appears in *The Canadian Settler's Guide*, as it was told to Mrs. Traill by her sister. Dandelion root coffee was a widely used substitute for the real stuff. Mrs. Traill notes that although her sister, Susanna, made the brew far better than she herself, the taste still was not equal to genuine coffee. Nevertheless, it makes an interesting beverage!

"The roots should be carefully washed, but not so as to remove the fine, brown skin which covers them, and which contains the aromatic flavour. The roots, when dry, should be cut up into small pieces, about the size of a kidney-bean, and roasted either in a Dutch-oven, before the fire, or on the stove, stirring them from time to time, to prevent burning; when they are brown through, and crisp, like freshly-roasted coffee, remove them, and let them cool; grind like coffee. Put a small cupful into the coffee-pot, and pour over it a quart of boiling water, letting it boil again for a few minutes."

Marble Cake

Any standard cookbook will supply a recipe, but there is a shortcut to do this, too. Buy one white and one chocolate cake mix, and follow the instructions for each. Fold the two batters together with a knife, creating marble-like swirls, and bake. Of course, it may be served with marble ice cream—often called chocolate ripple.

31 Peterborough
An Engineer's Picnic

The Peterborough Hydraulic Lift Lock, the highest in the world and the first to be built of concrete, opened in 1904. Since then, in addition to being a major tourist attraction, the lock has conveyed boats journeying up and down the Trent-Severn waterway. It is a tribute to the foresight and skill of the engineer designer, R.B. Rogers.

A public inquiry held in 1906 at the completion of the lift lock criticized the entire project as expensive and unnecessary. The inquiry found that a conventional set of locks would have cost only half as much, and could have been completed much more quickly. Further, the engineer was chastised for not supervising and directing the construction in a businesslike and professional way. As a result of this criticism, R.B. Rogers, the engineer responsible for the concept, design and construction of the largest and most innovative lift lock in the world, resigned his position as superintending engineer of the canal in disgrace.

In 1985 the Historic Sites and Monuments Board of Canada designated the Peterborough Lift Lock as a National Historic Site.

How to get there

Regardless of which highway you use to enter Peterborough, there will be signs bearing the Canadian Parks Service beaver symbol that will mark the way to the lift lock.

If you miss the signs and find yourself in the middle of the city, proceed as follows. From the town square in the middle of the city, head north on Water Street and over the Hunter Street Bridge. Stay on Hunter Street and you will soon be at the lock.

The selected picnic spot is at one of the tables in front

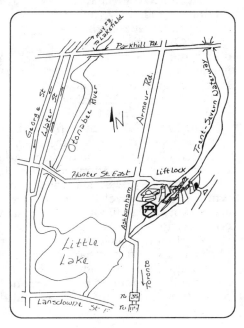

of the Lift Lock Visitor Centre. From this vantage point one can picnic while watching the boats being transported by the locks.

R.B. Rogers, Engineer

Canadian historians have not been particularly kind to the engineers who built this country. France remembers Eiffel's tower and his bridges, Britain remembers Telford's canals and bridges, and Americans know that Roeblings built the Brooklyn Bridge. In Canada the names of engineers such as Sir Casimir Gzowsky, Sir Stanford Fleming, Lt. Col. John By, Andrew McCulloch, and R.B. Rodgers are generally unrecognized, yet these are the men who built our canals and railways. Although the Peterborough Lift Lock is now a National Historic Site, few realize that without the imagination, determination and perseverance of R. B. Rogers, there would be no Peterborough Lift Lock.

Born in the Peterborough area, Rogers attended McGill University, receiving a degree in civil and mechanical engineering in 1877, and a degree in mining engineering in 1878. After several years surveying in Ontario and Manitoba, he returned to Peterborough in 1884 to take the post of superintending engineer of the Trent Canal.

The Lift Lock at Peterborough

The Trent Canal developed in a piecemeal fashion, as different sections were built to aid the early settlers with the transport of lumber and produce. The route, meandering through Rice Lake and the Kawartha Lakes from Lake Ontario to Lake Simcoe and then on to Georgian Bay, was established long ago by the Indians. The first white man to travel the route was Champlain in 1615. He was accompanying a Huron war party who were going to attack their enemies, the Iroquois.

Work started on locks and canals in Ontario in the middle 1830s but it was sporadic and haphazard and by the 1880s there was still no connection through from Peterborough to Lake Ontario. In 1887 a commission appointed by then Prime Minister John A. MacDonald recommended that the government finance the construction that would complete the canal system all the way from Georgian Bay to Lake Ontario.

Designing and constructing a canal was a challenging and exciting prospect for an engineer in the late nineteenth century. Concrete was replacing masonry, permitting the construction of deeper locks. The industrial revolution meant that the production of great machines such as canal bridges, marine railways and lift locks was now possible.

The first lift lock, which conveyed vessels up and down a lift of 50 feet (15.35 m), was built in 1875 by the British engineering firm of Clark and Stanfield on the Trent and Mersey Canal at Northwich, England. This lock had a major mechanical failure in 1882 and in spite of repairs and alterations continued to experience major difficulties. It was eventually modified and re-opened in 1908.

The second lift lock was in France. The French government accepted a proposal from the British engineers for a lift lock and in 1887 they built the second and improved lift lock, l'Ascenseur des Fontinettes, with a lift of 43 feet (13.1 m). The British then further refined their design on a 51 foot (15.4 m) lift lock they designed for the Canal du Centre in Belgium. This lock, at La Louvière, was completed in 1888.

R.B. Rogers had journeyed to England and Europe and talked with these engineers and studied their designs. He returned convinced that lift locks were the correct engineering solution for three Canadian sites — Peterborough, Kirkfield, and Healey Falls. He lobbied strongly with the Minister of Railways and Canals and when the Liberal government of Wilfrid Laurier approved the canal plan, it included the Peterborough Lift Lock.

Although the original concept was British, the Peterborough Lock was designed by Rogers and his associates, and the contracting was done by two Canadian firms: Corry and Laverdure of Ottawa did the excavation and concreting, and Dominion Bridge built the presses, rams and superstructure. The lock's completion was justly acclaimed as a great Canadian achievement.

Things to see and do

1. Allow lots of time for the visitor centre beside the lift lock. It contains a model that explains how the lift lock works, plus many historical photos, and a film of the operation. The centre is open daily from 10 a.m. until 5 p.m. year-round. The lift lock operates during the navigation season which is from Victoria Day weekend until Thanksgiving weekend.

2. Drive the scenic River Road from Trent University to Lakefield along the Otonabee River. There are five lock stations along the route, and these are the oldest known all-concrete locks in North America.

3. Take a boat cruise through the locks. Inquire in the visitor centre as to where and when the cruises leave.

Things to eat

Rogers took a European design and adapted and improved it and made it Canadian. For our picnic we concentrate on dishes that were originally European fare but have been enhanced by the truly Canadian additions of maple syrup, wild rice, and cheddar cheese.

MENU

Maple Syrup Chicken
Tomato and Wild Rice Salad
Cheddar Cheese Biscuits
Apple Cider

Maple Syrup Chicken

(Serves 4)

1 broiler-fryer chicken cut into eighths
100 g butter, melted
2 eggs, beaten
70 ml maple syrup
oatmeal

Combine the butter, eggs and maple syrup in a bowl. Dip the chicken pieces into the mixture and then roll them in oatmeal. Bake the coated chicken in a 350 °F (175 °C) oven until tender (about one hour). Cool and transport to picnic.

Tomato and Wild Rice Salad

(Serves 4)

250 ml wild rice, cooked
125 ml mayonnaise
1 green onion, chopped
dill weed,

4 tomatoes
50 ml yogurt or sour cream
salt,
white pepper

Cut a slice off the top of tomatoes. Scoop out pulp, seeds and juice and put the pulp into a blender. Add mayonnaise, yogurt, onion and seasoning and blend until smooth. Stir wild rice into mixture and chill.

At serving time put the mixture into the hollow tomato shells.

Cheddar Cheese Biscuits

125 ml cheddar cheese, grated
125 ml butter, melted
1 ml Worchestershire sauce
5 ml Branston sauce or chutney
250 ml all-purpose flour

Mix the first four ingredients until smooth and creamy. Slowly add the flour and continue mixing until a soft dough is formed. Wrap in waxed paper and chill in the refrigerator for at least one hour. Preheat oven to 400 °F (200 °C). Shape the dough into small balls and bake on an ungreased cookie sheet for about 10 minutes.

St. Lawrence - Lake Ontario

32 Sandbanks Provincial Park
The Rumrunner's Picnic

Smugglers, buried treasure, shipwrecks, and unmatched scenery characterize Prince Edward County. Our picnic is in Sandbanks Provincial Park, where once rumrunners landed late at night with their precious cargoes, but where now vacationers explore the magic landscape of the dunes.

How to get there

The park is at the southwest tip of Prince Edward County. Leave Picton on Highway 10, driving southwest. In 5 kilometres take the turn-off on Highway 11. When you come to the T-junction, turn left and enter the eastern section of the park. Follow the road along for 3 kilometres until you reach the parking lot by the amphitheatre. It is well marked. Park here, and you are in the picnic ground. The tables are sheltered from the wind off the lake by the dunes. If it is a sunny day, you may choose to spread your picnic blanket on the beach, just a short walk across the dunes.

Island or Peninsula?

When you look at a map you will see that Prince Edward County is an isthmus connected by a narrow neck of land to the mainland of Ontario at Carrying Place. This stretch of land is the two-mile portage that was traditionally used by Indians, voyageurs and fur traders instead of paddling all around the perimeter of the peninsula, avoiding the dangerous waters near Sand Point and Long Point. Further study of a map shows that the Murray Canal is just north of the Carrying Place, and it is seven miles long. There is a reason for the

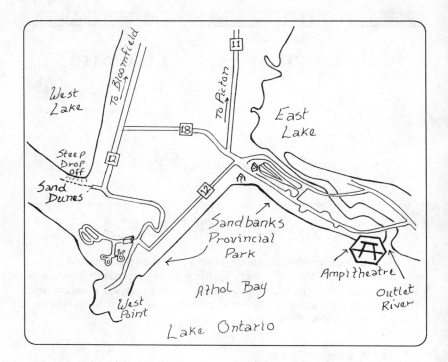

fact that the canal is where it is, and three times as long as it needs to be, and the reason has nothing to do with geography.

The need for a canal had been recognized early in the nineteenth century, when many of the other great canals of Ontario were being planned and built. Such a canal would markedly improve the efficiency of shipping along the northern coast of Lake Ontario. At that time Prince Edward County had elected a Liberal member to Parliament, while the County of Northumberland, to the immediate north, had chosen a Conservative representative. The party then in power was Conservative and so, despite the obvious reasons for building the canal at Carrying Place, it was built in Northumberland County. Begun in 1882, it was completed in 1889.

The Dune Trilogy

Around 1800 the coast of Prince Edward County was densely wooded, with a mixture of hardwood and conifer trees. The story of how it came to be a setting much like Frank Herbert's mythical planet, "Dune," is a story with three parts: the logging, the barley days, and the elements—a combination of irreversible forces.

When the American settlements south of Lake Ontario had used up most of their supplies of wood for construction and shipbuilding they turned their eyes to the north and began to harvest the shores of the Great Lakes. Similarly, the settlements of Montreal and Quebec extended their harvesting to the west, and these forests served the sawmills and shipbuilders of both sides of the border as long as they lasted. The pines near Sandbanks, between East and West Lakes, were much in demand for masts for the schooners. The tall trees were cut and hauled along what was called The Mast Road, to the shipyard at Milford. By 1850, most of the tall trees were gone.

The second stage of this county's history, the Barley Days lasted from 1860 until 1890. Because of a quirk in American law just after the Civil War, Prince Edward County turned to agriculture in a big way. The American government raised the tax on whiskey from 25 cents to $2.00 a gallon, causing the American drinking public to think much more kindly of beer. Further, American brewers believed that Canadian barley made better beer than American barley. The farmers of Prince Edward County obliged by adapting their recently cleared land to barley production, and for this they were amply rewarded. For a while the farmers, and the shipbuilders, who carried the cargo across the lake, flourished. More land was cleared, and more grain was grown. It was a dangerous venture for some, because harvest time coincided with the season of severest storms on the lake. Many a schooner was lost off the coast at Sand Point.

Monocropping has always been dangerous, especially when it is at the mercy of the economy of another country. In 1890 there were a number of internal changes in the American liquor industry, not the

least of which was a new protective tariff for domestic grain producers. The Barley Days in Prince Edward County were over.

The extensive clearing from logging and farming left nothing to hold down the sandy earth, which began to shift and creep, turning farmland into unproductive sandy areas and dunes. Commitment to environmentalism is a fairly recent development, and it took a while for those in power to accept the extent of the threat. Attempts at reforestation had been made, but many acres had been lost before a serious program was begun in the 1950s to stop the advance of the sands. Wind, waves and erosion created the fascinating landscape of Sandbanks Provincial Park, now a source of revenue once again, as tourists flock to the biggest sandpile in the province of Ontario. It is the fourth busiest day-use park in the province.

The Rumrunners

The eighteenth amendment to the constitution of the United States became law on January 16, 1920, effectively stopping the legal production of liquor for a decade. Prohibition was a triumph for the temperance people in the United States. They had managed to have the demon gin outlawed, and they were sure that the bars and nightclubs and other houses of sin linked with the liquor trade would be closed forever. How wrong they were! Instead, the American drinking public hardly noticed the change except for the increase in liquor prices. The reason for this was that the Canadian government did not outlaw the production or export sale of liquor. And so smuggling alcoholic beverages over the world's longest unprotected international border became a very lucrative occupation.

Prince Edward County was ideally situated to become a centre for the smugglers. It extends south into Lake Ontario, reducing the distance to the American side of the lake by some 30 miles, and was close to the distilleries in Belleville and Kingston. By the mid-1920s the trade had become an established, if unacknowledged, part of the county economy. Many farmers with land along the shore made quite a bit of money by leasing landing rights to the smugglers. Others increased their income by permitting their basements, barns or sheds to be used for storage of the contraband. Local fishermen made extra voyages across the lake to make deliveries to Oswego. The hotels in Picton did very well during those years, and always had a plentiful supply of liquor for important customers.

This boom, too, was dependent on the whim of the American government, and ended as suddenly as it began. By 1933 domestic production of alcoholic beverages became legal again south of the border, and the smugglers were forced to return to more honourable, if less lucrative, methods of earning a living.

What was once a source of embarrassment in tea-totalling Prince Edward County is now the source of amusing legends and anecdotes. It is said that the county interest in boat racing dates from the time when it was important to have a boat that could outrun the coast guard.

Poison Ivy

· This infamous plant, also referred to by its scientific name, *Rhus radicans*, resembles many other plants found along the trails and in the parks of Ontario. Remember the three-part compound leaves, and the two types of stalk formations: the low, brush form and the long stalks of up to 15 metres.

It is not only the fibres along the stalk and leaves of the poison ivy that cause the reaction which brings this plant its fame. The oily juice of these plants can be picked up simply by brushing against one of them. The result of contact is usually dermatitis. Reactions may be slightly delayed, but usually consist of an itchy, oozy rash of blisters.

If you wash with strong soap such as Fels Naptha immediately after contact with the ivy plant, the infection may possibly be avoided. Otherwise, mild cases of dermatitis are treated with ointments which are sold over the counter in drugstores. If the case is more serious, a physician should be consulted.

Things to do

1. Beachcomb and suntan on the exquisite white sandy beaches.

2. Play in the giant dunes. The east dunes are the place to picnic, but the west dunes are the place to play. Refer to our map for directions on how to find the unmarked parking lot off County Road 12. There is a short trail from there, and a 10-minute walk brings you to the giant dunes. Climb to the top of one, and survey the coastline of the bay.

3. Wander the dunes. Both the east and west areas of the park are protected by baymouth sandbars. The east lake dune system is stabilized, but the west dunes and sandbar are still shifting. Plant life is especially varied, ranging from fresh and salt water seaside plants to prairie plants—relics from the end of the last ice age—to the northern margin of the Carolinian deciduous forest.

4. Because of its geography the county is a stopping area for a wide variety of migrating birds, and an ideal place for bird-watching.

Unusual marsh birds can be observed at the north end of the park, such as long-billed marsh wrens and swamp sparrows. Twenty-one species of shore birds have been counted as they stopped over during migration. Goldeneye and buffleheads can be seen occasionally by the mouth of Outlet River at East Lake, along with a myriad of other waterfowl. Be sure to record your sightings in the record book at the Visitor Centre to aid the park naturalists in their continuing survey.

5. Visit Birdhouse City. This astonishing urban concentration of about 85 bird houses does not attract many of the migrating birds, although a number of locals have chosen to become tenants. But the rich variety of designs should soon begin to tempt up-market birds seeking sanctuary in the suburbs! The houses, many of them fashioned after historic buildings in the county, have been built and donated by organizations and private persons in the Picton area. The architectural detail of several of the bird homes signals a new era in bird housing design. The subdivision is on County Road 8, on the southeast side of Picton—just follow the signs, as the birds do.

6. Drive through Prince Edward County, visiting the many antique and curio shops. There are treasures to be had. A brochure describing several interesting tourist routes can be picked up at the Tourist Information Centre in Picton.

7. When driving through southern Ontario, and especially Prince Edward County, you will notice a wide variety of lawn ornaments. There are bambis, swans, ducks, horse jockeys, life-sized horses rearing up on their hind legs over the begonias, dwarfs (usually in sets of 7) and so on. Although our research has not yet reached the stage where we feel prepared to comment on the socio-anthropological significance of this quaint custom of property decoration, we highly recommend this topic as a diversionary strategy for long drives.

8. Look for buried treasure near the mouth of the Outlet River. It is said that long ago gold was buried here, but never found again.

Things to eat

Since the word rum, according to the Oxford Dictionary, is a generic word referring to any intoxicating liquor, rumrunners are those who smuggle it. Some of the following recipes includes hints of the very intoxicants which outraged the temperance movement not so very long ago.

MENU

Cheddar Cheese Rabbit*
Tomatoes in Raspberry Vinegar Dressing
Rum Pie

*Although this dish is often referred to as Welsh Rarebit, this is an Anglicism jocularly applied to the Welsh dish.

Cheddar Cheese Rabbit

(Serves 4)

This is like a cheese fondue, and should be served in a chafing dish at the picnic site. Bring the ingredients to the picnic, and mix together at the site. Dry ingredients can be pre-mixed at home, and the egg can be beaten and carried in a jar.

   2 cups medium Ontario cheddar cheese, grated
   1 1/4 cups flat beer
   1 egg, beaten
   1/2 tsp. dry mustard
   2 tsp. brown sugar
   dash cayenne
   salt to taste

Heat the chafing dish. Melt the cheese, stirring constantly. Gradually add the beer. Combine the egg with the remaining ingredients, then stir into the cheese mixture. When mixture is thickened, reduce heat to low and serve it with a platter of crisp buttered toast fingers.

Tomatoes in Raspberry Vinegar

(Serves 4)

Since raspberry vinegar was a staple of the Loyalist settlers who came to Prince Edward County in the nineteenth century, we offer this delicious salad. Make it ahead of time, so it has a chance to marinate for a few hours.

   5 large, ripe tomatoes   *1/4 cup raspberry vinegar (see below)*
   1/2 cup light vegetable oil   *salt*
   pepper   *thyme*
   oregano   *parsley*

Blanch and peel the tomatoes, and cut them into bite-sized pieces. Combine the remaining ingredients in a blender, and then toss with the tomatoes. (The quantities of spices are not specified—suit your own taste here, but use fresh herbs if you can.) Chill for several hours and serve cold.

Raspberry Vinegar

6 quarts of fresh raspberries
1 quart cider vinegar
sugar

Mash the raspberries in a large glass or plastic (not metal) bowl with a fork or potato masher. Pour the vinegar over them, and refrigerate overnight. Squeeze two quarts of the raspberries in a jelly bag that has been moistened with cider vinegar. Strain the vinegar back into the unused mashed raspberries. Discard the mash in the jelly bag and let the mixture stand overnight again. The next day strain another 2 quarts, and the third day, the last of the mixture. Once all the juice has been extracted, measure it and bring to a boil. Add an equal amount of sugar, and cook for 8-10 minutes, stirring constantly. Bottle and store. (This is also often served as a summer drink on ice.)

Rum Pie

(Serves 6)

This should be made a day ahead and well chilled. The meringue forms the pie crust, and the delicious rum cream is the filling.

5 egg whites
1/4 tsp. cream of tartar
1 cup sugar
1 cup whipping cream
1 Tbsp. icing sugar
1/4 cup rum
2 squares unsweetened chocolate or dark, semi-sweet chocolate bar

Beat the egg whites until foamy, and add the cream of tartar, continuing to mix. Slowly add the sugar, one Tbsp. at a time, and continue to beat until the mixture stands in stiff peaks. Spread the mixture in a 9-inch greased pie plate, shaping it like a hollow pie crust. Bake slowly at 250 °F for at least an hour, or until golden brown. Turn off the oven and let the pie crust cool gradually with the door partly open. It will be crisp and dry.

Whip the cream, and when it is stiff, add the icing sugar, and then the rum, 1 tsp. at a time, while continuing to beat. Place the cream in the cooled meringue pie shell, and garnish with grated chocolate. Chill well.

33 Kingston
A Birthday Picnic for Henry

No shot was ever fired in anger from the Citadel of Upper Canada. Although it was built to protect British North America from the United States, animosity between the two countries had faded by the time it was completed. With no convenient enemy, the soldier's life at the fort was one of perpetual drilling on the parade square and fighting boredom. Thus it was a major occasion and a reason for much rejoicing, when in May of 1838 the first baby was born on the post. He was christened, appropriately, Fort Henry Bates.

How to get there

Fort Henry is on the shore of Lake Ontario, on the southeast side of the city of Kingston. It can be reached by leaving the city centre on Ontario Street, following the signs for Highway 2. The fort is just over the Lasalle Causeway. The picnic spot is not in the fort proper, but instead is in a grove to the southeast which used to be the site of a military hospital. The hospital was built in 1830 and was used continuously until the 1870s. It burned in 1924. The picnic area is reached from a road at the back of the parking lot which leads over the brow of the hill to the picnic tables beyond.

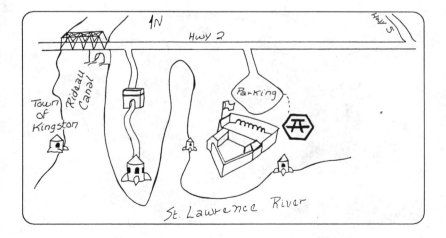

Fort Henry

It seems that many of the more interesting defensive constructions were built to fight a war that was already past, and are of questionable value in any war that might be yet to come. In the period following the first world war, the French built the Maginot Line to fight a fixed, trench war with Germany. The German tanks bypassed it when the second world war started. Similarly, in the 1950s, the Americans, not wanting to experience another sneak aerial attack, constructed the Distant Early Warning (DEW) radar line across northern Canada. It provided employment for some Inuit, and a fine telecommunications network, but this line is easily bypassed by today's ballistic missiles.

Britain was not able to send much help to her North American colony during the War of 1812-14, since at that time most of her resources were committed to fighting Napoleon. Thus the brunt of the defence of the colony fell on the shoulders of the local militia, and the thousands of Indians loyal to the British Crown. After the war, however, Britain proceeded to expend vast sums of money in Canada on the construction of defensive installations to protect us from another invasion from our neighbours to the south. The net result of this building boom was to provide Canada with some truly outstanding tourist facilities, specifically: the Halifax Citadel, the Quebec

British artillery officers and a nine pounder gun (circa 1867)

Citadel, the exquisite Rideau Canal system (see Jones Falls Picnic), and Fort Henry.

Although there was no fighting, from even before the fort's completion, Fort Henry was an outpost of the British Army and was continuously manned by troops of the line until 1867 when Canada became an independent nation. Over the 58-year period, 33 different regiments occupied these cold dark rooms, and kept watch from these ramparts.

But there was more to do in the fort than march on the parade square, and peer out over the ramparts searching for approaching Yankees. There were the mundane things such as cleaning, cooking, laundry, and the sewing on of buttons. Cook sergeants were only introduced into the British army after 1855, and the men were always responsible for the appearance of their quarters, uniforms and equipment. The practical result of these responsibilities, especially in a peacetime garrison such as Fort Henry, was that there were a large number of women in the fort—both soldiers' wives and women from the town. By army regulations the cooking remained a male preserve, but the men paid the women to do the laundry, mending and cleaning. The official position of the British army was that a few women on a post was a good thing, since they had a leavening effect on the enlisted men. The numbers were kept small; usually only 6 to 12 men per 100 were allowed to marry. It was possible to control this since a soldier could not get married without his commanding officer's permission. If, however, permission was granted, then the wife and subsequent children became part of the regiment, entitled to rations and quarters (such as they were). This was known as being married "on the strength."

The records indicate however, that on foreign postings, and especially at Kingston, the commanding officer permitted more men to be married "on the strength" than the regulations allowed and at Fort Henry in the 1860s, nearly half of the 150-man garrison were married. This increase in married men greatly reduced desertion rates.

The situation for officers was quite different. They often came from wealthy families, usually purchased their commissions, brought their furniture from England, and lived like young gentlemen on a country holiday. If they were married, their wives could accompany them, and often did so.

Fort Henry Bates

1838 did not start well for the Fort Henry garrison. In November of 1837, armed rebellion had broken out in Lower Canada and most of the regular soldiers had been sent to reinforce the troops there.

Thus in December, when the rebellion broke out in Upper Canada, only Major Richard Bonnycastle of the Royal Engineers and his civilian force of Irish labourers were present to defend the yet unfinished citadel. The rebellions were soon put down, and the troops returned to Fort Henry. Especially welcomed back was Lieutenant Bates, Adjutant of Second Lenox Militia. He returned to the fort just in time for the birth of his son, the first child born in Fort Henry.

The christening on May 4, 1838, was celebrated by the entire fort. With the permission of the commanding officer, the child was baptized Fort Henry Bates. The officers and soldiers took up a collection and gave the parents a purse containing £25. The father was presented with a special sword and sash to mark the occasion—it is not recorded whether the mother's role was acknowledged. The letter that accompanied the purse stated,

"The prayer of all is, that the First Born and scion of Fort Henry may never forget the circumstances under which he was born."

A historical footnote was added to this story when, in 1959, Fort Henry Bates's great grandson visited the fort. The circumstances indeed have not been forgotten and in each succeeding generation of the Bates family the oldest male child has always been named Henry.

Things to do

1. Visit Fort Henry and take the guided tour. The Fort Henry Guard is a non-military organization composed entirely of university and high school students. The Guard is patterned after the British Infantry and the Royal Artillery of 1867.

2. Learn the grim story of penal life and see instruments of torture and restraint, together with prisoner-made weapons at the Kingston Penitentiary Museum. Open year-round, by appointment only, phone (613) 547-4250.

3. Tour Bellevue House, the home of Canada's first prime minister and chief architect of Canadian Confederation, John A. MacDonald. Open daily, closed holidays.

4. The Pump House Steam Museum, at 23 Ontario Street, is a municipal water pumping station restored to full 1849 working order with the engines operating.

5. Royal Military College of Canada, Canada's oldest military academy, is on Point Frederick, immediately east of Fort Henry. The college museum is open daily from the last Saturday in June until Labour Day.

6. The International Hockey Museum, on Alfred and York Streets, traces the sport from its organized beginnings on the ice of Kingston Harbour, to the present.

Things to eat

The picnic should be the sort of thing that a young British gentleman, putting in his time in the colonies, might enjoy on a summer afternoon. No time or expense was spared since, in any case, his servant would be doing the work. There was, however, some difficulty in getting the correct ingredients so far away from civilization. The colonials just didn't seem to understand the need to raise sheep.

MENU

Barbecued Lamb, served cold with a mint sauce
Stuffed Nasturtiums
Pickled Beets
Pickled Onions
Cold Asparagus with Curry Mayonnaise
Hard Tack Biscuits (this is the army, after all)
Eccles Tarts
Syllabub

Barbecued Lamb

(serves 4-6)

one boned, flattened shoulder of lamb (about 3-4 lbs.)
1 cup fresh chopped mint leaves
1 tsp. dry mustard
pepper
2 Tbsp. lemon juice
1/4 cup melted butter
1 clove garlic, crushed
2 Tbsp. grated onion

Prepare a paste of 1/2 cup fresh mint, mustard, pepper, and lemon juice and rub into lamb. Let stand for at least two hours. Prepare charcoal and burn down until only embers remain. Prepare a sauce of the remaining ingredients. Place lamb on the grill over embers; brush often with sauce. Turn the meat after about 20 minutes and continue turning at about 15 minute intervals until done. Total cooking time will be about one hour.

Chill in refrigerator, and transport to the picnic wrapped in foil. Slice at the picnic table and serve with mint sauce.

Stuffed Nasturtiums

1 dozen nasturtium blossoms
1/2 cup cooked (tinned) salmon
1/4 cup cream cheese
1/8 tsp. marjoram

Make a mixture of the salmon, cheese and marjoram. Select nasturtiums in assorted colours. Carefully wash them and remove the stems and the pistils. Fill the cavities with the mixture and arrange on a white plate.

The pickled beets and onions are found in your larder or, if you were remiss last harvest season, at you local supermarket. Fresh asparagus, cooked until just tender, is lovely, but tinned asparagus will do (soldiers have to learn to rough it). Dress the asparagus with the following dressing.

Curry Mayonnaise

1 cup mayonnaise
1/4 tsp. ginger
2 tsp. curry powder
1 clove garlic, mashed
1 tsp. sugar
1 Tbsp. lemon juice

Mix together, spread on the asparagus. Note, the curry powder flavour can be improved by cooking the powder in a microwave for a minute before mixing it in.

Hard biscuits are found in your friendly neighbourhood quartermaster stores.

Eccles Tarts

pastry (see Aunt Nell's recipe)
15 ml butter
15 ml lemon juice
125 ml brown sugar

2 ml nutmeg
2 ml allspice
125 ml currants
125 ml candied fruit
white of an egg
confectioner's sugar

Preheat the oven to 425°F (220°C). Roll the dough into 5-inch (13-cm) circles. Scald the currants in water to soften them. Mix the butter, lemon juice, sugar, spices, currants and fruit together. Place a large spoonful of this mixture into the centre of each dough circle. Dampen the edges of the dough. Bring the sides of the dough up around the mixture and pinch together in the centre. Turn upside down and roll lightly. Make two or three gashes in the top of the pastry with a knife. Brush with egg white and sprinkle with sugar. Bake on an ungreased baking sheet for 10-15 minutes.

Syllabub

1/2 cup Madeira
2 tsp. brandy
1/2 cup white sugar
1 cup heavy cream or whipping cream
nutmeg

Make a syrup by boiling the sugar in 1/4 cup water for about 5 minutes. Cool and mix with the brandy and Madeira. At the picnic site combine the sweetened alcohol with the cream and nutmeg and serve at once in punch glasses.

34 Thousand Islands
An Environmentalist's Picnic

The St. Lawrence Islands National Park is comprised of 94.8 acres on the mainland, and eighteen of the Thousand Islands. (The islands can only be reached by boat.) The park is rich in wildlife and vegetation with several unique species, despite the danger of industrial pollution in the St. Lawrence River, and thus seems the right spot for an environmentally sensitive picnic.

How to get there

The mainland portion of the St. Lawrence Islands Park is at Mallorytown Landing. Take exit #675 from the 401. This is about 14 miles east of the Thousand Islands International Bridge at Ivy Lea.

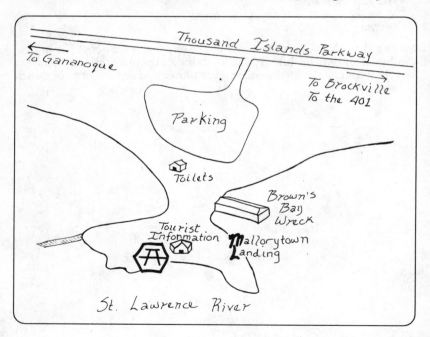

Playground of the Rich and Famous

Tourism, the major industry in the Thousand Islands district, began long ago, when people like Charles Dickens passed through. His observations, recorded in 1842, are still appropriate:

The beauty of this noble stream at almost any point but especially in the commencement of this journey, where it winds its way among the thousand islands, can hardly be imagined. The number and constant successions of these islands, all green and richly wooded; their fluctuating sizes, some so large that for half an hour together one among them will appear as the opposite bank of the river, and some so small, that they are mere dimples on its broad bosom; their infinite variety of shape; and the numberless combinations of beautiful forms which the trees growing on them present: all forms a picture fraught with uncommon interest and pleasure.

And so people came, bought islands, built castles, mansions, cottages, cabins and camps. George Pullman, of railway fame, bought one of the islands and the president of the United States, General Grant, rode in a sumptuous Pullman passenger car for a weekend visit in 1872. Castle Rest, the mansion on Pullman Island, remained in the Pullman family for several generations, but was razed when family interest waned as the cost of taxes and upkeep rose. Nevertheless, the president's visit was a great incentive for further settlement. Singer Island still has its castle. Also called Jordstat Island, it was owned by Frank Bourne, president of the Singer sewing machine company, who built *Towers*, a 28-room castle. It is now a summer school retreat. Heart Island's Boldt Castle, built in 1896, is probably the best known castle today, for it is a tourist attraction. George C. Boldt owned the Waldorf-Astoria hotel in New York. There is a tragic story behind this castle, which was never occupied by its owners. It was almost completed after two years of construction work, with $2 million already invested in luxurious fittings and furnishings, when Mrs. Boldt died suddenly. George halted the work forever, and the castle languished. It was rescued in 1925 by the chairman of the LifeSaver Company, who completed it and initiated the public tours which continue today.

You didn't have to be a millionaire to buy your own island, and many lesser souls have bought smaller islands for their family summer homes. The great era of the islands passed, though, as the automobile turned people away from the leisurely travel of steamers and trains. Over ninety percent of the islands have cottages on them, but most are only used in the summer time.

The Geology

St. Lawrence Islands National Park

About 1,000 million years ago the Thousand Islands region lay beneath a great sea. As sediments were deposited on the bottom, layers of various kinds were formed. Over time the effects of pressure and heat as the rocks moved deeper into the earth caused recombinations of the various elements, and new mineral forms were created. These formations eventually worked their way to the surface of the lake, creating a great range of mountains as high as the present-day Rockies. That was about 600 million years ago. These giants simply weathered away during subsequent millennia, leaving only the roots of the great mountains, now the Thousand Islands. The glaciers passed over the area several times, receding most recently about 12,000 years ago, and leaving behind the drainage channel from the great inland sea, which became the St. Lawrence River. Time, pressure, temperature changes, water and wind have left us with the fascinating landscape that is the Precambrian Shield.

Rockhounds will delight in identifying the Potsdam, Nepean, March, Oxford and Gull River formations, each the result of a particular set of environmental circumstances. A booklet can be obtained from the Visitor Centre describing the age, composition and location of these formations in the park.

God's Garden

Be that as it may, a more felicitous, if less scientific explanation is an Indian myth. It seems that once upon a time the lush region here was truly paradise, the garden of the Great Spirit, enjoyed by the animals and human occupants together in peace. But there came a time when dissension disturbed the idyllic tranquility, despite warnings from the deity. At last, despairing of the irresponsibility of humanity, the Great Spirit chose to remove paradise from those who had abused its peace. He gathered up the land in a great blanket, and put it over his shoulder for the return trip to the heavens. As he travelled, the blanket wore through in several places, and pieces of paradise fell back to the earth, landing here and there in the river below, creating a thousand islands.

We, as the present-day human occupants of paradise, have also been recalcitrant. The St. Lawrence River is polluted. There are traces of poisonous chemicals in the turtles and fish, and acid rain is a serious issue with far-reaching consequences. The pollution of paradise is being fought on several fronts in Canada, one of which is the stewardship of our parks. Where once we took the wilderness for granted as an unending resource, we now realize how quickly it can be spoilt, sometimes irretrievably. Conservation programs are springing up now, and the future looks much brighter than it did a few years ago, when the great expanse of Lake Erie was declared dead. There is life there again, and the lesson has been learned to some extent. Government controls are weak, but they are appearing at all levels. The greatest good—and harm—can still be done by visitors. Everyone who visits the wilderness knows now to leave nothing but footprints and take nothing but pictures. Low impact picnicking involves common sense practices like taking away everything you bring, unless there is a suitable container provided for refuse. Pouring your food remains on the ground can change the soil upon which it lands; feeding animals food which is not their normal diet sooner or later makes them sick. Old beer cans and enormous wads of pink chewing gum spoil the park for the next visitors.

And so, enough preaching—since our readers are already converted environmentalists!

Things to do

1. Visit the exhibit of the Brown's Bay Wreck at St. Lawrence National Park. It is housed in the building just off the main trail to the end of the point. The ship was likely built in 1817 as a gunboat, and served as a patrol boat for the British military until about 1830. There is some mystery surrounding the origin and career of the ship. Some researchers believe that the vessel may also have been used as a tow barge or a sail barge by a private company moving goods within the inland seas. Whatever her purpose, she sank in nearby Brown's Bay over a century ago, and her partly submerged hull has served generations of local residents as a duck blind, a place to put on ice skates, and a fishing platform. In 1960 the national parks staff raised the hulk, soaked it in a preservative solution, and placed it in its cradle in the display at Mallorytown Landing. Here it becomes the perfect theme for our shipwreck picnic.

2. Pick up a checklist at the Parks Canada office and see how many of the plants, birds, mammals and reptiles you can locate and identify in the park.

3. Study the excellent cross-section model of the ice age in the St. Lawrence region. The model is in a plastic case in the Visitor Centre.

4. Take a boat cruise through the Thousand Islands. You can take one of the commercial boat cruises offered in the nearby towns, or you may bring your own boat, or rent one of any size. You can even enjoy a day on a houseboat.

5. Visit Hill Island, one of the islands along the span of the International Bridge at Ivy Lea. The Thousand Islands Bridge is really five bridges which "island hop" from the Canadian to the United States mainland. It was built in 1938, using four types of bridge construction: suspension, steel arch, continuous truss and stone arch. The bridge was officially opened August 18, 1938, by President Franklin Delano Roosevelt and Prime Minister William Lyon MacKenzie King.

6. While on Hill Island, take the elevator up the 1000 Islands Skydeck. Visibility extends for about 60 miles on a clear day. An elevator takes you to a platform 400 feet above the St. Lawrence River.

7. Also on Hill Island is a grove of pitch pine, a very rare tree. The pitch pine, valued by pioneers for its durability, but now considered a weed tree, can also be found in St. Lawrence Islands Park. It is a scraggy, twisted medium-sized plant with old cones still clinging to the branches. The trees usually grow in open, dry places with southern exposure. Look for occasional needles coming out of the trunk. The twisted needles occur in bunches of three.

Things to eat

What would you eat if you were shipwrecked on one of the Thousand Islands a century ago? You might possibly catch a snapping turtle, and cook up a pot of turtle soup. Then you would look around and pick a few of the more appetizing looking plants to make a salad, which you would then dress with the Thousand Islands dressing you wisely rescued from your sinking ship. For the first few weeks you might catch a fish and cook it, though you would get tired of your limited selection of entrées after a while. As an alternative you could catch a few bull frogs—their legs are quite tasty. You would likely make a floating island dessert, and wash it all down with an ice cream float. You would, of course, suck LifeSavers while you prepared your repast.

MENU

Turtle Soup
Weed Salad
Thousand Islands Dressing
Frogs' Legs with Garlic
Floating Islands
Root Beer Float
LifeSavers

You can get a licence to catch your turtle and frogs from the Ministry of Natural Resources, should you want to hunt them yourself.

Turtle Soup

(Serves 6)

1 pound turtle meat, cut into pieces
3 cups water
3 cups stock
bay leaf
1/2 tsp. thyme
2 cloves
1/4 tsp. ground allspice
1/4 tsp. freshly ground black pepper
1/2 tsp. salt
dash cayenne

Combine the above ingredients in a saucepan, bring to a boil, and let simmer for 30 minutes.

Sauté:
  2 medium onions, chopped
  Purée in a blender:
  1 cup peas
  1 cup corn kernels
  1 potato, diced

Add to soup base and stir in:
  1 Tbsp. flour
  1 tin tomatoes, drained (about 1 1/2 cups)
  Cook for 10 minutes, and add to soup, along with:
  1 Tbsp. chopped parsley
  2 cloves garlic, minced
  juice of 1 lemon

Simmer for at least 2 hours, or until the meat is tender.

Weed Salad

There are many so-called weeds, the leaves of which are delicious and nutritious. Suggested plants are: dandelion, chickweed, thistle (remove the spines, of course), wild mint, and young shoots of milkweed. Young shoots of evening primrose will add a peppery flavour to your salad. The stems of young cattails also make a pleasant addition to your salad. You might gather wild mushrooms for the salad, but only do this if you know which ones are safe to eat! Select fresh, younger leaves of the plant, and rinse them. Tear into bite-sized pieces, and toss with a dressing.

Thousand Islands Dressing

Begin with 1 cup of mayonnaise, to which you add 1 Tbsp. chopped onion, 3 Tbsp. chili sauce, 1 chopped hard-boiled egg, a touch of dry mustard and 1 Tbsp. ketchup.

Frogs' Legs

(Serves 4)

  8 frogs' legs (hind legs of bull frogs)
  45 ml whole wheat pastry flour
  pepper
  salt
  paprika
  parsley
  1 medium onion, chopped
  200 ml clarified butter
  100 ml stock
  125 ml bread crumbs
  60 ml crushed almonds
  5 ml lemon juice or white wine

Mix together flour, pepper, salt, paprika, parsley and roll the legs in the mixture. Heat half the butter in a heavy frying pan. Add the onions and cook until golden; brown the frog legs in the butter. Reduce the heat, add stock and simmer for 10 minutes, covered. Meanwhile, mix remaining butter with the bread crumbs, lemon juice or wine and crushed almonds. Remove the frog legs from the stock, coat with the crumb mixture and place in a casserole dish. Brown gently under broiler until golden; serve hot.

Floating Islands

(Serves 4)

3 egg whites
1/2 cup sugar (to be used 1/4 cup at a time)
2 cups milk
3 egg yolks
1/8 tsp. salt
1 tsp. vanilla

Make the "islands" first.

Place the milk in the top of a double boiler and scald. Now beat the egg whites until stiff, and then gradually add 1/4 cup sugar. Drop the meringue like dumplings into the hot milk, continuing to cook for two minutes. Turn the meringues, and cook for another 2 minutes, without letting the milk boil. Remove the meringues and set aside on paper towelling.

Now make the custard. Beat the egg yolks and stir them into the milk slowly. Then add the sugar and salt, and continue stirring until mixture thickens. Remove from heat, add the vanilla, and continue stirring for a few minutes while the custard cools slightly. Let it cool completely, place the meringues on top like islands, and serve.

35 Jones Falls
A Rideau Canal Picnic

If one has the time and inclination it is possible to take a small craft from New Orleans, up the Mississippi, through the Great Lakes of Michigan and Huron, over the Trent-Severn canal system to Lake Ontario and the St. Lawrence River, up the Cataraqui River, down the Rideau River and Canal to Ottawa, and down the Ottawa River to Montreal. In that trip of many leagues you would probably notice that the most exquisite picnic spot along the way is at the locks and dam on the Rideau Canal at Jones Falls.

How to get there

Fortunately, it is not necessary to go on an extended, or even a short boating trip to reach Jones Falls, since you can easily get there by car. Proceed northeast on Highway 15 from Kingston. The turn-off to Jones Falls, County Road 11, is just past the village of Morton,

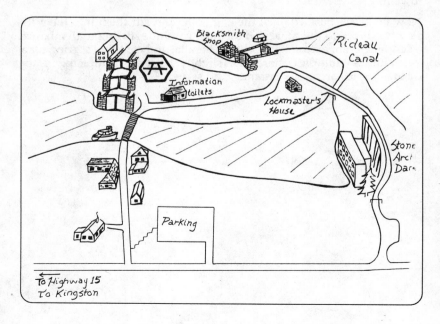

about 50 km (31 mi.) from Kingston. The Jones Falls parking lot is about 8 km (5 mi.) beyond the turn-off. From the parking lot walk down to the Hotel Kenney and across Long Bridge to the locks. The chosen picnic spot is at the top of the flight locks, on the basin.

Mosquitoes

The term mosquito, meaning little fly, refers to the small delicate insects that inhabit diverse environments the world over. The 74 species which inhabit different environments across Canada depend on a blood meal for their reproductive capability. Often this means *your* blood, especially on picnics. The species that commonly seek blood meals from humans are categorized as serious pests, and have been known to drive many a hardy picnicker out of the park. Some species do carry viruses which infect humans. The anophile species in Canada carried malaria in the early 1800s, but this parasite is now almost unheard of here. Other viruses can be transmitted by mosquitoes, but they do not commonly afflict humans. The largest threat from mosquitoes in Canada is discomfort from the bites of the females.

Mosquitoes belong to the order Diptera, and to the family Culicidae. They lay their eggs in moist ground or in standing water. The egg phase is one of seven phases the mosquito passes through before reaching adulthood. Most Canadian species will complete only one generation each year, but some complete two or three; the average life span of a mosquito is three weeks. Males feed on carbohydrates alone, and an autogenous female requires a carbohydrate meal—usually nectar—as well as a blood meal to initiate laying of her eggs. Usually females mate once, immediately after reaching adulthood, and then begin the search for a blood meal.

Approaching a warm-blooded victim, the female will first be attracted by concentrations of carbon dioxide, then she will sense the body heat. After landing on the host, the female will probe the skin with the proboscis in search for a capillary. She will consume up to three times her body weight and wait twenty-four to thirty-six hours for digestion and appropriation of the blood meal. Then the female seeks an appropriate spot to lay her batch of eggs. She may subsequently repeat the process of feeding and laying eggs up to five times in her short life-time—unless she is swatted.

The Rideau Canal

It was the Duke of Wellington, liberator of Spain and victor of Waterloo, who decided that the ancient Indian portage route via the Rideau and Cataraqui Rivers should become the largest civil engineering project in North America. The inconclusive War of 1812 (Mr. Madison's War) was over but the British colony of Canada was still reasonably apprehensive about the intentions of its neighbour to the south. The colony was particularly vulnerable since the main supply route for the interior forts and settlements, the St. Lawrence River, ran along the Canada-United States boundary.

Lieutenant Colonel John By of the Corps of Royal Engineers was selected by Wellington to build the 120-mile (190-km) canal. The Colonel established his headquarters on the Ottawa River near the Rideau Falls and across the river from Hull. Initially called Bytown, this settlement ultimately became the city of Ottawa and the nation's capital.

Canal building in England was quite different from canal building in Canada. In England the canals were primarily arteries of commerce which would wind through settled farms and urban areas to transport coal, iron and foodstuffs. The topography was known in detail and extensive reconnaissance preceded construction. In Canada, nature had provided the transportation network of lakes and rivers. Indeed the fur traders used the water networks to travel from Montreal west to the Rocky Mountains and north up the Mackenzie to the Arctic. Canal building in Canada, which was carried out in dense woodland, consisted of improving upon nature's work by providing locks and channels around rapids and falls, and connections between river systems.

Colonel By's reconnaissance consisted of travelling the proposed route by canoe in the company of Hudson's Bay Company voyageurs. From this survey, together with additional information provided by his junior officers, Colonel By proceeded to construct the 47 masonry locks and 52 dams that comprise the Rideau Canal system.

The work was done in five summer seasons under extremely difficult conditions. The heat and bugs of the Ontario forest caused intense discomfort and "swamp fever" (probably malaria) claimed the lives of many workmen. This, as well as inexperienced earthwork contractors and exorbitant demands of land owners, produced unwanted delays. However, five years and 800,000 pounds sterling later, on May 24th, 1832, it was finished. The engineering and masonry workmanship were of such quality that today, over 150 years later, all of the original masonry locks are still in use.

Especially significant is the masonry arch dam at Jones Falls. It rises 61 ft. (19 m) above the bed of the stream and is 350 ft. (107 m) long at the crest. When completed in 1831, it was the highest dam in North

America, and the third largest dam in the world. To see this dam follow the path up the basin to the crest (see map). Notice also the barrel-stave pipes that still carry the water to the powerhouse below.

Starting in Ottawa, the Rideau Canal uses 33 locks to climb 277 ft. (85 m) to Upper Rideau Lake. It then descends a total of 162 ft. (50 m) via 14 locks down the Cataraqui River to Lake Ontario at Kingston. Counting from the Ottawa River, the locks at Jones Falls are numbers 39, 40, 41 and 42.

Things to see and do

1. Relax on the banks of the canal and watch the many and varied pleasure boats as they lock through.

2. Go on the guided tour and visit the defensible lockmaster's house, the blacksmith shop, and the dam.

3. Plan a canal trip for your next year's vacation.

Things to eat

The men in the work camps of the 1830s probably existed mainly upon whole-wheat bread, beans, pea soup, the occasional haunch of bear meat and, in season, lots of blueberry pies. On the other hand the British always managed to bring a bit of gentility with them wherever in the Empire they were posted and, aside from referring to dinner as tea, tended to treat eating as a formal, serious matter. With this in mind we propose the following semiformal picnic menu.

MENU

Rabbit Pâté on Little Squares of Toast
Cold Bear (or beef) Haunch
Broccoli Salad
Scottish Potatoes
Gooseberry and Raisin Pie

Earl Grey Tea
or
London Dry Gin and Tonic
(if the malaria is bad)

Rabbit Pâte

(serves 6-8)

(If rabbit cannot be found, chicken livers can be substituted.)

200 g rabbit (or chicken) livers
2 green onions, finely chopped
115 g butter
pinch of thyme
salt and pepper
1 clove of garlic, crushed
75 ml Madeira
melted butter

Clean the livers carefully. Chop the livers into small cubes and sauté together with the onion in sizzling butter until they are light brown. Add the thyme, salt and pepper, and garlic and continue cooking for 5 minutes. Combine with the Madeira in a blender, adding sufficient melted butter to make a smooth paste. Put into a pot and seal with a layer of melted butter. Refrigerate, and serve cold at the picnic.

A Joint of Beef or Bear

A cold roast of beef, sliced and served at the picnic table, is always a welcome and delightful treat. Try to cook the roast a bit rare, as this will produce tender and moist slices when cold. Generally we would choose a standing rib roast and cook it in a 350 °F (175 °C) oven for 20 minutes per pound or until the meat thermometer reads 140 °F (60 °C). Serve accompanied with hot English mustard and horseradish.

Scottish Potatoes

Cold roast beef accompanied by cold potatoes! Take tiny new potatoes with their skins on (about 5 per person) and boil until they are tender but still firm (15 to 20 minutes). Drain and cool until tepid. Sprinkle with chopped chives and dry mustard, then chill. Before taking to the picnic, mix with 1 cup herb mayonnaise.

Herb Mayonnaise

To make the base mayonnaise, mix together in a blender at medium speed for about 70 seconds:
1 egg
50 ml lemon juice
2 ml salt
0.25 ml dry mustard

Then add 250 ml olive oil in a slow, steady stream through the opening in the top of the blender cap, while the blender is running. Ingredients will emulsify while the oil is being added. If, however, the ingredients fail to emulsify, pour mixture into cup, rinse out blender with hot water, put a new egg and lemon juice into it, and repeat the process, using the mixture in place of the oil, and this time pouring in a very slow, steady stream.

Blend in with a spatula:
    1 clove of garlic, crushed
    85 ml minced green herbs (parsley, chives, basil, marjoram, thyme)

Let stand in refrigerator overnight so that spice flavours permeate. This can be a dangerous food for picnics, since it has real eggs in it, so keep it well chilled until serving.

Cold Broccoli Salad

(serves 4)

According to Ogden Nash, "Broccoli, thought not exoccally, is within an innich, of being spinach." It also adds green to the meal, plus, like spinach, it is terribly good for you.
    1 kg fresh broccoli
    250 ml lemon juice
    125 ml olive oil
    2 ml cayenne
    2 ml salt
    1 clove garlic, crushed
    2 green onions, finely chopped
    2 hard-boiled eggs, chopped

Wash broccoli and remove leaves and tough part of stalks. Remove the florettes from the stalk. Then cut the stalks julienne fashion. Cook the broccoli either by steaming or microwaving, until tender but crunchy. Combine the lemon juice, oil, seasoning, garlic and onions into a dressing. Transport separately to the picnic and dress the broccoli just before serving. Garnish with the chopped eggs.

Gooseberry and Raisin Pie

(makes 1 pie)

500 ml fresh gooseberries	*150 ml raisins*
250 ml water	*2 ml salt*
350 ml sugar	*45 ml flour*
pie crust (see Wasaga Beach Picnic)	*15 ml lemon juice*

Soak the raisins in warm water for about 30 minutes. Mix together gooseberries, raisins and water over a medium heat. Stir in the sugar, salt and flour and continue heating until the mixture thickens. Remove from heat, add lemon juice, and pour into a lined pastry plate. Top with a lattice crust and bake for 30 to 40 minutes in a 425°F (220°C) oven. Cool, and serve with vanilla ice cream.

36 Morrisburg
A Loyalist Picnic

The Loyalists were the refugees of the American Revolution. Eighty thousand people who preferred to be governed by the British king, or who had simply chosen the wrong side, were driven from the Thirteen Colonies by the victorious Americans. Many went to England and the British West Indies; over ten thousand came to the British Colony of Canada during the years following the American Revolution. A number settled in the Indian lands west of Montreal, and this area came to be called Upper Canada, and eventually Ontario.

How to get there

The picnic site is on the banks of the St. Lawrence River just outside Upper Canada Village, between the Pioneer Memorial and the lighthouse. The Upper Canada Village entrance is on Highway 2, 11 kilometres east of Morrisburg. From the entrance follow the signs to the Crysler's Farm Battlefield Memorial, and then go to the parking lot beyond. The picnic site is just across the little railway track.

United Empire Loyalists

Upper Canada Village

The American War of Independence in 1776 was in part a civil war as some 30% of the population of the Thirteen Colonies—some 250,000 people—were opposed to the revolution. Some remained passive, but others actively joined the fray and formed Loyalist regiments which fought against Washington and his troops. After the war these people were not welcome in the land of their birth. They could no longer vote, sell land, sue debtors, or become lawyers or doctors; many were legally banished. In many instances they were actively persecuted and tales of mob violence, of hangings and burnings, of

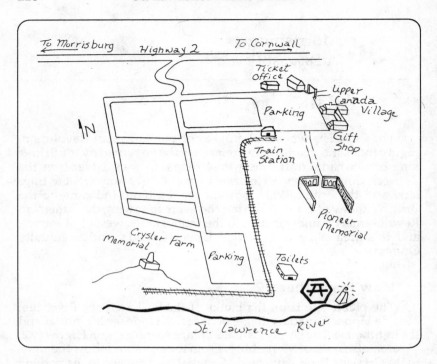

"tar-and-featherings," were not uncommon. For many the only choice was to leave their land and possessions and go into exile.

In the year 1783, Canada was a British colony of 150,000 mostly French-speaking people who had settled along the St. Lawrence between Montreal and the Atlantic Ocean. There were also some small British settlements in the eastern townships between Montreal and Quebec City, and in Nova Scotia.

Although some Loyalists were of pioneer stock, a number were lawyers, farmers, carpenters, craftsmen, clergymen, soldiers and slaves. They did not choose to go into the wilderness to farm, to live through Canadian winters in tents and shanties, to face drought, famine and disease. They came because they were refugees from a war, and although Britain acknowledged her debt to them, the British authorities in Canada were not prepared for the influx.

The Loyalists were promised land, but it had not yet been surveyed. They were expected to farm, but there were no axes with which to clear the land or ploughs to till the soil. They were to be provisioned by the British government but often the rations did not arrive, and were meagre when they did.

When the British defeated the French at Quebec in 1760 they had declared the vast land to the west of Montreal to be Indian reserve, closed forever to white settlement. In 1784, under pressure from the hungry Loyalists, and with the permission of the Indians, this area was opened to settlement and 5,000 Loyalists were transported in. These pioneers experienced famine, disease, and harsh winters but carried on and became the backbone of English settlement in Canada. They founded the cities of Toronto, Kingston, and Cornwall. By 1792 the new English-speaking province of Upper Canada had been created, with Niagara-on-the-Lake as its capital.

Loyalty to the British crown was what bound these early settlers together, and this loyalty was to become the binding force of the country's early elite (see the Family Compact Picnic at Hamilton). In 1789 Sir Guy Carleton, governor of British North America, encouraged this class distinction by granting to Loyalists and their descendants the right to put the prestigious initials "U.E." (United Empire) after their names. The Loyalists' contribution is recognized today in Ontario's Latin motto, *Ut Incepit Fidelis Sic Permanet* (Loyal she began, loyal she remains).

Flooding the St. Lawrence Lowlands

The construction of the St. Lawrence Seaway dams and locks upstream of Montreal in the mid-1950s resulted in the flooding of 38,000 acres, 20,000 of those in Canada. This region included seven Canadian villages and one-third of the town of Morrisburg. As a result, three new towns were created, and 525 houses and eighteen cemeteries were relocated to higher ground.

Things to do

1. Wander over Crysler's Farm Battlefield Park. One of the decisive battles of the War of 1812-14 was fought here. Four thousand American soldiers, travelling down the St. Lawrence River to attack Montreal, were defeated here by 800 British troops.

2. The building of the St. Lawrence Seaway (see Welland Canal Picnic) flooded many of the Loyalist farms and settlements. The Pioneer Memorial, north of the picnic site, contains hundreds of pioneer gravestones that were retrieved from the lowlands before the flooding.

3. Upper Canada Village itself is also a result of the seaway construction. The initial exhibits, houses and buildings, which would otherwise have been destroyed, were also retrieved from the lowlands. The village is a living museum of 1860s farm life in the St. Lawrence Valley. It is open daily from May until October.

Things to eat

Susanna Moodie, a sometimes humorous but always interesting chronicler of pioneer life, wrote in her 1853 book, *Life in the Clearings*:

"There are always regular pic-nics, each party contributing their share of eatables and drinkables to the general stock. ... hams, fowls, meat pies, cold joints of meat, and abundance of tarts and cakes..."

In keeping with the settler theme we suggest the following menu

MENU

Potted Fowl
Scotch Eggs
Garden Vegetable Salad with Pioneer Dressing
Fresh Baked Bread from the Upper Canada Village Bakery
Home-made Ginger Beer

Potted Fowl

This recipe was used by cooks in the 1800s to store leftover chicken (or any other fowl). Starting with the remains of a cold roast chicken, strip the meat from the bones, gristle and skin, and for every pound of meat add a thin slice of ham, 1/4 lb. of butter, 1 tsp. of powdered mace, 1 tsp. of nutmeg, and a dash of salt and cayenne. Chop the meat into very small pieces, sprinkle the butter and spices on top and pound all the ingredients together until they are reduced to a perfectly smooth paste. Put into a ramekin and cover with 1/8 inch of clarified butter. Store in the refrigerator, and serve cold.

Scotch Eggs

(6 servings)

6 eggs
1 kg sausage meat
breadcrumbs

Boil the eggs for 12 minutes until hard-boiled. Cool and peel. Wrap each egg in sausage meat about 1 cm thick. Roll the covered eggs in breadcrumbs and fry until the meat is cooked. Cool, slice in quarters and serve cold.

Ginger Beer

(makes 4 dozen bottles)

2 1/2 lbs. sugar
1 1/2 oz. ginger root, grated
1 oz. cream of tartar
2 lemons
3 gal. boiling water
2 Tbsp. yeast

Put the sugar, ginger root, and cream of tartar into a large earthenware crock. Squeeze and peel the lemons. Strain the juice and add the juice and the peel to the crock. Pour the boiling water into the crock and stir until the sugar is dissolved. Cool until it is just warm and then add the yeast. Cover the crock with a cloth and leave in a warm place for 24 hours. Skim off the yeast and siphon or decant the mixture into another container, discarding the sediment. Bottle and cap. The ginger beer should be ready in three or four days.

Pioneer Salad Dressing

1 tsp. dry mustard
1 tsp. sugar
2 Tbsp. salad oil
4 Tbsp. milk
2 Tbsp. vinegar
1 tsp. salt
dash of cayenne

Combine the first three ingredients, mixing well. Gradually add the milk and vinegar, stirring constantly to prevent curdling. Stir in salt and cayenne. When finished the dressing should be creamy.

Prepare a salad of chopped garden vegetables such as carrots, cauliflower, broccoli, green onions, and tomatoes. Pour the dressing over and toss just before serving.

Ottawa Valley

37 Ottawa
An Ottawanian's Picnic

On September 5, 1945, a cipher clerk left the Russian embassy in Ottawa with detailed documents describing Soviet spy rings in North America, including their acquisition of atomic secrets. He went from police station to newspaper office to government officials trying desperately to interest someone in his information. He found, as any casual visitor to Ottawa knows, that it's hard to get to see anyone in this town without an appointment. Eventually the Mounties listened to him, and Ottawa acquired the first attribute of an international capital—a spy scandal.

In our search for a suitable picnic spot in the city core we discovered that Ottawa has now acquired the second mark of an international city—there are no places to park! However, slightly removed from the confusion of Confederation Square, under the watchful eyes of the mandarins of the Department of External Affairs, where the Rideau flows over the cliff in the curtain-like falls that give the river its name, is a little oasis called Rideau Falls Park, and it is there we stopped to picnic.

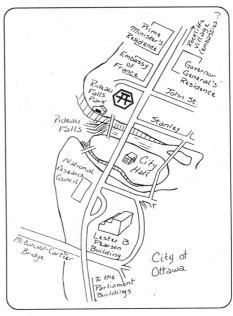

How to get there

The park is off Sussex Drive, immediately east of the Falls. It is about a five-minute drive from the War Memorial. There is adequate parking for cars within about 20 metres of the picnic tables. The view of the falls is superb and you can walk over the weir. The building beside the park is the French Embassy, the one on the island behind you is the Ottawa City Hall, the one west of the falls is the National Research Council, and the big one across the falls and kitty corner is the Lester B. Pearson Building, which houses the office of the Secretary of State for External Affairs.

Eminent Ottawanians

Here at the confluence of the Ottawa and Rideau Rivers, overlooking the falls, one can relax and enjoy a distinctively Canadian repast, and reflect on some of the interesting characters who have been there before you, such as:

Igor Sergeievich Gouzenko — the Russian cipher clerk who exposed the Russian spy ring. Igor and his family were given new identities and hidden somewhere in Canada for the rest of their lives. On his occasional public appearances he wore a hood to protect his identity. While in seclusion he wrote two books; one, entitled *The Fall of a Titan*, won the Governor General's award. He died in 1982 of natural causes. The Soviet Embassy is on Charlotte Street at Wilbrod Street on the western shore of the Rideau River, only a short distance upstream from the picnic spot.

John Buchan, First Baron Tweedsmuir, Governor General 1935-1940 — a poet, politician and author who had written six books of fiction, poetry, and history while he was an Oxford undergraduate. He continued writing at a prodigious rate throughout his life, his works ranging from historical biographies to fast-paced fiction such as the *Thirty-Nine Steps* (1915). In 1937 he instituted the Governor General's Literary Awards. He lived at Rideau Hall, two blocks north of the picnic spot.

Barbara Ann Scott — an Ottawa figure skater and one of Canada's best loved athletes. At the age of nine she started a training routine, skating seven hours a day. She was Canadian Woman's Champion at fifteen, North American Champion at seventeen, and in 1948, at age nineteen, won the Canadian, US, American, and European Championships as well as the Olympic Gold Medal. Canadians responded by making Barbara Ann Scott dolls and similar memorabilia a must on every little girl's Christmas list. The Minto Skating Club, where Barbara practised seven hours a day, is a few kilometres away on Lancaster Road.

William Lyon Mackenzie King — Canada's longest serving prime minister. He was the man who proved it is possible to govern this country by relying only on advice from your pet dog and your dead mother. Mackenzie King is remembered fondly by many as the prime minister who introduced Unemployment Insurance. King lived at Laurier House, 335 Laurier Avenue East, about three kilometres south of the picnic spot.

Queen Beatrix of the Netherlands — was born in Ottawa. Her parents were living here during the time when the Nazis occupied Holland. In order that the future queen not be born on foreign soil, a special Act of Parliament decreed the maternity wing of the Ottawa Civic Hospital temporarily Dutch territory. After the war the grateful Dutch government responded by providing all the tulips that grace the canals and driveways of Ottawa each spring.

Victoria — Queen of the United Kingdom of Great Britain and Ireland, Empress of India. She reigned over the British North American colonies from 1837 until her death in 1901. She is held in special regard by Ottawanians because it was she who, when asked to settle the feud between Toronto, Montreal, and Kingston as to which city would be the capital of Canada, chose lowly Bytown (now Ottawa) for the honour. She never visited Ottawa.

Charlotte Whitton — social worker, politician, feminist. She became Canada's first female mayor when she was elected mayor of Ottawa in 1951. She was re-elected in 1952, 1954, 1960, and 1962. Flamboyant and outspoken, she is clearly one of the more colourful and controversial women of this century. Her terms as mayor were notable for stormy verbal battles with hostile male colleagues. The city hall—her office—was built in 1958. It is across from the picnic site.

Things to see and do

Ottawa, as the nation's capital, has an incredible wealth of museums, galleries, and historic buildings, all deserving a visit. On a per capita basis, there are more parks, museums, galleries, and general interesting things to do here than in any other city in Canada. Information on what to do, where, and when can be obtained from the National Capital Commission Visitor Centre at the corner of Wellington and Metcalfe (just across the street from the Parliament Buildings) and at Canada's Capital Visitors' Information Centre at Confederation Square. All we suggest is that, as well as the obligatory tours of the Parliament, the Museum of Civilization and the National Gallery, you try to find time to stroll through the Byward Market (less than half a kilometre from the picnic site), to wander around the Chateau Laurier, walk down by the locks, and check out the cafés and bars across the river in Hull.

Rideau Falls

Things to Eat

Back in the 1950s, when people really cared about those things, the formal black-tie diplomatic banquets at the Chateau Laurier used to serve Canadian gourmet delights. A banquet menu consisted of such dishes as: pressed pheasant under glass, steamed wild rice, and asparagus with bernaise sauce.

Now generally we find pheasants a little hard to catch and harder to pluck and so we suggest the following substitutions to change the black-tie banquet into shirtsleeve finger-food.

MENU

Terrine of Chicken
Chilled Asparagus with Garlic Dip
Crusty Rolls
Wild Rice Pudding

All these items can be obtained at the Byward Market or, you can purchase only the rolls and use the following recipes.

Terrine of Chicken
(Serves 8-10)

1 chicken, 3-4 pounds, cut into pieces
1 cup onions, chopped
1/2 cup carrots, chopped
1/2 cup celery, chopped
3 lemons, thinly sliced
2 tsp. dried tarragon or 2 sprigs fresh
bouquet garni (see below)
1/4 tsp. freshly ground pepper
5 cups water
1 medium zucchini, cut into strips
1/4 cup tinned sweet pimento
2 Tbsp. unflavoured gelatin

Wash the pieces of chicken and place them in a large pot, along with the next eight ingredients. When it is boiling, reduce the heat and simmer for 1 1/2 hours on very low heat, until the meat falls from the bones. Remove the chicken meat and bones, drain and cool. Strain the stock and set it aside.

Steam the zucchini until barely tender, and immediately place in a bath of cold water to stop the cooking process. Dry with paper towelling.

Remove the chicken meat from the bones. Arrange one-third of the pieces of meat on the bottom of a loaf pan. Place a layer of zucchini strips on top, and then another layer of chicken, another of zucchini, and a top layer of chicken. Arrange the pimento pieces attractively on the top.

Soak the gelatin in 1/2 cup of the strained stock. Place 3 cups of the strained stock in a pot and bring to a boil. Stir the gelatin mixture into the stock until it is dissolved, and pour over the chicken/zucchini mixture in the loaf pan. Tap the bottom of the pan a few times on a hard surface to remove air bubbles, cover and chill until set (overnight is best). Place extra gelatin/stock mixture in another glass container and chill.

To serve, set the loaf pan in warm water for about 30 seconds, and upend on a platter of lettuce or watercress. Cube the extra gelatin and use for garnish. Slice and serve at your picnic.

Bouquet Garni

A bouquet garni is a small package of spices which is used to flavour a stock, but is not part of the final product. Find a small piece of cheese cloth, and place a bay leaf, some dried or fresh thyme, parsley, a couple of cloves, and 6-8 peppercorns, and tie up the cheese cloth with a piece of string. This remains in the pot until the straining.

Asparagus with Garlic Dip

Open a tin of asparagus or get fresh asparagus and either steam or microwave it until tender, then cool. The dip is the Spanish garlic mayonnaise, also known as Aioli, which is a supreme accompaniment to fish or vegetables.

Garlic Mayonnaise

125 ml lemon juice
3 ml salt
5 ml soy sauce
3 cloves garlic crushed
2 eggs
500 ml olive oil

Combine the first five ingredients in the blender and blend at high speed for 30 seconds. Then reduce the blender to medium speed and open the cap at the top. Pour the oil in a slow steady stream into the centre of the whirling mixture. Turn the blender off when the mayonnaise is thick.

Wild Rice Pudding

(Serves 4)

250 ml cooked wild rice
1 ml anise seed
2 cm ginger root
125 ml milk
1 cinnamon stick
3 egg yolks
125 ml sugar

Make a spice bag from cotton or cheesecloth and put into it the anise seed, ginger and cinnamon stick. Add the spice bag to the milk and heat almost to boiling. Simmer for another 4-5 minutes; set aside to steep for 30 minutes and then remove the spice bag.

In a large bowl beat the egg yolks and sugar together until light and fluffy; then add the flavoured milk in a thin stream, continuing to beat. Return the mixture to the saucepan and cook over low heat, stirring constantly until it thickens. Add the rice to this custard and continue cooking over low heat for an additional 5 minutes. Pour the pudding into a serving bowl and let cool.

38 Chalk River
A Nuclear Picnic

If you are admitted to a major hospital in Canada for a thorough examination, there is a 30% chance that one of the tests performed will have at its heart a radioactive isotope.

Enter the magic world of inner space and picnic in Canada's nuclear establishment of Chalk River. The site is fascinating. The exhibit in the visitor centre and the guided tour of the site pushes the visitor well into the twenty-first century. It is an opportunity to reassure yourself and your family about the safety of nuclear power, and dispel a few of the myths.

How to get there

The Chalk River Nuclear Laboratories and Public Information Centre are 8 km from the village of Chalk River on Highway 17. Stop and register at the Outer Gate, and then drive the eight km to the Public Information Centre. The picnic tables on the hill beside the centre offer a fine view of the Ottawa River.

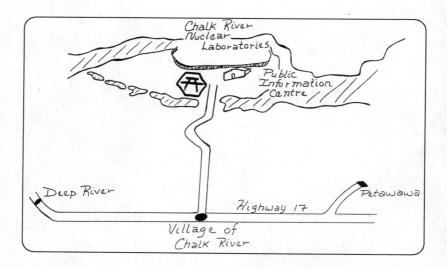

The Chalk River Labs

The first Canadian nuclear reactor, the third in the world, was built here in 1945. It is called ZEEP and it only produced one watt of heat. However, it provided the basis for the design of the current CANDU reactors which each produce 750,000,000 watts. You can see ZEEP below you, an older building on the left. It is no longer in use.

In 1952 the Atomic Energy Commission was created to pursue peaceful uses of atomic energy. The laboratories below your picnic site employ 2,000 people who are working to find applications of nuclear science in areas such as cancer research, environmental protection, and health and safety. The Chalk River plant produces 60 to 70 percent of the free world's medical isotopes.

Nuclear Confusion

The principal sources of acid rain are the fossil fuel power generating plants. The major source of greenhouse gases that cause the dangerous greenhouse effect is the burning of fossil fuels. Over 50 percent of the warming trend comes from this alone. Mining of fossil fuels, especially great open pit mines, defaces the landscape irreparably. Working conditions in underground mines are often unsatisfactory and mine disasters are frequently in the news. Miners in many coal towns still die early from "miners' disease, black lung" or pneumoconiosis, a coating of the lung tissue with carbon.

Nuclear power has none of these side effects. The waste from production is orders of magnitude less than that from mining and burning fossil fuels. Health conditions for workers are excellent, and accidents are fewer.

Nuclear power is cheaper and kinder to the environment than fossil fuel. In Canada we generate 18 percent of our electricity from fossil fuels, 67 percent from hydroelectric sites, and 15 percent from nuclear energy.

Canada continues to be a leader in the peaceful uses of atomic energy. Canadians pioneered in radiotherapy and developed the cancer-treating cobalt-60 units. These are now being replaced by another Canadian development, the Therac 25 linear accelerator. Together with the researchers at the Montreal Neurological Institute, atomic scientists have developed a positive emission tomography scanner which can observe organ functions within a patient's head. Radio-isotopes are used to scan the liver, the kidney, the lungs, and most cardiovascular organs. Radio-isotopes are also used to check welds in pipelines. The people who declared Vancouver a Nuclear Free Zone had better check their local hospitals, and their pipe line contractors.

The problem is that nuclear waste won't go away. Spent nuclear fuel must be kept under water for the first five years, then it must be

School children examine a nuclear fuel bundle

protected and shielded for the next 500 years. The amount of waste is not great. As of 1987 the entire amount of spent fuel in Canada would fill an ordinary skating rink to the top of the boards. However, 500 years is a long time and each CANDU reactor is producing about 3.3 cubic meters of used fuel per year.

Food irradiation, "zapping" food with gamma rays to destroy parasites and micro-organisms, is another use of nuclear technology. There are over 140 gamma irradiators worldwide, and the process is approved in 19 countries. Canada endorses the process for potatoes, onions, wheat, flour, herbs, and spices. Detractors claim that micro-organisms might develop resistance to radiation over time, or that dangerous new strains may mutate. They also claim that radiolytic products are created in the food which can cause blood abnormalities. Environmental groups are trying to have irradiated foods labelled as such so that consumers can make a choice.

Things to do

1. Tour the Public Information Centre. The displays and video presentations are well-prepared and most informative, and the staff members are extremely knowledgeable. Allow at least an hour for this.

2. Tour the laboratories. Guided tours are available daily from mid-June until September. Children under eleven are not allowed on the tour, but free baby sitting is provided. During the off-season you can still take the tour, but two weeks advance notice is requested, so that a guide can be arranged. Call (613) 584-3311, ext. 4429.

3. Visit the museums at Canadian Forces Base Petawawa. There are two: one featuring a history of military parachuting, and the other tracing the history of Petawawa since its establishment in 1905.

4. Walk in the Petawawa National Forestry Institute where forestry research began in Canada in 1918. There are trails, exhibits, tours, and a beach. The Forest Visitor Centre is on Highway 17, four kilometres east of Chalk River.

Things to eat

Microwave ovens have nothing to do with nuclear energy, but the fact that they heat food by making the molecules vibrate at 2,450,000,000 times a second does give them a certain space age flavour. Thus we prepared this menu in the microwave before transporting it to the site. The logical beverage would be heavy water but, since it is fairly hard to come by, substitute mineral water which, with its chemical content, is a little heavier than ordinary water.

MENU

Barbecued Chicken
Mexican Crêpes
Zucchini-Tomato Salad
Mineral Water

Microwave Barbecued Chicken

(Serves 4)

1 1/2 kg chicken, cut into pieces
125 ml tomato purée
60 ml vinegar
15 ml Worcestershire sauce
2 ml Tabasco sauce
2 cloves garlic, crushed

10 ml butter
1 bay leaf
2 ml ground ginger

To make the sauce combine all the ingredients except the chicken in a small bowl and cover with vented plastic wrap. Microwave on high for 2 minutes and set aside.

Arrange the chicken in a round baking dish with the meatier, thicker portions toward the outside. Cover with wax paper and microwave at high for 4 minutes. Drain and turn over.

Brush half the sauce onto the chicken. Return to the oven and microwave at high for 6 minutes. Turn, brush with remaining sauce, and microwave at high for 5 to 7 minutes, or until chicken is tender. Let stand for 5 minutes. Cool, then chill in refrigerator. Eat cold at your picnic.

Microwave Mexican Crêpes

(serves 4)

2 eggs
60 ml milk
15 ml jalapeño pepper, chopped fine
30 ml sweet red peppers, chopped fine
15 ml whole wheat pastry flour
2 ml oregano
cooking oil
150 ml cooked kernel corn
1 avocado, peeled and puréed in blender
125 ml Monterey Jack cheese, grated.

Make sure that the eggs and milk are at room temperature. Whisk together the eggs, milk, peppers, flour and oregano. Coat a nine-inch glass pie plate with a thin layer of oil (a quick heating in the microwave helps) and pour in 45 ml of the batter. Swirl the batter around until it almost covers the plate. Microwave uncovered on medium power for 2 minutes and 40 seconds. Flip the crepe out face side down on waxed paper and repeat the process with the remaining batter. This should make four crepes.

Spread the avocado over the crepes. Arrange the corn and one half of the cheese in rolls at one side of each crepe. Roll up and set each crepe seam-side down on the pie plate. Sprinkle with the remaining cheese and microwave at medium power for 1 minute. Cool and eat cold.

Zucchini-Tomato Salad

(serves 4)

2 small or 1 large zucchini, peeled and thinly sliced
2 large tomatoes, thinly sliced
15 ml chopped fresh thyme
120 ml olive oil
30 ml vinegar
15 ml dry wine
5 ml dry mustard
dash of salt and pepper
30 ml of mixed herbs—parsley, rosemary, chives

Place the zucchini in a shallow casserole and cover with vented plastic wrap. Microwave on high for 4 minutes. Remove and drain on paper towels. Cut the tomato slices into quarters and arrange with the zucchini in a shallow container. Sprinkle with thyme.

Combine in a blender all remaining ingredients and blend on low speed until the vinaigrette is creamy. Pour over the slices and chill in the refrigerator. Serve cold.

Northeastern Ontario

39 Sudbury
The Miner's Picnic

A long time ago a great meteorite hit the earth at great speed, creating the valley at the southern edge of which Sudbury lies, and the substantial veins of nickel and copper upon which the economy of the city is based.

How to get there

The entrance to Bell Park is on the east side of Paris Street, just north of Science North, which is well sign-posted. Carry your basket to the table by the little waterfall, just above the beach.

The geology

Sudbury Basin is the geological formation which resulted from the meteor. It is a depression 56 kilometres long and 27 kilometres wide, which contains four small lakes. Along the rim of the basin are deposits of minerals, sixteen of which are mined today. This is the richest deposit of nickel in the world, and Canada's largest copper-producing region.

Sudbury

The land around here was used primarily by the Ojibwa people for centuries, and then, beginning in the late nineteenth century, by the loggers from the lumber companies. The Canadian Pacific Railway line came through in 1883. This is when the settlement was named Sudbury, after the English birthplace of the wife of the construction superintendent, James Worthington. It was the construction crew that discovered the enormous deposits of nickel and

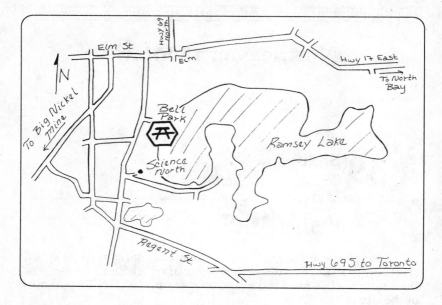

copper which were to become the economic base of the region for years to come.

By 1888 the Canadian Copper Company smelting operations were underway. International Nickel was the result of an amalgamation of Canadian Copper and Orford Refining in 1902. The other big company, Falconbridge Nickel, was formed in 1928. The two companies continue to be major employers here. Because Sudbury developed as a company town, there was almost no tax base for municipal development for many years, since there was no tax money from the mining industry. The city grew over the years, in spite of a low budget and the devastating effect that the mines had on the surrounding landscape. Sudbury is still Canada's most important mining community.

The Devastation

It took about a century to destroy the land around Sudbury. It wasn't only the mining. The way had been prepared by years of logging in the district. Once the big trees had been removed for the industries south of the border, the process of erosion began.

The techniques of the prospectors added to the destructive process. They would often burn off large tracts of land to get at the soil beneath. A more systematic way of getting rid of unwanted timber was the roast beds of the great mining companies, which burned slowly, sending their toxic gases into the air for weeks at a time. The roast beds, fed by wood unwanted by the loggers, burned lumps of nickel and copper ore to drive off some of the sulphur as sulphur dioxide. The burned ore was then smelted, discharging the gases and particles which permanently poisoned the soil for miles around the mines, until nothing grew there. Keith Winterhalder, a plant biologist who lives in Sudbury, summarized the results of 100 years of environmental carelessness:

"Plant death and the erosion, acidification and metal-contamination of soil, together with increased fire- and frost-action resulting from the openness of the landscape, had created a total environment so hostile that the cycle of plant establishment and growth was broken, possibly forever. We were left with a bitter legacy in the soil, and no amount of emission control could do anything to reverse the situation."

Reclamation

For decades Sudbury had the reputation of being the ugliest city in Canada, but in the 1970s one of the world's largest reclamation projects began. Professor Winterhalder, quoted above, was one of the people who initiated the re-greening of Sudbury. Miraculously, the grey wasteland is now a fascinating landscape. Rich patches of green dot what was once square miles of bare, blackened earth. The parks and residential landscaping have turned the rocky terrain into a beautiful background for community living.

First, the poisonous emissions had to be controlled. Inco built the super-stack—the 380-metre chimney which dominates the skyline. It takes the poisonous gases much higher before they are released, causing them to dissipate before touching the ground. The emission levels were reduced, and two of the smelting plants were also closed down in 1972, leaving the way clear for a new beginning.

Experiments had revealed that the soil around Sudbury was very acid, and further, that when ground limestone was supplied, plants began to grow again. Limestone appeared to neutralize the toxicity of the soil such that birch, poplars and willows, as well as grasses, could grow once more.

But how to apply limestone to such a vast area in sufficient quantities, and then, how to plant the seeds which might grow there, given a chance? This is when the community stepped in to solve their own problem. There were several trials, and some painful errors. The first wave of tree planting on unlimed soil failed as a result of toxicity. It was decided that liming was mandatory and that revegetation should begin with grass establishment. In 1975 school students were organized to sow grasses in newly limed soil, helping the seeds along with fertilizer. The grass grew, and the community, funded by government and the mines, took over the concept and applied it on a larger scale. Soon they had created many grassy areas where wild seeds could take root and flourish. Later tree planting projects were successful when the trees were placed in a more appropriate environment.

Now the drive through the Sudbury region is pleasant. Where once there was nothing but grey, dead soil, there are green embankments

Bell Park

by the road. But on the horizon you can still see signs of the past—just enough to underline the achievement of the people who managed to make Sudbury green again.

Things to do

1. Swim in Lake Ramsey, just below the picnic site. The lake was once called Bimitimigamasing, but it is easier to pronounce now.

2. Attend some outdoor theatre events in Bell Park. The amphitheatre that you passed on the hill below the parking lot seats 2,600 people, and features a wide variety of events through the summer season.

3. Tour the Big Nickel Mine. The enormous Canadian nickel coin dominates Sudbury's skyline. It is at the entrance to this most successful demonstration mine. The Big Nickel, billed as Canada's largest coin, is 30 feet high. Your tour takes place below the surface of the earth.

4. Tour the Inco mining-smelting-refining complex. It is the largest in the world. Bus tours last 2 1/2 hours, and cover the geology, history and process of mining nickel.

5. Spend a few hours in Science North, the museum that involves everyone. Lie on a bed of nails, or create a tornado—unusual experiences abound in this hands-on exhibition.

6. Take a one-hour cruise on Lake Ramsey. The boat leaves from the dock at Science North several times a day.

Things to eat

This is a miner's picnic. The meal really should be carried in black metal lunchboxes, one for each person, with a Thermos of coffee in each.

Fill Thermos with thickly brewed, strong, black coffee. Pour into the Thermos while still very hot.

Prepare 2 bologna sandwiches with mustard on white bread. Wrap in wax paper and place in lunch bucket.

Add:
1 jar of home baked beans
1 spoon.
1 large piece of apple pie

Carry lunch bucket to picnic site.

40 North Bay
The Quintessential Picnic

For at least 6,000 years this was Indian territory. The Nipissing Indians occupied this region when Champlain, La Verendrye, David Thompson and a host of other explorers came down the La Vase River on their way west in search of furs. Despite the historical importance of this route, it took five little girls to make the area famous. This picnic is set in Champlain Park where the La Vase River empties into Lake Nipissing. But the picnic excursion should also include a visit to the home where the Dionne quintuplets were born.

How to get there

To reach Champlain Park, drive south on Lakeshore Drive until you reach a fork. The right fork is a continuation of Lakeshore Drive, but is now called Premier Road. Follow it to the end, and find a parking place. We suggest that you walk down to where the river empties into Lake Nipissing, and spread your picnic blanket.

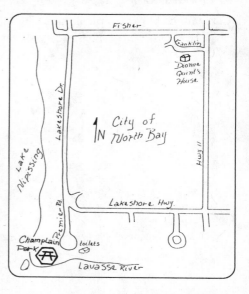

Champlain

There is a plaque by the river at the eastern edge of the park which lists many of the European explorers who passed this way in their canoes. The first on the list is Samuel de Champlain, a French cartographer, who came through twice, once in 1613 and again in 1615. The waterways from Quebec (where Champlain had founded a French settlement in 1608), and the western reaches of Ontario, were characterized by many rapids and waterfalls. Soon after his arrival in New France, Champlain had observed that the cumbersome French long boats were not suitable for the Canadian rivers. He noticed the canoe used by the Indian people, and decided that the French expeditions would require a similar conveyance. He had the Indians build an adaptation of their canoe, which could carry ten passengers instead of the usual three or four, and could also transport three or four tons of cargo. Such a canoe could still be carried around rapids and waterfalls when necessary. A few years later the French established a small canoe industry at Trois Rivières. With their more refined metal tools they could make sturdier canoes than the Indians, who still worked with flint and bone tools.

The adoption of the canoe was a major factor in the success of the French traders. A hundred and fifty years later, during intense competition for fur resources, the canoeing voyageurs were able to expand their territory more rapidly than the British traders in their York boats.

The Dionne Quintuplets

On May 28th, 1934, five identical baby girls were born near Corbeil, a village in northern Ontario. They were to become the focus of news and human interest stories in newspapers around the world, and to remain public property throughout their childhood. The publicity that attended the childhood of the quintuplets brought vicarious joy to millions of people during the depression, but was a mixed blessing to the five little girls and their family. The phenomenon of the quints—for such it was—is difficult to assess. Can Allan Roy Dafoe, the family doctor, be chastised for capitalizing on the babies at whose birth he had been present, when they were the only surviving quintuplets in medical history, a chance of 1 in 57 million? Can the government of Ontario be condemned for making the little girls wards of the province in order to promote them as a tourist attraction during the worst depression the nation had seen? Before we judge too quickly, we must remember—or imagine—the times. The world then was a dark and dreary place. Almost one-quarter of the Canadian work force was unemployed. Bad news prevailed: drought, crop failures, suicides and bankruptcies. Is it any wonder that the miraculous survival of five beautiful baby girls was welcomed everywhere as a relief from the daily tension and tedium?

Annette, Cecile, Marie, Emily and Yvonne Dionne were born in the home of their parents, Elzire and Oliva Dionne, who already had five children. They lived in a little log house on the edge of Corbeil, near Callender, just south of North Bay. Oliva Dionne registered the births of his daughters in the local newspapers, hoping to get the free hampers that were customarily distributed to new parents. He needed them—there was no extra money in the Dionne household,

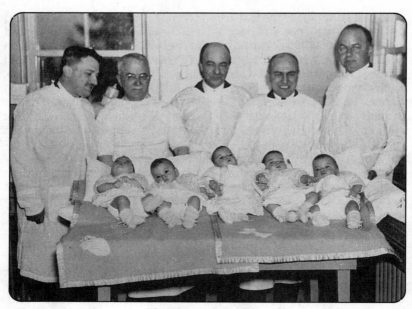

The Dionne Quintuplets

and five more mouths would be an almost intolerable strain. Once the North Bay reporters confirmed the unbelievable story it was picked up by other newspapers, and soon reporters gathered outside the Dionne home from all over the world. The family doctor, Dr. Dafoe, was at first dazed by the publicity surrounding his instantly famous charges. He had set up a nursery in part of the Dionne household, and arranged for special nurses to help with the babies. They needed constant care for the first few months—their combined weight at birth was only 13 pounds, 5 ounces. As the realization of the potential for personal fame dawned on Dr. Dafoe, it was also striking Mitchell Hepburn, premier in the Ontario government, who had an election campaign coming up. For the Dionne family, the next few years would bring fame, fortune—and heartache.

The government made the babies wards of the province, and built a special hospital for them across the road from their parents' home, with Dr. Dafoe in charge. The parents were allowed to visit only under the strictest supervision—Mrs. Dionne was not at first permitted to hold her babies. In a couple of years Quintland was built—a fenced yard with viewing areas where tourists could watch the little girls play. At first the girls were displayed to the public six times a day, then later twice a day. In the first year alone revenues for the government were estimated at $20 million. In the next few years the quint industry brought hundreds of millions of dollars into the province through the tourists it attracted, particularly from the United States. There was never an admission charge at Quintland, but people were anxious for souvenirs, and the hotel and restaurant business in the region experienced an unprecedented boom.

Deeply unhappy with the way his daughters were being raised away from the family, and away from traditional French Catholic values, Oliva began a law suit against the government. The battle was complex and took several years, causing the family severe emotional pain. The girls were eight years old by the time the government agreed to let them come home. Part of the settlement was the big home that was built to house the family, which by now had twelve children.

But it was too late. The quintuplets didn't really know their seven brothers and sisters, and were not used to the authority of their parents. They were used to being the centre of attention of a large staff in their special hospital. Now they had to adapt to being members of a large French Canadian Catholic family, still carefully protected from outsiders by their father. They had never had to help with housework; they had no idea of the conventional patterns of behaviour within a family. Their memories of this time are resentful. There was plenty of money, since some of the profits had been set aside for the girls. But they always remained somewhat separate from the family, and they all left home at sixteen, as soon as they had graduated from high school. Even their high school experience had been sheltered, since they attended a special school in what had been their hospital, with only eight other carefully selected students.

The girls had missed some of the essential lessons of growing up: getting along within a family, and getting along within a peer group at school. They had never shopped for their own clothes, or learned to manage their own money. The cost of this special upbringing was high. Three of the girls married, but their marriages ended in divorce. Emily died in 1954 during an epileptic seizure, and Marie died in 1970 of a blood clot. Oliva, their father, died in 1979. Mrs. Dionne still lives in a bungalow facing the mansion built so long ago for her special family. It is now a hospital serving the elderly. The three surviving sisters, now in their mid-fifties, live near each other in suburban Montreal, finally having acquired the privacy that eluded them for so many years.

Things to do

1. Visit the Dionne home where the quintuplets were born. It is now a museum of Quint memorabilia. The house has been moved to the junction of Highways 11 and 17 on the North Bay bypass.

2. Drive by Nipissing Manor in Corbeil about 15 km southeast of North Bay, and imagine it as it used to be when it was part of Quintland, with a large fenced-in playground, and several souvenir booths nearby. Follow Highway 33 south to Highway 94, and turn east. You will notice the manor before you reach the village of Corbeil.

3. Visit the home of Dr. Allan Dafoe, the doctor who delivered the quintuplets in Callander. It is now the North Himsworth Museum. Driving south on Highway 11, turn left onto Lansdowne Street, where you will find the museum.

4. Visit the biggest used bookstore in Canada, Allison the Bookman, at 342 Main Street East. The antiquarian room is especially interesting. Here you can look up that obscure book you can never find. Mr. Allison knows them all.

5. Rent a canoe, and paddle from Trout Lake down the La Vase River to Lake Nipissing, just as Champlain did.

Things to eat

For this picnic you are expected to have five people in your party. And of course, a quintessential picnic begins at 5 o'Clock in the afternoon. Since the quintuplets were born in the fifth month of the year, we shall have a spring picnic. You may choose to wash it all down with a little Five Star Brandy.

MENU

Lettuce Soup
Herb Biscuits with Cheese Spread
Green Salad
Tomato Aspic
Cold Sliced Chicken Breast
Rhubarb Crisp

Lettuce Soup
(Serves 4)

1 pound (about 2 cups, packed) freshly picked lettuce
1/4 cup butter
2 Tbsp. grated onion
2 Tbsp. flour
4 cups of stock (milk may be used here)
salt to taste
dash paprika

Wash the lettuce and place in a pot with just a little water. Steam for 5-6 minutes. Drain, and reduce to a liquid in the blender.

Sauté the onion in the butter until golden, then stir in the flour until the mixture forms a thick paste. Gradually add the stock or milk, stirring constantly. Add the seasonings, and the lettuce. Heat through, and place in Thermos for transport to the picnic.

Herb Biscuits

See recipe in Thunder Bay picnic.

Cheese Spread

1 cup cottage cheese
one 8-ounce package cream cheese, softened
2 cloves garlic, minced
1 Tbsp. fresh thyme
1 Tbsp. fresh basil
1 Tbsp. fresh chives
1 tsp. fresh oregano
freshly ground pepper
dash cayenne
1 tsp. Worcestershire sauce
dash tabasco sauce

Process in a food blender until smooth. Keep chilled till serving. Spread on herb biscuits.

Green Salad

Gather a mixture of fresh greens from the garden—various sorts of lettuce, dandelion greens, nasturtium leaves, endive, or whatever you have; or purchase a similar variety of interesting leafy vegetables. Wash, chill, and tear leaves into bite-sized pieces. Keep chilled until serving. Toss at the picnic site with your favourite dressing.

Tomato Aspic

(Serves 5)

Here is a quick way to make the old classic.

1 envelope unflavoured gelatin
2 1/2 cups spicy Clamato juice

Mix the gelatin in 1/2 cup of the juice, and let stand. Meanwhile, heat the rest of the juice in a pot. Just before it boils, stir in the gelatin mixture. Pour into a mold and chill. Serve with a bowl of mayonnaise.

Rhubarb Crisp

(Serves 5)

5 cups rhubarb, cut in 1/2-inch pieces
1/3 cup sugar
1/2 tsp. nutmeg
1/4 tsp. allspice
2/3 cup quick-cooking rolled oats
1/4 cup whole wheat flour
1/2 cup brown sugar
dash salt
1/4 tsp. grated ginger*
1/3 cup melted butter

Spread the rhubarb in an 8-inch square pan, and sprinkle with sugar, nutmeg and allspice. Mix together the oats, flour, brown sugar, salt, and ginger, and then stir in the melted butter to make a crumble. Place the topping evenly over the rhubarb/spice mixture, and bake at 350' F for 35 minutes. Cool and take to the picnic.

*We always keep a piece of ginger root frozen in a plastic bag in the freezing compartment of our refrigerator. It grates easily this way, without thawing.

41 Temagami
The Trapper's Picnic

When Grey Owl took the stage, dressed in fringed Indian buckskins, the audiences of England and North America were enchanted by stories of his life in the wilds of Northern Canada. The books he wrote about his experiences with the animals he came to know so well were widely read by an adoring public. When he died in 1938, however, the British aunts who had raised him, and several ex-wives and their children, claimed Grey Owl was a fraud. He was really just Archie Belaney, an English schoolboy whose fantasies about Indians had become his adult reality.

Years have past since his unmasking, and Grey Owl is now seen as the avid conservationist that he was, a leader—albeit ahead of his time. Fraud or hero, Grey Owl is one of the fascinating characters in Ontario history. He spent several years camping on the shores of Lake Temagami, where this picnic takes place.

How to get there

The entrance to Finlayson Point Provincial Park is on Highway 11, just south of the town of Temagami. Drive right through the park to the western end, where you'll find the picnic area.

Grey Owl

Growing up with his two maiden aunts and his grandmother in the south of England, Archie Belaney sought his adventures in books. Although his aunts encouraged him to get a good education, Archie was a loner and rarely took part in many of the normal exploits of young boys. But his books told him stories of animals and of Indians with great courage who harvested the wilderness, hunting what animals they needed while continuing to live in harmony with them. The wilderness became his dream, and as soon as he was finished with school he left England for Canada.

Archie was 17 when he first came to Temagami. He assisted Bill Guppy, an expert trapper, in order to learn firsthand about the Canadian wilderness. Guppy was a professional trapper in the early days of tourism in the north, when white men were a rarity, and some of the Indian people still lived as they had always done. Tourism was in its infancy 1907. Archie helped to build one of the luxurious lodges

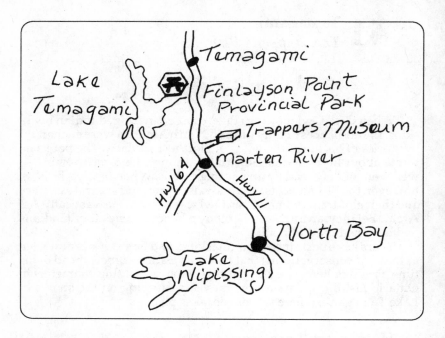

on Lake Temagami, and served as a guide to wealthy American tourists.

After a season of working with Guppy, Archie knew a lot about professional trapping. He decided to spend the winter of 1908 with the Bear Island Band of the Ojibwa, who had a permanent camp across the lake from the lodge, on Bear Island. Because of his patience and eagerness to learn, the elders taught him much of his knowledge of the bush. He trapped with them, adding his knowledge of their techniques to what he had learned from Guppy. He took a wife, Angele, and their daughter Agnes was born. However his lifelong pattern of running from family restrictions was about to begin. Archie had accomplished what he wanted—he understood the native ways in the wilderness, and so in a couple of years he left Bear Island and his family, much to the chagrin of the elders. By then his skin colour had deepened to a rich tanned brown, his hair had grown long, and he was indistinguishable from his Indian friends except for his intense blue eyes. This is when he began to alter the story of his past just a little, so that it would fit with his new identity. Grey Owl was emerging, and Archie Belaney was fading into the mist of an unhappy past.

He moved back and forth for a few years between Biscotasing and Temagami. There are those who recall him as an awkward but willing young Englishman, and there are those who remember him as an Indian with mixed blood who said something about a Scottish father and an Apache mother. Also, there were a few who heard both stories from him, shrugged, and accepted Archie—or Grey Owl— just as he chose to present himself. As Archie became more at home in the wilderness his new identity became more natural. There were still anomalies in his behaviour—the Indian guide who could play classical music on the piano; the trapper who quoted Tennyson late at night.

As a boy his aunts had encouraged him to write. His grandfather had been a writer, as had several of his uncles. It was natural for Archie to try to express his wonder, his confusion and his joy in his new universe in writing. There were several attempts, but eventually he sent the manuscript for *The Men of the Last Frontier* to a publisher back in England. His writing style is compelling, and his stories of the Indian people of the northland was published in 1931. Grey Owl's career as a writer and lecturer was launched. Soon *Pilgrims of the Wild* (1935), *The Adventures of Sajo and Her Beaver People* (1935), and *Tales of an Empty Cabin* (1936) followed. He was an excellent speaker, and so was much in demand on the lecture circuit of two continents.

Grey Owl feeding a beaver kitten

Much had changed for Grey Owl. No longer did he trap or hunt. Although he had spent many years as a guide and trapper, he had come to believe that indiscriminate killing of animals was wrong. He became a conservationist instead, and capitalized on his ability to befriend wild animals so that he could learn about them. He became an expert on many wild animals and birds, making pets of two beaver kittens. He wrote many books about these experiences, and they remain classics. This is the Grey Owl who was revered by the public in the 1920s and 30s.

His career ended abruptly with his death in 1938, apparently from exhaustion from his speaking tours and writing schedule. Returning to his cabin following an extensive tour, he became ill with

pneumonia, and died at the age of 50. When he died, another side of
Grey Owl was exposed: the man who had abandoned several wives
and children, whose wanderlust had prevented him from (or ex-
cused him from) the responsibilities of his several families. Yet his
wives all spoke fondly of him after his death, with a deep understanding of his need to leave them.

He is remembered in Temagami and Biscotasing as a trouble-
maker by some—and it is true that he was frequently drunk and
rowdy. During his twenties Archie cultivated a reputation for wild-
ness and for imposing his own brand of justice on others. He ran away
from an attempted manslaughter charge. But there were mitigating
circumstances; he clearly should not have thrown the knife, but he
was furious at the victim, who had raped a child. The old-timers, the
men who worked as guides and packers with Archie Belaney, are
gone now. But they remembered him as one of them. He was not to
develop the skills which set him apart until after he left Temagami.
His reputation for violence faded as he became fully established in his
identity as Grey Owl, the naturalist.

Hero or fraud, then? Was the Grey Owl image merely a pose for
publicity purposes to gain a wide audience for his ideas? Or did
Archie Belaney really become Grey Owl, an unusual man with
unusual convictions? Certainly he was one of the more committed
men of the wild frontier, and one whose literary skills permit us to
understand a bit about what drove him to the bush, what he found
there, and why he spent much of his life convincing others to cherish
the wilderness as he did.

Trapping in Northern Ontario

Trapping is Canada's oldest industry. Long before the coming of
the Europeans the Indian people practised efficient conservation and
harvesting of this renewable resource. Trapping, for the aboriginal
peoples, is an integral part of their religions and economy. Because
they are dependent on the animals for food, clothing and as trade
items for acquiring other commodities, their respect for animals is
strong, and governs their balanced harvesting.

By the sixteenth century fur-bearing animals had become scarce
in Russia and Europe, and other sources were sought. Traders came
to North America, and with the Europeans came a new pattern. The
motivation for trapping was no longer based on respect for the
animals, but on the desire to maximize economic returns, with no
regard for supply or conservation. The result was imbalance, and
extinction of some wild animals. For two centuries trapping was
practised by many with no concern for the suffering of the animals,
with the result that the entire industry and its products have been
brought into question.

In recent decades this situation has been corrected. Controls have been set in place, and the 75,000 Canadian trappers, about half of whom are aboriginal people, can go about their business with the support of several associations providing them with continuing education, and protecting their interests. These associations are strong advocates for humane trapping and sponsor research into improved techniques as well as the enforcement of stringent regulations to protect the stock of various species of fur-bearing animals. According to the Fur Institute of Canada:

Animal species produce more young than the habitat can ultimately support. This "surplus" production is what aboriginal hunters saw as the animals' "gift," available to support human life as long as it was used wisely. It is true that nature doesn't need us to maintain the balance; surplus populations will be brought under control, one way or another. Starvation, disease, predation, intra-species fighting and cannibalism will do the job equally efficiently—but they are not necessarily more "humane" than hunting and trapping. They are, however, hidden away in the bush, where most of us don't see them.

The old ways still hold among the aboriginal peoples. Trap lines are still regulated by traditional ownership and community controls on harvests. There are also a number of additional controls which have been imposed on all trappers to maintain the balance, such as licensing and collection of royalties. The royalties are applied to scientific research and biological monitoring of species. Further, the trapping season is regulated to protect the animals; for example, when too many females are being harvested the trapping season can be altered to protect them during breeding season. Quotas also limit trapping to surplus numbers as measured by wildlife experts. This is especially important for the beaver, easily harvested because of its sedentary life in stable colonies. Lynx have "zero" quotas in many parts of the province just now, to allow them to increase to a healthy margin beyond a sustaining population.

Through education of trappers, legislation and research, trapping methods are increasingly humane. For example, daily inspection of each trapline is now mandatory. Harvesting of this renewable resource is once again practised responsibly, and endangered fur-bearing species are no longer hunted in Canada. Thanks to conscientious wildlife management, there are more fur-bearing animals in Ontario now than there were when the Europeans first came.

Things to do

In the early decades of this century the north was the focus for Canada's resource development; now it is the focus for those who seek to experience the remaining Canadian wilderness, and to explore our nation's history. To accommodate the influx of tourists, the government, in partnership with northern communities, has developed a series of well-serviced parks, and some excellent museums, which enrich any visit to the area.

1. Fish in Lake Temagami from the shore, or launch your canoe just beside the picnic site in Finlayson Point Provincial Park, our favourite picnic site. A historical marker beside the lake commemorates Grey Owl's years in the region. The building nearby houses local historical displays, and is open daily during the summer season.

2. You can walk in the footsteps of Bill Guppy and Archie Belaney by taking the walking trail to the fire tower on top of Caribou Mountain. The start of the trail is just opposite the entrance to Finlayson Park, on Highway 11. The first part of the trail is recognizable as the old highway. Interpretive brochures for the Tower Trail are available at the park gate, and the walk is about 2 miles along a fire road.

3. Visit the Trappers Museum and Gift Shop at Marten River. It is operated by the Ontario Trappers Association. Well informed attendants will answer all your questions about the history, techniques and principles of trapping. Displays of trapping devices show how committed the trappers' associations are to humane trapping. Displays of animals help you to learn to identify them in the wild, or when they are part of someone's fur coat. The museum is on Highway 11, 4 miles north of the junction with Highway 64, and about 12 miles south of Temagami. It is open daily from mid-May to mid-October.

4. You can visit an authentic logging camp from the 1930s era at the Marten River Provincial Park, just 2 kilometres south of the junction of Highways 11 and 64. Many buildings have been renovated, including a well equipped blacksmith's shop, and tours are offered during the summer season. The park offers hiking trails and a beach, too.

5. Driving north from Temagami for 20 miles to Latchford, you can visit a superb museum—considered by many to be the best museum in northern Ontario. It features exhibits on mining, logging, and the impact of the railway on the hinterland.

6. Continuing north for another 15 miles, you will reach the town of Cobalt. In 1910 the region was the fourth largest producer of silver in the world. Traces of old mines can be seen on the landscape and the Cobalt Mining Museum displays the history of this cradle of Canadian mining. The technologies developed here were integral to the

subsequent development of the mining industry in northern Ontario. Pick up a brochure at the museum or the tourist office and wander the "Silver Trail," two fascinating miles of mining history. It is a self-guiding trail, and an excellent educational resource.

MENU

Sweet Pickled Beaver
Beaver Tail Beans
Wild Rice
Chickweed Salad
Berry Pudding

Beaver was often on the menu for Grey Owl's dinner when he was living alone in the bush. Beaver can only be caught by licensed trappers now; sport hunting is forbidden. But if you want to try some of the following recipes, you can probably obtain beaver meat by contacting a trapper through the Trappers Museum at Marten River (see Things to Do). These recipes are from *The Hunter's Kitchen*, by the Western Guides & Outfitters of British Columbia, and appear with permission from Gateway Publishing.

Sweet Pickled Beaver

1 beaver, skinned and cleaned
1/2 cup vinegar
1 Tbsp. salt
2 tsp. soda
1/2 cup dry white wine or apple juice
1 cup pineapple juice
juice and grated rind of 1 lemon
1 tsp. cinnamon
1/2 tsp. cloves
1/2 cup brown sugar
2 Tbsp. dry mustard

First, wash the beaver thoroughly with salt water, then let soak overnight in enough cold water to cover, adding 1/2 cup vinegar and 1 Tbsp. salt to the water. The next day, remove the beaver from the brine, wash and cover with a solution of 2 quarts of water to 2 tsp. soda. Bring to a boil, reduce heat and simmer for 10 minutes. Drain and rinse the beaver, and place it in a clean pot. Add water just to cover. Sprinkle mixed pickling spice on top, bring to a boil, reduce heat and simmer for 20 minutes. Drain and rinse the beaver again. Pat dry, and place in a roaster. Mix the mustard, spices, sugar, wine and fruit juices and spread over the beaver. Cover and roast at 325 °F until tender, and baste frequently.

Beaver Tail Beans

(Serves 2)

Blister beaver tail over fire till skin loosens or dip in boiling water for a couple of minutes. Pull skin off and discard. Cut up meat and boil with a pot of beans. Add salt and pepper to taste. Some chopped onion adds to the flavour. Beaver tail is also good roasted over a campfire or in the oven.

Wild Rice

(Serves 4)

Wild rice is usually gathered in canoes by the Indians in some parts of Ontario. Grey Owl would have eaten this occasionally when he lived with the Ojibway Indians on Lake Temagami.

1 cup wild rice
1 1/2 cups water
1/2 tsp. salt

Wash and sort the rice carefully. Bring the water to a boil, and add the rice slowly, so that the water continues to boil. Cover tightly and continue to cook over medium heat for about 30 minutes, or until rice is tender. Let rice stand for a few minutes until all water has been absorbed. Dot with butter and serve.

Chickweed Salad

Whether you are preparing for a picnic in the wilderness, or in your own backyard, you are likely to be able to find this tasty plant. Chickweed leaves and stems are a delicate vegetable, and the seeds are used by the Indians for bread, or for thickening soup.

Pick enough chickweed for your party, and wash and sort it. Cut the leaves and stems into pieces, and place in a salad bowl. Add some freshly cooked bacon bits for flavour, and toss with a pungent dressing—we suggest white wine vinegar and olive oil, with a touch of celery salt. Serve immediately.

Berry Pudding

With Grey Owl's English heritage unmasked, we should conclude this meal with a pudding, albeit made from wild berries.

Pick a mixture of wild berries: raspberries, huckleberries, blueberries and strawberries will all work well. Sort them and just barely cover them with water. Cook over medium heat for about ten minutes, or until soft and popped. Add sugar to taste, and continue cooking until thick. Pour into a casserole.

Prepare the following topping.

1 1/2 cups flour
1 Tbsp. baking powder
1/4 tsp. salt
1/2 cup brown sugar
1 tsp. cinnamon
1 egg, beaten
1/2 cup milk or cream
1/2 cup melted butter or shortening

Combine wet ingredients and dry ingredients in separate bowls. Then add the wet ingredients to the dry, stirring until just moist. Pour over the stewed berries, and bake at 400 °F for 15-20 minutes. It's great served hot with ice cream or whipped cream. You can bring the berries and the topping ingredients to the picnic and bake this on the fire.

From the rocks at Kirkland Lake came $15 billion worth of gold, the Toronto Globe and Mail Newspaper, and an international murder mystery. There was a mile of gold along the shore of Kirkland Lake but it took an English immigrant, Bill Wright, and an American prospector, Harry Oakes, to find it and mine it. Here, where miners toiled deeper into the earth than man had ever gone before, where the streets are literally paved with gold, in a small town that has produced 40 hockey players for the National Hockey League, we celebrate our northern miners picnic.

How to get there

The picnic site is on the lawn in front of the Sir Harry Oakes Chateau. If you are entering the town of Kirkland Lake on Highway 66 from Swastika or Chaput Hughes, the chateau is on your left, a block east of the Journey's End Motel. It is signed as the Museum of Northern History at the Sir Harry Oakes Chateau.

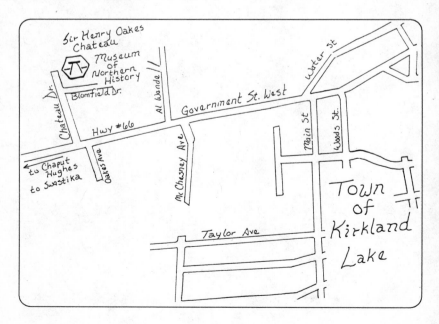

Sir Harry Oakes' chateau

The Yankee and the Englishman

Bill Wright was born in 1876 in northern England and started his working career as a butcher's apprentice. He joined the British army and served in India, and later in the Boer War. There, Bill Wright bought the veteran's land grant of a Canadian soldier for 160 acres in northern Ontario, and emigrated to Canada at the age of 31. To learn farming, Bill went to work for a farmer. However, the farmer had worked as a prospector in the Klondike gold rush, and his stories inspired Bill to try his luck in search of this elusive metal.

A few years later, in July 1911, Bill was prospecting with his brother-in-law Ed Hargreaves about 60 miles north of Cobalt. Hargreaves was out hunting rabbits and lost his way. He fired a rifle shot, the pre-arranged signal which brought Wright off his camp stool and into the bush to guide his partner. On the way a promising outcrop caught Bill's eye. Closer examination revealed visible gold—and the first great mine of the "golden mile" was discovered. Bill and Ed could only stake three claims, because it cost $10 to record each claim and they only had $30. Even though subsequent investigation revealed a rich vein eight to nine feet wide, Hargreaves did not believe that they had found the bonanza and so he sold his interest for a few thousand dollars.

The Wright-Hargreaves mine that started with those three claims went on to produce 4,000,000 ounces of gold, a value exceeding $157,000,000 at the gold prices of the day. Wright managed to remain a major shareholder in the company, an unusual feat for a prospector, and later bought two Toronto newspapers, the Toronto Globe, and the Mail and Empire, which he combined to form today's Globe and Mail.

Headframe of the Lakeshore mine

Harry Oakes was born in Sangerville, Maine, on December 23, 1874. His father was a land surveyor and sometime schoolteacher, and his mother was a schoolteacher and school supervisor. He had a good upbringing, as was fitting for a young middle-class Yankee. He attended prestigious Bowdoin College, and spent two years at Syracuse Medical School. But the worlds of commerce and medicine were not for him, because Harry had a dream. He wanted to make a million dollars, but he did not want to do so by exploiting anyone else. Thus, when news of the Klondike gold rush filtered through to the young medical student, he knew he had found his calling. Harry was 23 years old when he left for the Klondike. In the years to come he would prospect in the Yukon, Alaska, Australia, New Zealand, Death Valley, South Africa, and finally, less than 1000 miles from his home, in northern Ontario.

It was a poor Harry Oakes that arrived in Swastika in the summer of 1911. He had chased his elusive fortune for 14 years and all he had to show was an ability to work 16 hours a day, seven days a week. He could survive forever on bannock and beans, and he had accumulated an encyclopedic knowledge of geology and rock formations. He still relied on money sent by his sister and brother to survive. He remained optimistic and knew his skill and talents would eventually serve him well in his search for a million dollars.

All of the promising area around Swastika was already staked. Eventually Harry found some claims that, owing to incomplete development work, would come vacant at midnight that night. When Harry discovered this, he had only $2.65, not even sufficient to record one of the claims. He wandered into the general store and fell into conversation with the four Tough brothers—George, Tom, Bob, and Jack. Soon a deal was set; Harry would show them the claims and the brothers would pay to record them. Off into the minus 52-degree night the five partners went.

Each wearing four and five pairs of pants, and coats over jackets over sweaters to fight the cold, the five men worked through the night. By three in the morning they had staked the claims. At six o'clock, while huddling around a fire, they were greeted by Oakes' friend Bill Wright who, together with his partner, had just arrived, hoping to stake the same claims. Wright was too late.

One month later Oakes and his partners found the first vein on the Tough-Oakes, and three months later, another one. In the next thirteen months they mined and shipped 101 tons of ore worth $46,000.

The Tough-Oakes Mine, for all its fabulous showing, was not enough for Harry and his dream of a one-man mine. Harry's knowledge of geology helped him for he knew that what many other prospectors considered red granite was actually porphyry, an intrusive rock often bearing gold. He came to the conclusion that the most favourable formations would be in the bedrock beneath the waters of Kirkland Lake—so he set about acquiring the claims below the lake. Wright, who was still smarting from being beaten to the Tough-Oakes claims, was watching Harry carefully. Once Wright figured out what Harry was doing he got the four claims alongside Harry's underwater group thus preventing Harry from claiming it all. Such was the rivalry between the two friends.

Fourteen years in the gold fields had taught Harry more than just geology. For years he had watched as the prospectors were paid small amounts for claims that were later developed into wealthy mines. The skills of mining are different from prospecting, and large amounts of up-front capital are needed to develop a hardrock mine. Nevertheless, Harry the prospector undertook to develop his own claims into the Lake Shore Mine.

The development was difficult: although the Oakes brothers and sisters supported him, Oakes had to sell out his share of the Tough-Oakes mine, and Charlie Chow, who ran the boardinghouse, had to accept mine shares from Harry instead of money. From 1913 until 1920 Harry fought law suits, war-time labour shortages, and material and equipment shortages. He begged for investment money, to drive his mine workings farther under the lake.

By 1921 he was a multimillionaire, and the largest stock holder of the Lake Shore Mine, the second richest gold mine in the western hemisphere. And everybody else who had helped him was also rich: Bill Wright, who was vice-president of the mine, Harry's mother, brother and sister, the miner who first struck the vein, and Charlie Chow.

Harry went on to attain a certain level of international notoriety: in 1935 he left Canada for Nassau to avoid Canadian income tax. In 1939 he became Sir Harry, and that same year became friends with the Duke and Duchess of Windsor. The Duke was at that time the governor general of Nassau. Harry was murdered in Nassau in 1943 and the investigation was so badly handled that his murderer was never found.

Discovery after discovery occurred at Kirkland Lake, and soon there were twelve major gold mines along its shore. The miners achieved the distinction of working in the deepest mines in the world as the Wright-Hargreaves and the Lake Shore mines both pushed their shafts to below 8000 feet. (South Africa's mines are deeper, 10,000 feet, but they start at 5,500 feet above sea level whereas Kirkland Lake's elevation is only 1,000 feet above sea level.) The streets of Kirkland Lake were literally paved with gold when road crews accidentally used ore instead of waste rock as ballast to build up a road.

Things to do

1. The Sir Harry Oakes Chateau is built on the site of Harry's first log cabin which burned in 1929. The architecture was designed to harmonize with the earlier log structure and used some mining construction methods. When the house was being constructed, Harry would have the men coming off shift from his nearby mine urinate into a large tub. The urine was subsequently used by the house builder to polish the copper roof of the chateau to a rich-looking green. After Oakes and his family moved away the building was used as a guest house and for directors' meetings. The headframe of the Lake Shore Mine is visible from the back balcony. The house contains some interesting mining exhibits and photographs, and some memorabilia from the Oakes family.

2. Although all the old mines have gone, a new mining process has made an appearance on the shores of Kirkland Lake. Dredges now pull up the waste rock from the original mines and pipe it to the new Macassa mill where it is reworked. Check at the Museum to learn if the mine is offering tours in the summer months.

Things to eat

Prospector's food was pretty basic—bannock, beans and lentils. The appropriate picnic food therefore is a big pot of lentil stew.

Lentil Stew

Lentils, or dry pulses, were a staple of mining camps because they were easily transported and kept indefinitely. Their high protein and vitamin content still make them a popular choice for a meal.

Combine in a kettle:
  1/2 pound lentils
  5 cups water
  2 carrots, cut into chunks
  1 small onion, cut into quarters

Cook until the lentils are tender, about 45 minutes.

Add:
  6 green onions, chopped
  1 clove garlic, crushed
  1 1/2 cups tomato juice
  1/2 cup minced parsley
  1 Tbsp. vegetable oil
  1 tsp. salt
  1/2 tsp. freshly ground pepper
  1/2 tsp. oregano

Simmer until the soup reaches the desired thickness—it will vary from soup to stew over time, or with neglect. Stir in 1 Tbsp. wine vinegar or lemon juice just before serving. Provide a side dish of yogurt for dollops. Insulate the pot with newspapers for transporting to the picnic site, or take a Coleman stove and reheat it.

Loaves and Fishes or Feeding the Multitude

This chapter is for that fortunate individual who has just been elected or appointed Social Convenor, or equivalent, of a group or club and is now responsible for the planning and conduct of the annual picnic.

Companies, unions, churches, communities, families and lots of other groups hold picnics for their members. The planning required for such events is quite detailed, but with reasonable care you can indeed keep everything under control—except, of course, the weather.

In this chapter we will describe the generic large-group picnic, covering a variety of concerns, such as theme, supplies, games and activities, recipes for preparing large quantities of food, and provide answers to that worrisome question: "how many potatoes in a potato salad for 100?" The chapter is mainly one long and involved checklist, with some games and recipes tacked on. You have undertaken an awesome and daunting task, one that would overcome a lesser individual, but we hope that we have provided enough suggestions that you might enjoy the afternoon and even volunteer to do it again!

1. What happened last year

Did everybody enjoy themselves? Was the location OK? Who booked it and from whom . . . is she still in town? Was Mrs. Brown's potato salad the hit of the picnic, or the basis of the food fight that broke out? Will you be a hero by just repeating what was done before, or were many people dissatisfied? Organizations are often very bad at this sort of thing, but some conscientious digging can probably head off a lot of hurt feelings, and make the picnic fun for all.

2. The occasion

Picnics are often associated with an event, such as the completion of spring planting in rural communities, or a harvest festival. Certainly the fall bazaar or fair is still a common occurrence in many rural and urban communities. Work parties are another good reason for a picnic—it used to be barn-raising, but now it is sometimes garage-raising or developing the community ball field. Many hands do make light work, so have another look at your job jar—there might be a good excuse for a picnic in there.

Picnics can be planned around a theme, although this is not at all necessary. Here are some suggestions to spark your imagination:

Canada Day	summer solstice
Christmas in July	50th birthday
a wedding	retirement
end of school	end of summer

3. The group

The first step is to recognize the composition of the group since this will influence all the other factors: the food, the activities, the facilities, etc. With old, established picnics this is fairly well understood, but with new groups, watch out. This may be the group of boys that you bowl with Wednesday night, but the picnic includes their families ... what do you know about them? What are the ages of their children? Do they like a primitive but beautiful site, or are they happiest in an urban park? Do they have teenagers or little kids, or is this an adult group which, on a picnic, can be counted on to behave as aging adolescents? This last group is especially hard to deal with as you can expect several bad sprains and possibly a broken bone or two as the picnickers try to convince their 40-year-old bodies that they can still play football like they did when they were 20. Even if it is the same group as last year, remember that a year has gone by, and while it may not have changed you or your friends much, the children might have metamorphosed from fun-seeking kids to very self conscious teenagers.

4. Facilities: Where to hold the picnic

Municipal and provincial parks usually provide pleasant settings for large picnics, and some provide special places and facilities for large groups. Once you have selected a likely spot, visit the site and check to see that there is enough space for the activities you are planning, shelter in case of rain, sanitary facilities and a water source. If these are missing, portable toilets can be rented, and a water supply can be carried in, but both of these eventualities require lead time and planning.

If you intend to serve alcoholic beverages, check first to make sure that this is legal in the site you have selected. The consumption of alcohol is usually forbidden in public parks, but sometimes you can obtain a permit, particularly if you are using a community hall as a base.

It is a good idea to notify the local police department about the event, as well. You may need assistance with traffic control, or help in dealing with unruly guests—or you may need nothing at all. This is just part of the ounce of prevention which beats a pound of cure.

If you are booking a park as the site of your picnic, you might wish to be weather-safe, and book an alternative venue, such as a community hall or church, in case of rain. Sometimes groups set up an alternate date, assuming that if the first day is rainy, the second won't be. For example, the invitation or announcement would read, "Social services department picnic at Kinsmen Park on Saturday, July 6th, or, in case of rain-out, Saturday, July 13th." Make sure you book both dates with the parks department, or appropriate authority.

5. Equipment

You will need supplies for decorating the picnic site, such as balloons and streamers. In larger centres these can be found by checking the Yellow Pages under "balloons, helium or giftwares". Helium machines can be rented for a nominal fee, and even outdoor sites look more festive when there are brightly coloured balloons flying from the trees and telephone poles.

You will need prizes for any contests or races—and make sure that you have plenty. We usually give at least three prizes for all children's contests, and, if possible, a prize to everyone. Ribbons for first, second, third, fourth, and so on are often available at the same place where you buy the balloons.

You will need to buy, borrow or make the equipment for any races or contests; for example, barrels for barrel races, strong ties for three-legged races, bags (green garbage, perhaps) for the sack race, eggs for an egg toss, and so on.

Finally, there will be the cleanup after. Rakes, brooms, shovels, or maybe just a lot of garbage bags, but do remember them — and line up your work crew ahead of time.

6. First aid equipment

We have found that the best arrangement is to bring a complete industrial first aid kit. These can be purchased from any industrial supply store, and come in a waterproof metal box.

Alternatively, you can put together a kit for yourself with a minimum of the following:

Band-aids of various sizes	sterile 2" and 4" gauze pads
low-allergy adhesive tape	skin disinfectant
lots of cotton balls	scissors
elastic bandage for sprains	sling
safety pins	burn ointment
insect repellent	

In any case, make sure that you do have an adequate first aid kit at the picnic.

6. Activities

Games
Think back to the picnics of your childhood—what games did you play? I'll bet that you, like us, have trouble remembering the rules. Later in the chapter are the rules for some of the games we remember, but we have found that there are regional variations, so alter them to suit your own recollection.

Contests
Contests are fun, if they are not taken too seriously. Pies seem to offer the most versatility for contests: there are pie-baking contests, pie-throwing contests, and pie-eating contests. There are barrel-rolling contests, where the contestants line up with their barrels (empty oil barrels are fine) at the starting line, and the prize goes to the person who walks the barrel to the finish line first without touching ground - or the person who goes the farthest. There are arm wrestling contests. There are spelling bees. Prizes can also be given for the best decorated bike, the scariest costume, and the most lovable dog. If you are at a beach for your picnic, there could be a sandcastle building contest.

Searches
Treasure hunts of various sorts are lots of fun, and work well as team activities. Each team is given a list of things to find, and the winner is the team which collects everything on the list first. Alternatively, quantities of a particular item, for example, eggs, or specially wrapped candies, or tokens of some sort, can be secreted about the picnic site, and the prize goes to the team or individual who finds the most.

Team Sports
The old reliables — the baseball game, touch football, horse-shoes, or for some groups, a rousing round of croquet always go better if someone remembers to bring the bats, balls, mallets, hoops, and base sacks. Delegate the responsibility to someone, and then check up on them.

Kite flying
If your picnic site has a big enough field, with no power lines nearby, you can ask people to bring their kites; alternatively, you can

supply some. This only works in a big space, and only a few people can fly kites at the same time, since the strings easily become entangled. Alternatively, if the picnickers know and understand kite fighting, that is also is an interesting pastime.

Balloon rides

Hot-air ballooning has become very popular in the last few years. Many balloon owners are willing to attend community events or private functions to provide balloon rides, for a fee. Some groups have even rented helicopters for the afternoon, and sold rides to the picnickers.

Guided hikes

If the picnic is in a rural setting, a park just outside town, or even some of the larger city parks, guided hikes for groups of picnickers can be a welcome diversion, especially for senior citizens. Identify someone in the group who has special knowledge of birds, plants and/or animals. Ask your guide in advance, so that he or she can brush up if necessary. Limit the hikes to no more than an hour, and perhaps less, depending on whom you expect to participate.

Campfire sing-songs

Most effective after dark, sing-songs provide a quiet ending to an exciting afternoon. Everyone slows down and relaxes, little children fall asleep on blankets by the fire, and adults feel that sense of warmth and companionship which can only happen by a fire. Make sure that you provide at least one guitar or accordion player who has a wide repertoire appropriate to the ages of your group. Consider having song sheets available, if you think people will be able to see them. Alternatively, brainstorm with your accompanist in advance, and prepare a list of tunes for which most people already know the words, so that awkward silences and false starts will be avoided.

Fireworks

Fireworks have made a big comeback in the last few years, much to the chagrin of many parents. Nonetheless, they make a marvelous display when carefully selected and responsibly detonated.

7. Things to eat

Donations

There are many factories in most cities and larger towns which will be happy to donate some of their product for your picnic, in exchange for recognition in the announcement or invitation. Others will donate, but prefer to remain anonymous to stem the tide of subsequent requests. Some may prefer to give a small cash donation. Think about what you will need in the way of food, and then consider which companies are represented in your community. Most have a public relations officer to respond to such requests. It is certainly worth a try.

Supplies

If you are using a community hall or equivalent as a base for your food preparation, arrange to visit the place to assess the number and capacity of mixing and serving bowls, pots and pans, and so on. If you are going to be working in a park, preparing hot dogs and hamburgers, make sure that you book enough barbecues and frying pans, or whatever else you will need. Nothing is worse than a bottleneck in the food production area when everyone is hungry. The easiest way of all is to select cold foods, and have them prepared by individuals in their homes in advance. This is the ideal time for a potluck dinner, in true "picnickian" style, with everyone contributing to the feast. We have found that it isn't even necessary to direct people about what to bring—you will get several potato salads, but this is a popular dish anyway, and most of it will be eaten. You will also get some of the specialty salads that people like to make for such events, and the variety is endless. The most direction we have ever given is to request either a salad, casserole, dessert or bread. Usually the picnic organizers provide the beverages, in the form of juice or pop. Have water on hand for those who want it.

Most important, make sure you have enough. Err on the side of too much! To help you, we provide selected recipes.

Chicken Salad

(100 Servings)

Mix together:
>8 qts. cooked chicken, cut into small pieces
>8 cups chopped celery
>2 Tbsp. salt
>2 Tbsp. pepper
>2 qts. mayonnaise or salad cream
>6 green peppers, chopped
>16 hard-boiled eggs, sliced

Keep chilled until serving. It is best to prepare this the day of the picnic. You can maintain a safe room temperature by placing the serving bowls in a tub of ice on the picnic table.

Salmon Loaf

(100 Servings)

Mix together:
  20 one-pound cans of salmon
  6 qts. bread crumbs

Scald:
  8 qts. milk
  And mix with:
  3 cups melted butter
  5 1/2 cups flour
  1 tsp. paprika
  4 Tbsp. salt
  Cook for 15 minutes.

Combine the sauce with the fish, blend together, and pour into greased loaf pans. Sprinkle with buttered bread crumbs and bake at 350 °F for 30 minutes.

Coleslaw

(100 Servings)

  10 lbs. cabbage, shredded
  3 lbs. carrots, shredded
  3 lbs. celery, diced
  1 pt. mayonnaise or salad cream
  1 cup salad oil
  1/2 cup vinegar
  celery seed, salt and pepper to taste.

Combine, and chill until serving.

Potato Salad

(100 Servings)

  28 lbs. potatoes, cooked and diced
  10 doz. hard-boiled eggs, sliced
  2 cups onions, finely chopped
  5 sweet red peppers, chopped
  5 green peppers chopped
  salt and pepper to taste

Dress with:
   2 cups salad oil
   1/2 cup vinegar
   2 tsp. dry mustard
   1 qt. mayonnaise

Mix ingredients together and chill well until serving.

GROUP PICNIC CHECKLIST

This can be used as a rough guide, or as a plan of action, assigning committee members to each task, and setting scheduled dates of completion.

Select date for picnic, and alternate date, if appropriate.
Select site.
Visit site to check for:
water
toilets
number of picnic tables
shelter
cooking facilities - type of stoves
firewood
ball diamond
games/races area
electricity
nearest telephone
nearest hospital
Book site.
Get liquor permit, if needed.
Develop supply list:
prizes
ribbons
safety pins
string
rope
tape
fireworks
paper cups
paper plates
plastic cutlery
serviettes
garbage bags
garbage buckets
lawn chairs for seniors
barbecues

fuel
pots and pans
cooking implements
pot holders, oven mitts
first aid kit
water buckets
List food requirements:
snacks
main course
salads
buns or bread
casseroles
desserts
cookies
pies
List beverage requirements:
drinks for little kids
drinks for teenagers
drinks for adults
coffee, tea, cocoa, milk
cups to drink from

Games for groups

Elves, Giants and Wizards
Materials: none
People: ten, to a large crowd

Directions:
Two roughly equal groups of people should be formed. They should then be taught the three basic positions of the game:

-an elf is little with two little horns on his head (so the person squats with hands behind head, fingers pointing up)

-a giant is huge (so the person puts their arms way above their heads and goes on tiptoes.)

-wizards are sneaky fellows, always shooting rays of magic lightening out of their fingers. A wizard sort of person therefore, looks sneaky and is always pointing his arms at the other group.

To play the game, each group has a secret meeting and decides which of the three characters it will be. A first plan and a backup plan should be chosen. Then the groups face each other, about five metres apart, on a large field. There should be designated safe zones at each end of the field since the participants are going to chase each other up and down the field.

Once facing each other, and conducted by the gamesmaster, they all chant together three times in a row, "elves, giants, wizards" with the action for each word. After the third chant each group then chants its planned word. The result will be the two groups yelling the same, or different characters. This seems pointless unless you know that:

-elves can run under wizards' cloaks and pull the hair on their legs;

-wizards can shoot magic rays that will destroy giants;

-giants can stomp on elves' heads.

Thus whenever the first planned word called out by each team is different, there will be a winner (a chaser) and a loser (who will get chased). For example, if one side calls elves, and the other wizards, the elves are the winners and get to chase the wizards. So also, wizards chase giants, and giants chase elves. Any one tagged before getting to a safe zone has to join the other team. If the first planned word is the same for both teams, then each should immediately chant their backup plan word.

Kick-the-Can

Material: one can
People: four to a crowd

Directions:

This is a fast-paced game a lot like hide-and-go-seek. One person is chosen to be It. The can is kicked by someone and this is the signal for everyone except It to race off, within the prescribed boundary, and hide. The It retrieves the can, takes it home, and then with closed eyes, counts slowly to 60 out loud. It then goes to find the people without letting anyone get home undetected. When a person is discovered It runs to the can and says, "one, two, three on (name)." The correct name of the person should be called, but with a large group, when maybe someone doesn't know all the names, this rule can be relaxed. There will often be a race to the can, and if the hidden person gets there first, they shout, "home free," and are safe. Once a lot of people are at the can, both caught and safe, the last people out can try to sneak home and "kick the can." This action would free all the people at home to run and hide again. If no one kicks the can, then the first person caught is It for the next round. No one can be It more than twice in a row.

Dragon

Materials: a blindfold, and a treasure (shoe, box, $$)
People: about seven or more

Description:

Millions and hundred of years ago, dragons roamed the earth . . . and these dragons had great treasures. Now it seems that not all the dragons died off; one still lives and he is the richest dragon of them all. This dragon has been collecting money and jewels for centuries and has caves full of treasure. He is a very ferocious dragon, but he is blind. However, his hearing is especially good. Now the question is, is there anyone in the group who is stealthy enough to steal the dragon's treasure?

Select one person to be the dragon and blindfold them. Sit the dragon on the ground with his or her legs spread out, and with the treasure on the ground. The treasure is close to, but not touching the dragon. Have the group sit in a circle around the dragon. Then the leader will point to one person who will try to steal in and take the treasure. If the dragon hears something it will point at the sound, and the intruder will be zapped by magic dragon fire. The dragon can only point at sounds. The group should be very quiet, and only one person can try at a time to steal the treasure. Sometimes, the group can make rain noise by rubbing hands together. When the treasure is stolen, appoint a new dragon and continue.

References

Allan, Ted and Sydney Gordon 1952 (1974) *The Scalpel and the Sword*. Toronto: McClelland & Stewart.

Anahareo 1972 *Devil in Deerskins: My Life with Grey Owl*. Toronto: New Press.

Anderson, Frank 1979 *"Grey Owl." Sagas of the West* Vol. 4: 5-30. Saskatoon: Frank W. Anderson.

Armitage, Andrew 1979 Owen Sound: *The Day the Governor General Came to Town and Other Tales*. Chelterham, Ontario: Boston Mills Press.

Bailey, Melville 1943 *The History of Dundurn Castle and Sir Allan MacNab*. Hamilton: Board of Park Management.

Baird, Elizabeth 1974 *Classic Canadian Cooking*. Toronto: James Lorimer.

Barss, B. 1980 *The Pioneer Cook*. Calgary: Detselig.

Bassett, John M. and A. Roy Petrie 1974 *Allan Napier MacNab*. Don Mills: Fitzhenry & Whiteside Limited.

Beard, James 1959 *The James Beard Cookbook*. New York: Dell.

Beer, Donald R. 1984 *Sir Allan Napier MacNab*. Hamilton: Dictionary of Hamilton Biography.

Benoit, Jehane 1970 *The Canadiana Cookbook*. Toronto: Pagurian Press.

Benoit, Jehane 1980 *The World of Food*. Toronto: McGraw-Hill Ryerson.

Berglund, Berndt and Clare E. Bolsby 1971 *The Edible Wild*. Toronto: Pagurian Press.

Berton, Pierre 1977 *The Dionne Years: A Thirties Melodrama*. Toronto: McClelland & Stewart.

Berton, Pierre 1988 *Flames Across the Border: 1813-1814*. Markham: Penguin Books Canada Ltd.

Bramble, Linda *1988 Black Fugitive Slaves in Early Canada*. St. Catharines: Vanwell.

Breckenridge, Muriel 1978 *Every Day a Feast*. Toronto: McGraw-Hill Ryerson.

Bruce County Historical Society Yearbook 1984.

Bocca, Geoffrey 1959 *The Life and Death of Sir Harry Oakes*. Garden City, New York: Doubleday & Company, Inc.

Buswa, Ernestine, Margaret Fox and Patricia Ryan, Eds. 1978. *Ojibwe-Odawa People: Yesterday-Today*. Manitoulin Island: Ojibwe Cultural Foundation.

Canada: Tourist Guide 1982. Quebec: Michelin Tires (Canada) Ltd.

Canadian Book of the Road 1979. Toronto: The Canadian Automobile Association and The Readers Digest.

The Canadian Encyclopedia 1988 Edmonton: Hurtig.

Canadian Living Magazine 1984 *The Great Canadian Cookbook*. Toronto: Telemedia.

Carter, Charles A. 1969 *The Gallant Knight*. Hamilton, The MacNab Circle.

Chapple, William N.D. *The Story of Uncle Tom*. Dresden: Uncle Tom's Cabin and Museum.

Cole, Jean Murray, Ed. 1987 *The Peterborough Lift Lock*. Peterborough: Friends of the Trent-Severn Waterway.

Colombo, John Robert, Ed. 1978. *Colombo's Book of Canada* Edmonton: Hurtig.

A Concise Dictionary of Canadianisms 1973 Toronto: Gage Educational Publishing Limited.

Cooper, John Irwin 1978 *Ontario's First Century: 1610-1713*. Montreal: The Lawrence Lande Foundation, McGill University.

Cosens, Donald L., Ed. *The Donnelly Tragedy 1880-1980*. London: Phelps.

Crichton, William 1977 *The Donnelly Murders*. Markham: Paperjacks.

Dickson, Lovat 1973 *Wilderness Man: The Strange Story of Grey Owl*. Toronto: Macmillan.

Edmunds, R. David 1983 *The Shawnee Prophet*. Lincoln and London: University of Nebraska Press.

Fink Cline, Beverly 1979 *The Guy Lombardo Story*. Don Mills, Ontario: Musson.

General Electric Microwave Guide and Cookbook. 1977 The General Electric Company.

Gibson, Nancy and John Whittaker 1989 *The Lone Pine Picnic Guide to Alberta*. Edmonton: Lone Pine Publishing.

Gibson, Nancy and John Whittaker 1989 *The Lone Pine Picnic Guide to British Columbia*. Edmonton: Lone Pine Publishing.

Greene, Bert 1988 *The Grains Cookbook.* New York: Workman.

Grey Owl 1936 *Tales of an Empty Cabin.* Toronto: Macmillan.

Hall, Roger & Gordon Dodds 1978 *A Picture History of Ontario.* Edmonton: Hurtig.

Hawkes, Christopher 1974 *Sainte Marie Among the Hurons.* Canada: Ginn and Company.

Heath, Frances 1988 *Sault Sainte Marie: City by the Rapids.* Burlington: Windsor Publications.

Henson, Josiah 1965 (first published in 1849) *The Life of Josiah Henson, Formerly a Slave, Now an Inhabitant of Canada as Narrated By Himself.* Dresden: Uncle Tom's Cabin Museum.

*Heritage of Canada.*1978 The Canadian Automobile Association in conjunction with The Reader's Digest Association (Canada) Ltd.

HMS Nancy *and the War of 1812.* 1978 Ontario Ministry of Natural Resources.

Herron, Shaun 1988 "Archaeologists dig Halton." *The Spectator.* Burlington-Halton, October 22, p. T7.

Horner, Gary 1989 *The Bicycle Guide to Southwestern Ontario.* Edmonton: Lone Pine Publishing.

Howard, Victor and Mac Reynolds 1986 *The Mackenzie-Papineau Battalion.* Ottawa: Carleton University Press.

Hunt, C.W. 1988 *Booze Boats and Billions: Smuggling Liquid Gold!* Toronto: McLelland & Stewart.

1989 "Smugglers of the County." County Magazine 11(52):32-35, 59-61.

Johnson, E. Pauline 1911 *Legends of Vancouver.* Toronto: McClelland and Stewart Limited.

Johnson, E. Pauline 1912 *Flint and Feather, The Complete Poems of E. Pauline Johnson.* Toronto: The Musson Book Co. Ltd.

Johnston, Jean 1973 *Wilderness Women.* Toronto: Peter Martin Associates.

Keller, Betty 1981 *Pauline: A Biography of Pauline Johnson.* Halifax, Goodread Biographies.

Kelley, Thomas P. 1986 *The Black Donnellys.* Toronto: Pagurian Press.

Kelley, Thomas P. 1988 *The Vengeance of the Black Donnellys.* Toronto: Pagurian Press.

Knap, Alyson Hart 1979 *Wilderness Harvest*. Toronto: Pagurian Press.

Leacock, Stephen (1931) 1960 *Sunshine Sketches of a Little Town*. Toronto: McClelland & Stewart.

Leacock, Stephen 1965 *The Leacock Roundabout*. New York: Dodd Mead & Co.

Lewis, Henry T. 1982 *A Time for Burning*. Occasional Publication #17. Edmonton: The Boreal Institute for Northern Studies.

Legget, Robert F. 1976 *Canals of Canada*. North Vancouver: Douglas, David & Charles Ltd.

McDowall, Duncan 1984 *Steel at the Sault*. Toronto: University of Toronto Press.
McGivern, James S., S.J., Ed. 1975 *In the Early Dawn*. Toronto: Mission Press.

Michelin 1982 *Tourist Guide Canada*. Strasbourg: Manufacture Francaise des Pneumatiques Michelin.

Mika, Nick & Helen Mika 1985 *The Shaping of Ontario from Exploration to Confederation*. Belleville: Mika Publishing Company.

Miller, Orlo 1962 *The Donnellys Must Die*. Toronto: Macmillan.

Mitcham, Allison 1981 *Grey Owl's Favourite Wilderness*. Moonbeam, Ontario: Penumbra Press.

Moodie, Susanna 1970 (First published in 1871) *Roughing It in the Bush*. Toronto: McClelland & Stewart.

Morton, Arthur S. 1944 *Sir George Simpson: Overseas Governor of The Hudson's Bay Company*. Toronto: J.M. Dent & Sons.

Newman, Peter C. 1985 *Company of Adventurers*. Markham, Ontario: Viking.

Nihmey, John and Stuart Foxman 1987 *Time of Their Lives The Dionne Tragedy*. Toronto: McClelland-Bantam.

Nute, Grace Lee 1953 "Journey for Frances." *The Beaver* December.

1954 "Journey for Frances." *The Beaver* March.

Pioneer Cooking in Ontario 1988. Toronto: NC Press.

Piva, Michael J. 1988 *A History of Ontario*. Toronto: Copp Clark Pitman.

Ragueneau, Rev. Paul, S.J. 1972 *Shadows Over Huronia*. Midland, Ontario: The Martyrs' Shrine.

Robinson, Helen Caister 1981 *Laura: A Portrait of Laura Secord*. Toronto: Dundurn.

Roden, Claudia 1984 *Everything Tastes Better Outdoors*. New York: Alfred A. Knopf.

Rogers, Edward S. 1970 *Iroquoians of the Eastern Woodlands*. Toronto: Royal Ontario Museum.

Rombauer, Irma S. and Marion Rombauer Becker 1975 *The Joy of Cooking*. Toronto: Thomas Allen & Son.

Scargall, Jeanne 1980 *Canadian Homestead Cookbook*. Toronto: Methuen.

Sewell, John and Charlotte Sykes, 1988 *Rowland Travel Guide to Toronto*. Toronto, Rowland & Jacob Inc.

Smith, Susan Weston 1976 *A History of Recreation in the Thousand Islands*. Parks Canada.

Soltys, Phillip 1989 "The Teaching Rock." *Leisure Ways*, June pp.14-18.

Staebler, Edna 1966 *Sauerkraut and Enterprise*. Toronto, McClelland and Stewart Limited.

Staebler, Edna 1968 *Food that Really Schmecks*. Toronto McGraw-Hill Ryerson Limited.

Stewart, Roderick 1973 *Bethune*. Markham, Ontario: Paperjacks.

Stewart, Roderick 1977 *The Mind of Norman Bethune*. Toronto: Fitzhenry & Whiteside.

Sullivan, Alan 1972 *The Rapids*. Toronto: University of Toronto Press.

Traill, Catharine Parr 1969 (First published in 1855) *The Canadian Settler's Guide*. Toronto: McClelland & Stewart.

Trigger, Bruce 1969 *The Huron: Farmers of the North*. New York: Holt Rinehart.

Tyrell, J.B., Ed. 1916 *David Thompson's Narrative on His Explorations in Western America 1784-1812*. Toronto: The Champlain Society.

Vastokas, Joan M. and Romas K. Vastokas 1973 *Sacred Art of the Algonkians: A Study of the Peterborough Petroglyphs*. Peterborough: Mansard Press.

White, Randall 1985 *Ontario 1610-1985: A Political and Economic History*. Toronto: Dundurn.

Winterhalder, Keith 1983. "The re-greening of Sudbury." *The Canadian Geographic* 103(3):23-29.

Photo Credits

John Whittaker
Skeletons from Kenora 23 p.28, Pither's Point Park p.34, Fort St. Pierre Bastion p.35, Middle Falls on the Grande Portage p.40, The Canada Goose at Wawa p.46, Replica of the 1789 figurehead of the *Nancy* p.61, The Corran, 1989 p.66, The *Norisle* p.71, An Auld Aquaintance p.76, Donnelly Tombstone, St. Patrick's cemetery p.82, Stratford p.87, Elora Mill p.96, Mohawk Chapel p.101, The First Commercial Oil Well p.104, Josiah Henson's Cabin p.109, Nathan Phillips Square p.127, Dundurn Castle p.140, Secord Home at Queenston p.144, Dufferin Island p.152, Leacock Home, Old Brewery Bay p.171, Catherine Parr Traill's House p.178, The Lift Lock p.184, The Dunes p.191, St. Lawrence Islands National Park p.206, Upper Canada Village p.219, Rideau Falls p.228, Bell Park p.242, Sir Harry Oakes Chateau p.261, Headframe of Lakeshore Mine p. 262

Archives of Ontario
Pauline Johnson. S-17721, p.100
Oil Springs. S-4748, p.105
Group of Seven at Toronto Arts and Letters Club. B-12842, p.122
Early picnickers on Toronto Island. S-12764, p.131
Hanlan's Point lighthouse. H-1999, p.131
Laura Secord's Grave. S-90886, p.145
Caterine Parr Traill and Susanna Moodie with a neice. B-8364, p.177
Dionne Quints, 1935. S-803, p.246
Grey Owl feeding a beaver kitten. S-17966, p.253

Atomic Energy of Canada
Chalk River p.234

McGraw Hill Ryerson, C.W. Jefferys
Meeting of Brock and Tchumseh p.113
Pallisaded Huron-Iroquois Village p.136

Bethune Memorial House
Norman Bethune in China p.162

National Army Museum
Officers and Cannon p.198

Scugog Museum
Early Picnickers at the Falls p.151

Canadian Parks Service, J.R. Graham
Yellow Warbler p.117

Sault Ste. Marie Museum
Francis H Clergue p.51

Horace T. Martin
Beaver Hats p.41

St. Lawrence Seaway Authority
St. Lawrence Seaway p.157

About the authors

The search for the perfect picnic has been an all-consuming passion of the Gibson-Whittaker family. The search has been conducted on five continents and included mountaintops in India, riverbanks in Africa, castles and olive groves in Spain, and buffalo jumps and ghost towns in Canada. Nancy is a cultural anthropologist, gardener, management consultant, author and university lecturer. John is a cook, management consultant, author and professor of engineering management.

Recipe Index